The Latest Ca

MW00346041

The Latest Catastrophe

History, the Present, the Contemporary

HENRY ROUSSO

Translated by Jane Marie Todd

The University of Chicago Press

CHICAGO AND LONDON

The University of Chicago Press gratefully acknowledges the generous support of the France Chicago Center toward the translation and publication of this book.

HENRY ROUSSO is a senior researcher with the Institut d'histoire du temps présent at the Centre national de la recherche scientifique in Paris. JANE MARIE TODD is the translator of many books.

The University of Chicago Press, Chicago 60637
The University of Chicago Press, Ltd., London
© 2016 by The University of Chicago
All rights reserved. Published 2016.
Printed in the United States of America

Originally published as *La dernière catastrophe: L'histoire, le présent, le contemporain.* © Éditions Gallimard, Paris, 2012.

25 24 23 22 21 20 19 18 17 16   1 2 3 4 5

ISBN-13: 978-0-226-16506-6 (cloth)
ISBN-13: 978-0-226-16523-3 (paper)
ISBN-13: 978-0-226-16537-0 (e-book)
DOI: 10.7208/chicago/9780226165370.001.0001

Library of Congress Cataloging-in-Publication Data

Rousso, Henry, 1954– author.
[Dernière catastrophe. English]
The latest catastrophe : history, the present, the contemporary / Henry Rousso ; translated by Jane Marie Todd.
pages cm
"Originally published as La dernière catastrophe : l'histoire, le présent, le contemporain. Éditions Gallimard, Paris, 2012"—Title page verso.
Includes bibliographical references and index.
ISBN 978-0-226-16506-6 (cloth : alkaline paper) — ISBN 978-0-226-16523-3 (paperback : alkaline paper) — ISBN 978-0-226-16537-0 (e-book)
1. Historiography. 2. History, Modern—Historiography. 3. History—Philosophy. I. Todd, Jane Marie, 1957– translator. II. Title.
D16.8.R87213 2016
907.2—dc23
2015028395

In memory of Peter Novick

Contents

Acknowledgments

This book was a long time coming to fruition, and it is therefore impossible to cite here all those who contributed to my thinking at one moment or another. The Institut d'Histoire du Temps Présent (IHTP) has always been my intellectual and professional environment, and I am grateful in the first place to its founder, François Bédarida, who died prematurely and whose memory I associate with that of Michael Pollak, Michel Trebitsch, and Karel Bartosek, all of whom also passed away too soon. I would also like to mention Marianne Ranson, who was there from the beginning, as well as Robert Frank, Denis Peschanski, Jean-Pierre Rioux, and Danièle Voldman, in memory of the early days, in addition to Jean Astruc, Gabrielle Muc, Anne-Marie Pathé, and Éléonore Testa. In the writing phase these last few years, I have benefited from day-to-day exchanges with Christian Ingrao, the current director of the IHTP, Fabrice d'Almeida, Vincent Auzas, Alain Bancaud, Rémy Besson, Anne Boigeol, Olivier Büttner, Juliette Denis, Catherine Hass, Anne Kerlan, Anne Pérotin-Dumon, Malika Rahal, and Fabien Théofilakis. My thanks to Caroline Chanteloup, Valérie Hugonnard, Morgane Jouve, Nicolas Schmidt, and Boris Videmann for their assistance.

For our many discussions about the practice of history, I owe a special debt of gratitude to Christian Delage and Peter Schöttler. Also to Christian Delacroix, François Dosse, and Patrick Garcia (who was kind enough to read through the manuscript); their seminar on historiography provided fertile soil for this book's development.

I have benefited greatly from the close and regular ties with my friends at the European Network for Contemporary History (EURHISTXX), which

I coordinate within the CNRS: Peter Apor, Paolo Capuzzo, Martin Conway, Norbert Frei, John Horne, Constantin Iordachi, Michael Kopecek, Konrad Jarausch, Pieter Lagrou, Marie-Claire Lavabre, Thomas Lindenberger, Guillaume Mouralis, Peter Romijn, Mariuccia Salvati, and Dariusz Stola.

Then, too, I would like to mention a few people who directly or indirectly contributed to this book: in the first place, Stéphane Audoin-Rouzeau—who was also kind enough to be one of its first readers—and Annette Becker, with whom (along with Nicole Edelman) I have long conducted a seminar at the Université de Nanterre. My thanks as well to Marc Abelès, Ora Avni, Jean-Pierre Azéma, François Azouvi, Omer Bartov, Leora Bilsky, Nathan Bracher, Bruno Chaouat, Myriam Chimènes, Jean-Marc Coicaud, Éric Conan, Olivier Dumoulin, Marc Ferro, Étienne François, Valeria Galimi, Antoine Garapon, Richard J. Golsan, François Hartog, Gerhard Hirschfeld, Bogumil Jewsiewicki, Alice Kaplan (who helped me so much for the American edition), Gerd Krumeich, Gérard Lenclud, Jocelyn Létourneau, Michael R. Marrus, Bertrand Muller, Pierre Nora, Michel Offerlé, Pascal Ory, Robert O. Paxton, Philippe Petit, Krzysztof Pomian, Renée Poznanski, Donald M. Reid, Philippe Roussin, Jean-François Sirinelli, Zeev Sternhell, Benjamin Stora, Susan Suleiman, Nicolas Werth, and Eli Zaretski.

I also wish to express my gratitude to Francis Hofstein, with whom I was able to find a few words to express the weight of the past.

Finally, to Hélène, who suffered stoically through the ordeal of a constantly unfinished book, and to Linda, because the future is not only an illusion of yesteryear.

"You Weren't There!"

The scene: the Institut d'Histoire du Temps Présent (Institute of History of the Present Time), a unit of the Centre National de la Recherche Scientifique (CNRS). On that day in 1989, the director, François Bédarida, was presiding at a meeting devoted to preparations for an international colloquium to be held the next year on "the Vichy regime and the French." A disagreement over content arose between him and two young researchers: the first was Denis Peschanski; I was the other. A renowned historian, the sixty-three-year-old Bédarida had lived through the Occupation as a student and Resistance fighter in the Témoignage Chrétien movement. Peschanski and I were both thirty-five and had committed ourselves to that institution, created a decade earlier to organize and develop a historiography of the contemporary. The discussion became heated, and tensions mounted. Suddenly, Bédarida exclaimed with authority and a touch of annoyance: "You didn't live through that period, you cannot understand!" An abrupt silence fell, the participants hesitating between laughter and astonishment.

And yet there was nothing unusual about that remark in a laboratory where different generations worked side by side. Researchers who as adolescents or adults had lived through Nazism, World War II, decolonization, Stalinism, or the barricades of spring 1968—all episodes that, among others, formed the object of the institute's research during that period—sometimes clashed with younger scholars, whose view of things rarely coincided with their elders' experience, even when that experience was reinterpreted through the prism of a historian's work. On that day, however, Bédarida's reaction hit me hard. I suddenly found it out of place, almost absurd, given that "not having been part of it" was in principle a characteristic proper to the historian. But the remark seemed all the stranger in that it resounded in a place that had taken up the task of working on the near past, defending the idea that such work was not only possible but also necessary at a scientific, political, and ethical level. And the foremost trait of the near past is precisely the presence of actors who have lived through the events the historian is studying and may be able to bear witness to them, to engage in a dialogue with younger people regarding already relatively distant episodes. Historians of the present time, if they have not directly experienced everything within their field of observation, can at least speak with those who have. They are witnesses to the witness. Historians may even be the first to speak to the witness, if they have taken the initiative to question him or her; or they may be the last to have been able to speak to the witness while he or she was still alive. Bédarida's reaction therefore made complete sense: of the historians present, he was the only one to have actually lived through the events under discussion and thus had an apparent advantage over everyone else, to which he laid claim and which he intended to make known.

For historians, coping with the exclamation that they are "not part of it" means learning to deal with two prejudices that are antinomic and at the same time well rooted in the public's mind. The first is that good history is possible only with the passage of time, or even that the historian cannot come onto the scene until all the actors being studied have already made their exit. In that conception of their craft, historians observe a bygone past, a history that is over; they act only in the time of the dead, even if, in so doing, they bring the dead back to life on paper. Over those who have come before, historians possess in this view the absolute advantage of claiming the last word, by virtue of an interpretation that purports to be objective, distant, and cool, of facts that have become historical because their effects have ceased to affect the present. That prejudice still had some legitimacy in the late 1970s, especially in higher education, where choosing to focus on contemporary history could mean giving up the prospect of a prestigious career: the real historian was personified by the medievalist or the modernist. The development or creation at that moment, everywhere in Europe, of institutions charged with working on the near past was an indication of a change in attitude in that respect. The second prejudice takes almost the opposite tack: it holds that experience prevails over knowledge, that historical narration will never really be able to replace direct testimony (*témoignage*), and that the professional's claim to tell the truth about the past is a scientistic illusion.[1] It is the individual who took part who must first contribute in person to an authentic discourse about the near past, before yielding the floor to others, who will have nothing more than traces and the direct testimony of others. Bédarida knew better than anyone the impact of that belief, since he was immersed in an environment where the war-veteran witness, the Resistance fighter witness, the former-deportee witness occupied a growing place in debates and controversies about the recent past. More precisely, this was a time when historians were beginning to become cognizant of the presence and contribution in the public space of these witnesses, moral figures and social actors who first made their appearance in the days immediately following World War I. Frictions sometimes arose between them and historians, even those who were close to the witnesses. The situation also gave rise to controversies among historians themselves, between—to take the two extremes—those who rejected a priori any evidential value to oral testimony and those who, on the contrary, felt an almost religious awe for the witness, especially the victim witness. Bédarida was thus in an ideal position to assess the difficulty of that confrontation between acquired knowledge and reconstituted memories, even as, by virtue of his life's journey and his age, he was torn between these two major modes of representing the past. On that day in 1989, he forgot for an instant his professional habitus and gave free rein to his subjectivity, yet without ceasing to be a historian of the present time. More than that, he seemed to be intimating that the only true historian was one who had been a witness to the events being studied, thus adopting the same posture as the Greek historian Thucydides. The difference was that, during the events—the period of the French occupation—the young Bédarida could not have known that he would one day become a historian of that period. And there is a great distance between the direct and ingenuous experience of a historical moment and the production of an informed narrative of the event. It is one thing to observe one's time consciously, with the aim of producing a narrative account, as Thucydides had done, and another to appeal to one's memories of youth long after the fact and use them as elements in a credible historical narrative.

Although still somewhat green at the time, I began with that episode to understand that the history of the present time that we were purporting to found entailed an approach marked through and through by the tension, sometimes even the opposition, between history and memory, knowledge and experience, distance and proximity, objectivity and subjectivity, researcher and witness. All these cleavages can exist within the same person. Like other ways of doing history, that branch of the discipline must take into account different temporalities and a particular dialectic between the past and the present. The time it examines belongs primarily to the realm of the imaginary. In the real, different generations, different perceptions of what is remote and what near, diverse approaches to what is experienced and transmitted, exist side by side. The present time is in that respect a scientific fiction, in the same sense that there are literary or legal fictions. Amnesty, for example, erases a prison sentence by a formal decision that functions "as if" the conviction had not taken place, but without seeking to efface the memory of the crime itself, even less to oblige the victim to forget. The fiction here makes it possible to act in the present—to forgive or to empty out the prisons—without being entirely dependent on the weight of the past, which in any case will continue to produce its effects. Historians of the present time, for their part, act "as if" they could seize hold of time as it passes, freeze an image, and observe the transition between present and past—slow down the process of time's retreat and the oblivion that lies in wait for any human experience. The fiction consists, therefore, of not considering the present a single moment beyond reach, like Heraclitus's river—into which one never steps twice—but of conferring on it a substantiality, a perspective, a time frame, as all historians engaged in periodization do. The difficulty is not insurmountable: even for contemporaries of the events studied, the present time cannot be reduced to a fleeting instant. Their consciousness, their unconscious (which supposedly knows nothing of time), and their memory confer on it a time frame, which is more a perception than a tangible reality but which alone allows them to give meaning to the events experienced. That time frame, that specific temporality, can be identified as a "contemporaneity," a term that applies to everything we recognize as belonging to our own time, including the tradition, the traces, the recollection of bygone eras. Contemporaneity, as it happens, is not unique to recent periods. Since the first appearance of forms of culture, societies have lived in a present marked by the weight, sometimes the burden, of the past, a present open as well to the possibilities, even the uncertainties of the future. The perception of time, however, may well have evolved considerably. When historians observe a historical actor of that bygone past, they must constantly keep in mind the "having-been" of that actor, who lived and acted in a present time that no longer exists but that has to be reconstituted, as we are enjoined to do by an entire epistemological tradition from Raymond Aron to Reinhart Koselleck to Paul Ricoeur. The particularity of the history of the present time is that it takes an interest in its *own* present, in a context where the past is not over and gone, where the subject of one's narrative is a "still-there." Inevitably, there will be a few pitfalls.

It has been the ambition of the history of the present time, a movement that arose between the 1950s and the 1970s (depending on the place) and that reinvented a tradition dating back to the Greek origins of historiography, to understand and overcome these pitfalls. The object of this book is to retrace the evolution, to grasp the driving forces, to explain the paradigms and presuppositions of that branch of the historical discipline, which within a few decades has moved from the margins to the center. Has the history of the present time really always existed? Does it have properties peculiar to itself, or is it only one aspect, without distinctive traits, of a general historiography? What changes occurred in the last third of the twentieth century that made it appear that the discipline as a whole had been transformed? Those are a few of the questions I wish to raise here. The notion of a history of the present time has found a place in the international historiographical landscape precisely because it has a history and specific characteristics that can answer questions both conjunctural and universal. Although its legitimacy has now been acknowledged, that form of history continues to give rise to reservations and criticisms, less about its feasibility as such (that was the case in the nineteenth century) than about the epistemological choices that a part of that movement has made in the last two decades. As I will show at length in this book, the term "history of the present time" is, in this sense, not the same as "contemporary history." Every national tradition has its own way of characterizing the near past. That diversity reflects sometimes long-standing, sometimes recent traditions and different epistemological choices, historical objects, and stances in the public space. The polysemy of the notion of contemporaneity is not the least difficulty historians face, whether they are seeking to understand times past or their own time. That notion not only refers to a temporality, it not only signifies a proximity in time (and hence a curiosity about one's own time); it also refers to other forms of proximity: in space, in the imaginary. The presence of the most remote past can sometimes have more weight than events closer in time. In addition, it is possible to have very little in common with one's fellow living creatures and, on the contrary, a great proximity to ancestors of another time or even another place, assuming they are rediscovered and given an actuality in the present. That observation, apparently banal, raises countless questions. They are the object of this book, whose epistemological orientation is relatively well defined at both the intellectual and the institutional level: that of a history that has come face to face with the tragedies of the last century and, already, with those of this century, still in its infancy. That movement—or, rather, that practice of history—has attempted to outline empirically a way of doing and thinking about history when it reaches or even exceeds the limit of the comprehensible and the acceptable. It can be found anywhere that the recent past has seared its brand into bodies, minds, territories, objects.

In an article published in 2006, the historian Antoine Prost proclaimed that "the history of the present time is one history among others," denouncing a "pseudo-concept" forged for purely circumstantial reasons.[2] The astonishingly vindictive tone of this seven-page text lies in the claim that this movement, having won the battle of legitimacy, must now abandon the standard under which its victory was possible. No new banner is proposed, however, as if that branch of the discipline had to be dispossessed of its name and identity in the interest of epistemological imperialism, or perhaps out of resentment—neither of which is declared openly. And yet that historiographical practice does in fact possess a few singularities, which cannot be wiped out by the stroke of a pen. Of the four major periods of Western historiography—antiquity, the Middle Ages, the modern era, and the contemporary age—only the parameters of the last are constantly shifting and in dispute. Depending on the place and the national tradition, the contemporary may begin in 1789, 1917, 1945, or even 1989. As for its end date, it is by definition always moving, another banal but important difference. Of these four periodizations, contemporary history is the only one to be the object of recurrent disagreements, not about the interpretation of the temporal sequences themselves—there are debates about the end of antiquity or of the Middle Ages, just as there are about the beginning of contemporary history— but about its feasibility, its significance, even its name. Furthermore, the question "What does it mean to be contemporary?" belongs to an inquiry that arose in the nineteenth century and is not confined to historical reflection. It is pervasive in philosophy, anthropology, art history, and musicology, each of which uses the adjective "contemporary" in its own way. There is an epistemological question here on which historians must take a position, as I attempt to do here, by inquiring into the long evolution of a practice that purports to do the history of its own time; into the conjuncture specific to the twentieth century, which ultimately gave it a particular configuration; and, finally, into the variables and invariables that make it possible to identify the singularities of that way of thinking about history within the discipline as a whole.

Rather than take at face value the clichés that tell us time and again that "all history is contemporary" and that the practice dates back to the origins of the discipline, I first seek to understand what the term "contemporary" and the notions of contemporary history or history of the present time might mean concretely over the *longue durée*, starting from my own experience (the study of the history and memory of major recent conflicts) and moving backward in time. Then I focus my attention on the twentieth century, which gradually saw the emergence of an institutionalized history of the present time, with its own methods, paradigms, debates, and detractors within a historical profession that has itself profoundly changed. My intent in that section is not to propose a scholarly history of contemporaneity, but rather to situate within the longest time frame possible the generally accepted hypothesis that contemporary history has been gaining prominence since the 1970s. I linger on the last third of the twentieth century, because there is currently a debate about whether it introduced a change in the "regime of historicity," an expression that has become quite popular in French historiography in the last few years but is little discussed elsewhere. The term "historicity" (*Geschichtlichkeit* in German) came into being at the same time as the philosophy of history, within the context of the debate on historicism. Taken in its most basic meaning, it designates the specifically temporal—hence evolving, variable, limited, and mortal—character of human beings and societies and implies that the knowledge they may produce about themselves also has a limit, a finitude, especially when compared to traditional metaphysics. The meaning of the term changed at the impetus of anthropology, which designates by that term both "a wealth of events" (a phrase coined by Claude Lévi-Strauss) in a given society and a means of differentiating societies from one another, notably through the famous distinction between "hot" and "cold" societies, or between "cultures that move and those that do not." Added to this meaning is the essential idea that historicity is a self-consciousness or a self-perception, a subjective image that human beings or societies have of their own temporal dimension. In the 1960s historians such as François Hartog and anthropologists such as Gérard Lenclud, themselves influenced by Marshall Sahlins, used the question of the "regime of historicity" to form a bridge between their two disciplines so as to put an end to a decade of contentiousness regarding the question of the historical versus the structural. The notion took on a broader sense within the context of the 1980s–2000s, when an intense debate developed about the respective place in present-day societies of the past, the present, and the future:

> Consequently, the expression "regime of historicity" refers first—at least logically—to the type of relation that any society maintains with its past, to the way

it treats and deals with the past before using it (and in order to use it) and constitutes the sort of thing we call history—the way a society treats its past and
deals with its past. In ascending order of activism in treatment: the way a society
arranges the cultural frameworks that lay out the means by which its past af-
fects it (beyond what the fact that it has a past implies for every society), the
way that past is present in its present (more than it might necessarily be), the
way it fosters or buries it, reconstructs it, constitutes it, mobilizes it, and so on.
There would thus be an entire range of attitudes linked to cultural variability:
in one place, the past is a *magistra vitae*, a "life guide," in another, an unbearable
burden, elsewhere, an inexhaustible resource, a rare asset. . . . The regime of
historicity defines a culturally delimited, hence conventional form of relation to
the past; historiography is one of these forms and, as a genre, an element symp-
tomatic of an all-encompassing regime of historicity.[3]

That notion, beyond its theoretical interest, has sparked research on the
history and sociology of memory, on the representations and uses of the
past, on the history of history, since it postulates that not only are societies
historical, but also that their way of thinking about themselves in time and
space has a history, a variability. Hence the use of the term "regime," which
conjures up the idea of several different types of relation to time, which
may follow one after another or may coexist in a single place or at a single
moment. To work on regimes of historicity is thus not simply to focus on
historiography—the evolution of historians' writings—but also to postulate
that the way of envisioning time, in this case the present time, constitutes
an essential element for understanding a given society at a given moment.
Hartog, for example, has recently developed the hypothesis that since 1989
we have been living in a "presentist" regime of historicity, which succeeded
a "futurist" regime that began in 1789. The domination of the future as cultural horizon (progress, revolution, growth), including its worst variations
such as totalitarian millenarianism, has been supplanted by the domination
of the present: "without a future and without a past, [the present] generates
from day to day the past and future it needs day after day and valorizes the
immediate."[4] I share that view in great part, but with a few differences and
variations, which I explain later in this book. They have to do with the link
between presentism and the emergence of a new history of the present time,
which I see less as a symptom than as a reaction, and concern the moment
when one regime of historicity ceded to another: in my opinion, the evolu-
tions in the relation to time in the Western world, and especially the question of contemporaneity, began in the 1970s (hence before the fall of the
Berlin Wall) and can therefore be explained by factors other than the end

of the Cold War and of the Soviet system. Finally, though the present now indisputably constitutes a dominant and even invasive category, though it influences in particular the way we view recollections of the near past, it is nevertheless true that these recollections, that memory, unfold for the most part under the rather traditional regime of a burden of the past, a haunting past, even if the solutions proposed for facing them often entail a form of presentism.

In that respect, I was struck to discover—after others—the degree to which, since the French Revolution, the phenomenon of war has marked the historical time of the modern West. The frames of reference used by the actors and historians to delimit the contemporary era are usually the ends of wars or sometimes the beginnings of wars: the end of World War I, the end of World War II, the end of the Cold War, to which could be added the two major revolutions of 1789 and 1917, the first having led to a long string of wars in Europe, the second having resulted in part from World War I. At a deeper level, most of the ends of wars or revolutions gave rise to a strong increase of interest in contemporary history, when they did not purely and simply create a new regime of historicity (as after 1789). Interest in the near past thus seems ineluctably connected to a sudden eruption of violence and even more to its aftereffects, to a time following the explosive event, a time necessary for understanding it, becoming cognizant of it, but a time marked as well by trauma and by strong tensions between the need to remember and the temptation to forget. That, in any case, is the hypothesis I develop here, relying on the lapidary and compelling definition that all contemporary history begins with "the latest catastrophe," or in any case with the latest that seems most telling, if not the closest in time.

When, then, does the respective present of an age begin? It begins with the latest constitutive event, the one that determines its existence. For a happy couple, the present originates on the wedding day. If we begin with that example, we could say that every present of a given age begins with the latest catastrophe. Granted, that term might mask the essential. Almost every people—to confine ourselves from this point forward to the history of peoples—has experienced the same latest catastrophe, World War II. But it is not the mere fact of having been subjected to catastrophes, however violent they may have been, that on its own marks the origin of the present. The present does not begin everywhere in 1945, but the present of the historical structure of those subjected to the catastrophe begins with it.[5]

In this text, which is rather difficult stylistically, the definition of the history of the present time—*Zeitgeschichte* in German—swings back and forth between a joke and an erudite assertion. Its author, Hermann Heimpel, was a member of the academic establishment of postwar Germany and, notably, the director of the Max Planck Institute for History in the late 1950s. His writings and life story illustrate the ambivalence of contemporary German historiography, which is undoubtedly the paradigmatic model for some of the problems I try to raise in this book. Heimpel, after demonstrating his allegiance to the Nazi regime and being named to the Reichsuniversität installed in Strasbourg after the defeat of France, was also one of the first after the war to confront the question of German guilt. He may even have contributed, in the 1950s and later, to forging the ambiguous concept of *Vergangenheitsbewältigung*, the need to come to terms with the Nazi past, a notion that would occupy a central place in the history of the Federal Republic of Germany (I consider this point in chapter 3).[6] In that sense, the term "catastrophe" has a long history in the post-Nazi context. It was used in the late 1940s to dilute the specific responsibilities of the Germans in a euphemism that encompassed both the victims of the Nazis and the suffering of the German people in general. In the 1980s it became widespread in its Hebrew version—*Shoah*—following Claude Lanzmann's film by that name. It now designated the uniqueness and singularity of the extermination of the Jews, though without really managing to replace the term "Holocaust," used in the English-speaking world. By imitation or in reaction, the word "catastrophe" subsequently spread as a means to designate the original and founding tragedy of the identity of certain peoples: for example, the Palestinian term *Nakba* refers to the mass expulsions of 1948.

The term "catastrophe" must therefore be understood here in its etymological sense, both as an "upheaval" and an "end" in ancient Greek, often with insurmountable consequences; but also, in Latin, as a "denouement" and "coup de théâtre" in the literary and dramaturgical sense of the term. That historiographical conception, the premises of which date back to 1917–18, emphasizes that the catastrophe is a provisional origin of a present time whose fleetingness it accepts. In that respect, it belongs to a discontinuous view of history, deviating from the logic of revolutionary modernity, which rested instead on the idea of a continuity, a linearity, a fulfillment, moving in the direction of progress in particular. But that modernity itself arose from a major rupture in the course of history, or at least Western history: "Whenever an event occurs that is great enough to illuminate its own past, history comes into being. Only then does the chaotic maze of past happenings emerge as a story which can be told, because it has a beginning and an end. . . . What the illuminating event reveals is a beginning in the past which had hitherto been hidden; to the eye of the historian, the illuminating event cannot but appear as an end of this newly discovered beginning. Only when in future history a new event occurs will this 'end' reveal itself as a beginning to the eye of future historians."[7]

Granted, the notion causes a few difficulties, since it is unusual for a historical human catastrophe to be perceived unanimously and universally as such. At least it can be said that the catastrophes of the twentieth century that serve as our points of reference stem from a relatively novel situation: over time, both the victors and the vanquished of the two world wars ultimately came to believe that they were in the presence of calamities unprecedented in the history of humanity, even though the responsibility borne by each is sometimes still a matter of debate. In making that remark, I concur with Jean-Pierre Dupuy, whose defense of an "enlightened catastrophism" cannot fail to resonate with the view developed here. Parallel to the need to think lucidly in the present about future catastrophes, there may be a need to think just as lucidly, and just as much in the present, about the historical catastrophes of the recent past that served as a starting point: "It was in the last century that humanity became capable of destroying itself, either directly by nuclear war or indirectly through the deterioration of the conditions necessary for its survival. The crossing of that threshold had been in the offing for a long time, but it made manifest and critical what had until then been only a potential danger."[8]

There is thus a certain consensus that the catastrophes of the twentieth century, and in particular World War II, inaugurated a new contemporaneity marked not by optimism, as some believed in the 1960s (they made the year 1945 the starting point for a new world full of promise: Europe, growth, peace), but rather by pessimism. That spirit of the time gives precedence, in the matter of collective memory, to the most lethal moments of the near past, those that have had the most difficulty "passing away." The project of a new history of the present time has not been to go along with that obsessive, traumatic vision of the past, but rather to promote an understanding of it, to regard that history with detachment despite its persistence in memory. That historiography has had to provide interpretive keys, though these have often been incomplete and uncertain. It has had to confront the major phases of the anamnesis of the Nazi past and of the history of decolonization, even as it sought its own epistemological foundations. That is one of its principal characteristics and no doubt the greatest source of its fragility. Moreover,

by dating the present time from the latest catastrophe, we define the contemporary in structural terms (certain catastrophes have always punctuated
historical time) as much as we delineate a particular conjuncture: our own
regime of historicity is defined in great part by the difficulty of getting over
the memory of the recent major catastrophes, hence of reestablishing a certain historical continuity of longer duration. That is the last point taken up
in this book, in which I seek to understand the respective share of invariables that allow us to define "contemporaneity"—for example, the presence
of living actors who can bear witness in person—and of variables, especially
periodizations, that differ from one author, one culture, and one country
to another and are often dependent on ideological or intellectual a prioris.

I first conceived of this book as a manifesto, an offensive. Over time, the
project mutated into a more open inquiry. In this book, which is neither a
treatise on epistemology nor a normative essay on the proper way to write
history, I propose more simply a reflection on a certain way of thinking
about the history of the present time. The book became possible only because of my practical research in the field and my habit of studying sensitive periods, which led me to regard my discipline in a particular manner.
I do not claim in this book to represent all the possible modes for writing a
contemporary history: it belongs to the very conjuncture it analyzes. I analyze present-day societies in terms of the relations they maintain with the
past, on the basis of the historiographical situation in France, Germany, and
the English-speaking world. For lack of time, space, and competence, I have
been unable to include elements from Italian and Spanish historiography
and from certain Latin American countries, whose situations fall to a degree
within the perspective developed here. In all those places, contemporary history has assumed an incomparably greater role than it previously had, both
in academia and in the public space. It now attracts a large proportion of the
history students, courses in history, and resources allotted to the discipline
as a whole in many countries. That was unthinkable thirty years ago, when
the present time belonged almost exclusively, at best, to the other social
sciences, and at worst, to enlightened journalism. In addition, recent history
has attracted a growing number of writers, feature and documentary filmmakers, and artists of all sorts. Countless blogs, Web sites, and forums are
devoted to it, from the wackiest to the best informed. That evolution signals
the emergence of a new curiosity and of an expectation about the intelligibility of the recent past.

At the same time, the place of history in general has changed in nature. The notions of memory and heritage have invaded scholarship and the public space. Testimony has taken on the appearance of a social and moral imperative. To judge political crimes sometimes half a century old, temporal justice systems have been turned into "tribunals of world history." Nation-states have devoted a great many resources and a good deal of energy to setting in place national or international "public policies of the past." In the public mind, in ordinary language, the past has become a problem to be solved. It is now common to hear that societies, groups, or individuals must "face up to," "confront," or "cope with" the past; or that one must "come to terms with" or "master" the past. It is a strange metaphor when you think about it, since, literally, it means either that we put the past in a place that is in principle not its own, namely, in front of us; or that we constantly have our backs turned to the future in order to face the past, a concrete illustration of Walter Benjamin's prophetic vision upon viewing Paul Klee's *Angelus Novus*. Vis-à-vis history, and especially recent history, contemporary societies thus seem to maintain a relation deeply marked by conflict: personal or collective conflicts originating in insuperable traumas; wars of memory, public polemics, and scientific controversies, often all mixed up together. History no longer unfolds in the first place as traditions to be respected, legacies to be transmitted, knowledge to be elaborated, or deaths to be commemorated, but rather as problems to be "managed," a constant "work" of mourning or of memory to be undertaken. That is how deep-seated the idea has become that the past must be wrested free from the limbo of oblivion and that only public or private mechanisms can exhume it. The past has thus become a substance that can and even must be acted upon, adapted to the needs of the present. It is now a realm of public action. The imperative for truth characteristic of the historical method has turned into a social imperative for recognition, into policies of atonement, apologies, and expressions of "repentance" directed at the victims of the recent major catastrophes. It is within that context that a new history of the present time has developed, one that— barely on its feet—is summoned to respond to the challenges of the anamnesis of a near past in its lethal version, to the need for atonement (involving the mass consumption of expertise), to the imperatives of an omnipresent discourse on "memory," a term that has gradually lost some of its clarity even as the phenomenon has increased in importance. These historians of the present time, sometimes against their will, sometimes caught up in the exaltation of actions far removed from their training as detached observers, have themselves become actors in a history still being made.

CHAPTER ONE

Contemporaneity in the Past

AN OLD PROBLEM?

Every school and current of contemporary history has for the past thirty years undergone a development that was still unforeseeable in the 1970s. But that does not mean that the field is an innovation with no antecedents. "The history of the present time is an old story!" writes Antoine Prost.[1] That remark comports with one of the most widespread obsessions in the historian's craft: that of reducing every innovation to something we have already seen before and providing an inexhaustible list of antecedents that point out how pretentious it is to see the brand-new where there is only repetition. But the affirmation also expresses a certain reality that not only has never been disputed but, on the contrary, has often been invoked to ground the new history of the present time in a long tradition. For historians, the practice of writing the history of their own time is as old as their appearance on the scene as scholars, at least at first glance. It has been a key characteristic of their art or discipline, whatever their status over the ages. Once we are reminded of that obvious fact, there would be no reason to inquire about the particulars of that history; on the contrary, there would be good reasons to fall back into line without further delay.

There is a great distance, however, between what appears to be obvious and a more precise observation. Thucydides and Eric Hobsbawm may have both written about their own eras, but they did so with a few differences: after all, classical Greece and post-1945 Europe provide dissimilar contexts. Likewise, the place of contemporary history in scholarly studies and in its relation to power and society has not remained so immutable over three millennia that we need only point out a permanence, an invariability. As for the obvious—so far as it goes—historians have always focused on the history of their own time but have not done so in the same manner, with the same methods, or to the same ends. To this day, there is no comprehensive scholarly study on how the history of the near past has been conceived and received, intellectually and socially, across time. Although there has long been an interest in the history of the perception and measurement of time, there are no or very few systematic studies on the specific history of contemporaneity, a problem rarely raised as such in historiographical studies. In his *Douze leçons sur l'histoire* (1996; *Twelve Lessons on History*), one of the key works in French on the epistemology of history, Antoine Prost does not say a word about the notion, even though the emergence of the history of the present time constituted an important phenomenon in European historiography during the writing of the book and gave rise to a number of debates and controversies, especially after the fall of the Berlin Wall.[2] It is therefore pointless to maintain that the practice of a history of the present time has existed for all eternity, unless one is prepared to outline, at least sketchily, a history of the notion of present time itself. A tall order, to be sure, given the erudition required, even if one limits oneself to the Western world.[3] There are too many differences in the conceptions and perceptions of time over the *longue durée* for the notion of contemporaneity to be easily compared from one age to another. Yet that digression is indispensable for understanding certain recent debates, or in any case, for situating them within the *longue durée*. In what follows, I shall respond in part to the reproach sometimes made of historians of the present time, namely, that they never take into account that *longue durée* and situate themselves almost exclusively within the short term of the event.[4] That reproach can sometimes lead to odd accusations: if we are to believe the report commissioned in 2008 by the Ministry of Culture, a preliminary version of the plan (eventually aborted) for a "House of French History" desired by President Nicolas Sarkozy, the history of the present time, merely by virtue of its existence, has slowed the development of research on the *longue durée*. Supposedly, it is even one of the causes of the difficulty the French have had "in taking on their history in its entirety": "Research and debates on 'the history of the present time' have sometimes overshadowed analyses of phenomena over the *longue durée* and have given rise to epistemological and methodological disputes. The transfer to all historical periods of the methods specific to the 'history of the very contemporary,' especially in the case of political and social history, has tended to render null and void the old frames of reference: chronology, epistemology of sources, historical geography, and so on."[5]

Philippe Pétain's negative legacy has thus allegedly overshadowed the positive legacy of Joan of Arc, and the history of the present time has made us lose interest in chronology. As for epistemological debates, they are said to constitute in and of themselves a threat to national history. The argument could be shrugged off if that report had not served as the basis for one of the most controversial cultural projects of recent years on the part of the French government, and if it were not an example of recurrent criticisms of the history of the present time, which struggle to come up with serious arguments.

The adjective "contemporary," taken from the Latin *contemporaneus—cum* plus *tempus*, "pertaining to a single shared time"—appeared in about 1475, if we are to believe the *Trésor de la langue française* (*Treasury of the French Language*). The term "contemporary history" seems to be of later date, at least in its modern sense: an instance of it can be found, notably, in Pascal's *Pensées*, a point to which I will return. The term became widespread much later, however—in the nineteenth century, after the cultural and cognitive shock of the French Revolution. Balzac's novel *L'envers de l'histoire contemporaine* (*The Wrong Side of Contemporary History*) appeared in 1848, and Taine published his *Origines de la France contemporaine* (*Origins of Contemporary France*) beginning in 1875. It was then that the meaning now familiar to us emerged, namely, the study of a time that is the observer's own and of a distinct historical sequence that gradually came to complete the tripartite scheme of Western historiography (ancient, medieval, and modern) articulated around two major breaks: the fall of the Western Roman Empire and the Renaissance. Although the respective dating of these two events continued to change depending on the school or author, the demarcation itself assumed the dimension of a canonical periodization.[6] It emerged in the midfifteenth century among the Italian humanists, who wanted to mark the clear distance of their own age from a past they called the "Middle Ages," a term that appeared in 1469 in the writings of the pontifical librarian Giovanni Andrea dei Bussi. That division was popularized in historiographical studies of the late seventeenth century, notably in the writings of the German Cristoph Keller, known as Cellarius.[7] It is therefore a long tradition that has survived to our time, having been complemented in the nineteenth century by a fourth period—"contemporary"—it too elaborated to create distance from a "modernity" that had grown old and changed in nature after the Revolution of 1789. That traditional periodization, however, has been subject to constant criticism. Reinhart Koselleck, for example, sees it as an illusion of a linear and a homogeneous time, which keeps us from seeing "the contemporaneity of the noncontemporary in history" even though "every one of us can see that we still have contemporaries living in the Stone Age."[8] Jack Goody denounced that demarcation and its global interpretation of history as having been imposed by European civilization on the rest of the world, especially during the phase of colonial expansion.[9] Hence the other illusion: that civilizations existing in a single time, even though they are dissimilar, must inevitably go through the same evolution toward progress, democracy, and the market. They are required to "catch up," thanks in part to the aid of the Western world, which is supposed to show them the way. That illusion has sometimes had lethal consequences, including, quite recently, in Iraq and Afghanistan. The very notion of a regime of historicity has had the effect of deconstructing the idea of an equivalence among biological, social, and cultural time while further accentuating the ambivalence and ambiguities of the word "contemporary." A single time does not mean a single space; a single era does not cover a single cultural universe; and within a single age, structures, ideas, and practices that have evolved differently with respect to a past stand side by side, and that past itself must be analyzed in terms of a differentiated evolution.

In spite of all that, the traditional periodization persists in the discipline of history. In addition to suiting the professional habitus, it undoubtedly responds to a more general need, as Michel de Certeau writes: "Historiography first separates its present from a past. But everywhere it repeats the gesture of dividing. Hence its chronology is composed of 'periods' (for example, Middle Ages, Modern History, Contemporary History), between which the *decision* is made to be *other* or *no longer* what has been until then (the Renaissance, the Revolution). One by one, every 'new' time has given rise—has give a *place*—to a discourse that treats as 'dead' what preceded but which receives a 'past' already marked by prior breaks."[10]

We are undoubtedly contemporaries with individuals or groups still living in the Stone Age, but the very act of identifying them as such, hence of casting them back to an *other* time because of their differences, illustrates the need for a distinction between *today* and *yesteryear* that characterizes modern historicity. Although doing the history of one's own time is a practice that appears very old at first sight, the singularization, then the conceptualization, of an explicitly contemporary history—not to mention of the very notion of contemporaneity—in reality developed in the nineteenth and twentieth centuries.

It may seem presumptuous to retrace the history of these notions over the *longue durée*, even in broad outline, but I believe it is necessary if we are to understand the emergence of a new history of the present time in the late 1970s. The question then arose whether a new practice, a new way of doing history, had to be invented from whole cloth within a context where the entire discipline was in intellectual turmoil, or whether an abandoned tradition had to be revived. Some sought legitimacy for that practice in a tradition as old as history itself, while others insisted on its innovative character. But both claimed a place for it within a profession that assigned to it a certain institutional marginality, when it did not view it with suspicion. In 1978 a collection was published on the "new history," a coinage by the publishers that designated the profusion at the time of a constantly changing historiographical practice but one that continued to embrace the Annales School. In that collection, both Jean Lacouture and Pierre Nora argued for the constitution of a historiography of the contemporary, but they adopted different attitudes.[11] In the article devoted to "immediate history," another new term to designate contemporary history (also the name of a collection brought out by Éditions du Seuil, to which I shall return in chapter 4), Lacouture invokes Thucydides and Julius Caesar, Ibn Kaldūn and Charles de Gaulle, and the chroniclers Joinville, Froissart, and Commynes, as well as Michelet and Lissagaray, authors who all produced works "openly rooted in the present, a present they had experienced not only as witnesses but also as actors, sometimes as protagonists."[12] He nevertheless defends the idea that this form of history is truly novel, even as he recalls that understanding history in general (and not just contemporary history) as "a science of the past [that] finds its raison d'être, its nobility, and its justification only in the laborious extraction of its resources from the mountain of archives," is itself "a rather recent dogma," having appeared near the end of the French Second Empire. Nora, in his article "Présent" (an original choice of subject in the historiographical context of the time) takes little interest in contemporary history as it may have existed before the nineteenth century: "Was there a 'contemporary history' in the past? Saint Augustine, the Renaissance humanists, and Voltaire certainly had the sense they were living in a new era, but without its being linked, as it is for us, to the consciousness of a particular historical outlook."[13] He reminds us that the practice was in fact partially excluded from the field of history, which, by the 1870s, was becoming a full-fledged scientific discipline. Paradoxically, he identifies this as a founding moment, so as to better situate his own approach a century later. The debate attracted new interest in the 1970s and 1980s, when that exclusion became the negative reference point par excellence for the new history of the present time, which justified itself first and foremost by challenging the arguments on which the exclusion had relied. Nora even adopted a hypothesis to which I shall return in more detail: it was at the very moment when the notion of contemporaneity began to take root in the mental universe of the nineteenth century that the discipline of history, in the process of being professionalized, decided to separate contemporary history off from the rest of history, granting it a singularity because the identity of the discipline itself was reinforced by that act of exclusion.

In retrospect, and with the experience of a history of the present time now comfortably installed in the historiographical landscape, I believe the question needs to be asked differently. Why, in the late 1970s, did the development of contemporary history constitute an innovation within a discipline that was rapidly expanding and being rapidly reconfigured, whereas, a century earlier, in a more or less comparable context of innovation, contemporary history was instead perceived as a break, so much so that it was exiled into a sort of purgatory? Why did what seemed innovative in the late twentieth century arouse mistrust in the late nineteenth? Why, within a century, did contemporary history move from the margins to the center of the discipline? How, in the evolution of that practice, are we to sort out the structural elements linked to the position of historians working on "their" time, and the conjunctural elements belonging to different and changing contexts?

"EVERY HISTORY WORTHY OF THE NAME IS CONTEMPORARY"

The famous formulation by the Italian historian and philosopher Benedetto Croce that every history worthy of the name is contemporary has become almost a cliché. It means that any historical writing, whether about the recent or the remote past, has its source in the present: "If contemporary history springs straight from life, so too does that history which is called non-contemporary, for it is evident that only an interest in the life of the present can move one to investigate past fact. Therefore this past fact does not answer to a past interest but to a present interest, in so far as it is unified with an interest of the present life. This has been said again and again in a hundred ways by historians in their empirical formulas, and constitutes the reason, if not the deeper content, of the success of the very trite saying that history is *magistra vitae.*"[14]

Croce points out one of the characteristic traits of any historical approach, which contemporary history is not alone in taking into account:

the exemplary role of history and the fact that knowledge of the past must guide the actions of the present. Cicero had identified that trait nearly two thousand years before: "History . . . bears witness to the passing of the ages, sheds light upon reality, gives life to recollection and guidance to human existence [*magistra vitae*], and brings tidings of ancient days."[15] That idea of history as life guide created an inextricable link within the tradition between the past and the present. But that link also has a history. The formulation thus points out the degree to which history, as a process of knowing and understanding the world, is not a gratuitous, disinterested activity located outside the time of the person writing. It gives primacy to the historian over the historical object. Croce establishes a distinction between what he calls the "chronicle" and history: "The truth is that chronicle and history are not distinguishable as two forms of history, mutually complementary, or as one subordinate to the other, but as two different mental *attitudes*. History is living chronicle, chronicle is dead history; history is contemporary history, chronicle is past history; history is principally an act of thought, chronicle an act of will. Every history becomes chronicle when it is no longer thought, but only recorded in abstract words, which were once upon a time concrete and expressive."[16]

To write history is thus an intellectual act that extends beyond the mere narration of the facts and takes as its object the general; history stands opposed to the chronicle, which confines itself to the particular. Croce is defending an idealist conception in which, by virtue of traces—themselves living and present by definition—history *precedes* the chronicle ("first comes history, then chronicle") and even gives it a semblance of consistency: "external things do not exist outside the mind."[17] Robin G. Collingwood comments that Croce's notion is "a perfect synthesis of subject and object, inasmuch as the historian thinks himself into the history, and the two become contemporary."[18] Based on a reading of that famous passage from Croce, one can therefore conclude that history in general (and not only contemporary history in the strict sense) is contemporary in three ways. First, it is founded on traces accessible to observation and analysis, which, in their present state, provide the historian with a view of past entities whose original integrity is by definition inaccessible—even within the positivist conception, which postulates that this reality existed before the historian observes it. Second, it is an act of thinking that unfolds in the present, thanks to the work of an informed narrator who recounts the past. And third, it allows the historian to revive the past in the present and to *re-present* it, as Paul Ricoeur would later say, and even (if we follow Croce's rather radical position) to give it life in the first place, since in his view history does not exist outside the thought that produces it and gives it form after the fact.

Croce's theses are modern in that they were informed by the recent development of history as a scientific discipline, but they defend the primacy of the historiographical act over the illusion that history can be grasped "objectively," "as it really happened"—a dogma of nineteenth-century historicism. In spite of everything, however, they adopt an ancestral definition of history in the Western world, expressed in more or less constant form from the historians of antiquity to those of the modern age, a definition that does not separate the past from the present. We must not forget that the relation between the two was not the same before the break of 1789 and after it. Before, every history was contemporary, not because "historians of the present time" and "historians of times past" would, in spite of their differences, begin from the same premises or the same stance, but because history itself could not be conceived outside the present, because the history of a bygone past distinct from, even cut off from, the present time did not really have any meaning. Before the shock of the French Revolution, writing the history of one's time did not constitute a singular practice with respect to writing history plain and simple. In a certain way, the opposite was true, since there was practically no history except contemporary in the first sense of the term, a writing whose argument, structure, aims, and objects were essentially oriented by and through the present. Conceptions of time changed profoundly between the classical period and the modern period, but the distinction between a near past and a remote past, between the contemporary period and what preceded it, was a demarcation of the Revolution. For example, the Revolution created the notion of the ancien régime to designate a suddenly bygone past, though one still near and inscribed within a long tradition that had, in effect, to be destroyed. Inquiries that now appear to belong to the practice of contemporary history in the strict sense, such as the role of the witness or the weight of living memory, were raised from the start about history in general, whereas the question of "contemporaneity" quite simply did not arise—or, in any case, not in the terms familiar to us. "Modern Western history begins with the difference between the *present* and the *past*," writes Michel de Certeau, for whom the historiographical operation per se consists of a separation, a demarcation, a distinction.[19] History, in gradually emancipating itself from the religious tradition, became a scientific practice oriented toward understanding otherness, that of the men and women of the past, of change itself, of loss. Its mission was "to calm the dead who still haunt the present and to offer them scriptural tombs."[20] Over the course of the nineteenth century, history became the settling of a debt toward the dead, an entombment that therefore separated them from the living. Certeau identifies that break as occurring with Michelet. But what about before? How could historians conceive of a present time, a "contemporary" sequence, if they did not have the idea that a part of the past may be over and done with? What meaning could the term "contemporary" have in a historical time that was not thus split in two?

THE PRESENT TIME IN ANTIQUITY

If we adopt Hartog's view of the Greek and Roman period, which produced the first great historical narratives, the history of the "present," not the history of the "past," was truly the only one possible. We must keep in mind, however, that those terms did not have the same meaning they have now. The historian Herodotus, unlike the bards and reciters of epics, took as his exclusive area of competence "what happened because of men." In his *Histories*, he distinguishes between the time of the gods and that of men, which is to say, his own time. In that new conception of narrative, "the time of the gods and that of heroes," writes Hartog, "are 'pasts' that certainly took place, but they elude the knowledge of the historian looking back from the present." And he adds: "From the outset the historian, caught up in time and grappling with it, draws a line between past and present but does so on the basis of his own present, on the basis of the proper name he sends out into the world as he begins and which allows him to establish distance between 'now' or 'in my time' and 'before,' 'in times past.'"[21] Subjectivity, including temporal subjectivity, conditioned historical writing from the start: from the first sentence of the *Histories*, Herodotus of Halicarnassus takes the stage. The narration is the result of a direct observation of what he has seen, an *autopsis* (etymologically, "seen with one's own eyes"). It sets out to speak for posterity and distinguishes between two temporalities, since the history recounted is not only "contemporary" in the sense that it speaks of the historian's own time, but also establishes his authority by positing as inaccessible to observation a time other than the present time or the time of human beings.

That centrality of the eye can be found even more clearly in Thucydides:

Whereas the poets' *muthoi* are ageless and the *logoi* of the logographs [those who record in writing the narratives of the oral tradition] are of several different ages, the will to truth implies confining oneself to the present: there is no "true" history except in the present. Hence the (future) historian of the Peloponnesian War set to work just as hostilities were beginning. Of the two paths to historical knowledge, the eye (*opsis*) and the ear (*akoē*), only the former can lead (provided that good use is made of it) to a clear and distinct knowledge (*sáphos eidenai*): not only what I myself saw and what others say they saw, but on the condition that those observations (my own and that of others) withstand close analysis.[22]

Thucydides, despite his differences from Herodotus, thus expresses a similar position, so much so that some have seen him as a "historian of the present" who "set to work," in his own terms, "beginning from the first symptoms" of the war between Sparta and Athens and invented the fiction of a "history coming to you live."[23] To be as close as possible to *akribeia*—the truth, or rather, conformity to the facts reported—Thucydides too focuses on "his own time." On the very first page of *The War of the Peloponnesians and the Athenians*, he writes: "In respect of the preceding period and the still remoter past, the length of time that has elapsed made it impossible to ascertain clearly what happened; but from the evidence I find I can trust in pushing my enquiries back as far as possible, I judge that earlier events were not on the same scale, either as regards their wars or in other respects."[24]

Hartog points out, however, what might appear to be an original contradiction in that founding work. He reminds us that Thucydides "carries off the tour de force of giving both 'the clearest' exposition of Greece's past and the most clear-cut demonstration that 'true history' in the past tense is impossible."[25] He shows that the former Athenian general, by virtue of his quest for truth—which gives the expression "true history" its full meaning—was able to serve as a point of reference for the founders of positivist history in the nineteenth century, who were themselves in search of a method to capture history "as it actually happened." "But whereas the positivist historian thinks that the truth, in order to reveal itself, requires the silence of the archives and that history is therefore written in the past tense, Thucydides set out to demonstrate that 'true history' could be done only in the present."[26] Historians of the present time would not go so far as to make the Greek historians the inventors of "contemporaneity," which would not make much sense; nor would they reduce these texts to the single question of the relation between past and present. But the relationship thus established between an investigation of the world as it is, conducted by a singular subject writing about his own time, putting to use his own perspective and direct experience of the events, and situating his remarks within a search for the truth rooted in the present and oriented toward the future, has strong resonances for those now working on the history of the present time. So too that original link between history and politics, observation and action, between the one who "makes history" and the one who "does history," to borrow Certeau's distinction. For Thucydides, "the two activities find sustenance in the same material, the present, and assign themselves the same aim: utility for the future."[27] History is written for the good of the commonwealth, and there is no clear difference between what was, what is, and what shall be: the past is a repository of experiences for understanding the present and deciphering the future. "Perhaps the absence of the element of fable in my work may make it seem less easy on the ear; but it will have served its purpose well enough, if it is judged useful by those who want to have a clear view of what happened in the past and what—the human condition being what it is—can be expected to happen again some time in the future in similar or much the same ways. It is composed to be a possession for all time and not just a performance-piece for the moment."[28] Thus contemporaneity also signifies the historian's capacity to act on the present, either as an actor in the events described or because the act of narration itself has a political utility.

The importance of personal experience and the organic link between history and politics, past and present, can be found two centuries later in Polybius, then in the Roman tradition of exemplary history as *magistra vitae*: "Plato, as we know, tells us that human affairs will then go well when either philosophers become kings or kings study philosophy, and I would say that it will be well with history either when men of action undertake to write history, not as now happens in a perfunctory manner, but when in the belief that this is a most necessary and most noble thing they apply themselves all through their life to it with undivided attention, or again when would-be authors regard a training in actual affairs as necessary for writing history. Before this be so the errors of historians will never cease."[29]

Denis Roussel, translator of the French edition, cannot resist remarking that, "in general, the memoirs published by statesmen and generals, from Caesar to Winston Churchill, do not confirm Polybius's opinion."[30] That is undoubtedly true, and experience alone, even in the heat of action, is no guarantee of good history—far from it. All the same, the idea that the historian's direct experience, which by definition constitutes an element of contemporaneity in historical writings, can play a decisive role in the understanding of history is somewhat suggestive of the positions of Lucien Febvre and Marc Bloch. Despite the impossible comparison to Caesar and Churchill, Polybius's writings (like those of Thucydides), when read somewhat anachronistically, may find an echo in the historian of the present time writing today. That historian, in fact, constantly comes face to face with the legitimacy of the actor turned historian, an ancestral figure, to be sure, but one who is now able to use the same scientific methods, spend time in the archives, gain a familiarity with historiography, and thus not only match at times the professional researcher's own ability to produce knowledge, but also draw on an irreplaceable experience to write a contemporary history that is at once credible and "true."

History, then, originally constituted itself as a gaze and an action directed at the living, not as a study or recollection of the dead or as a debt to be paid to them. Contemporaneity in the strict sense was not singled out, because it was inherent in the historical method itself and there was thus no reason to establish it as a special category. In spite of everything, however, the practice of a history of one's own time gave rise to reservations about history itself, a history—we may note in passing—where war, violence, and sound and fury were omnipresent. To narrate history (close at hand) was neither without risks nor without effects, as the poet Horace expressed it in his famous ode to Asinius Pollio, a contemporary of his and the historian of the fratricidal struggle between Caesar and Pompey:

> Your theme is civil warfare, since Metellus
> Was consul. To describe its causes, phases
>   And crimes, Fortune's caprice,
> The doomed alliance of triumvirs,
>
> The blood-smeared weapons still unexpiated,
> Is to traverse a field sown thick with hazards,
>   Pollio: you tread on fire
> Still smouldering underneath deceptive ash.
>
> Yet do not leave our theatre long deserted
> By your stern tragic Muse. Soon, when the history
>   Is ordered on the page,
> Renew your high vocation, don again
>
>   The Attic buskin.[31]

The above excerpt could be used as an epigraph to many current historical works on the present time. It expresses the tension between a history judged to be still raging, its memory still raw—in this case, a civil war—and the wish in spite of everything for a respite, a latency period, the possibility of forgetting momentarily, which will allow contemporaries to breathe a little and the historian to make sense of the events, to order them on the page, before once again assuming the elevated, tragic, even pompous tone that befits historical narration. That is the meaning of the expression "don again / The Attic buskin," which alludes to the high-heeled cork boots worn onstage in Athens. That tension has pervaded all contemporary historiography, and, moreover, all contemporary culture of the last thirty years. Alongside the question of the historian's relation to political action and the importance of one's own subjectivity and one's own experience, that tension constitutes a constant element of all contemporary history.

THE ETERNAL PRESENT OF THE MIDDLE AGES

A first sight, it seems even more inappropriate to speak of contemporaneity within the context of the medieval West than for the classical period, in that conceptions of time changed radically with the advent of Christianity and then the development of urban mercantile societies in the early thirteenth century. "Pagan historians saw world history as cyclical. Civilizations flourished, they were born and died one after another. History studied times that were forever starting over again. But Christianity imposed a linear conception of time. The entire history of the world from its creation to its end unfolded within a single time. A rational Christian historian thus had to follow the whole history of the world in a single movement, from its creation to its end. . . . There was no difference in nature between history and prophecy, [and] strictly speaking, for a Christian historian there was truly only one time."[32]

The linearity of time can also be found in the dynastic chronicles, which inscribe the current sovereign's action within a long lineage that may date back to the Old Testament and within an eschatological perspective where his actions, divine in nature, can be understood only in terms of the promise of salvation, with no division between past, present, and future. Jacques Le Goff, commenting on Saint Louis's reparations of the royal necropolis of Saint Denis, to which the remains of the sixteen Merovingian, Carolingian, and Capetian kings and queens had been relocated, writes: "The simultaneous gathering together of all these kings and queens, whose lives were spread out over six centuries, each of whom did not know most of the others, now brought them together in an eternal present."[33] Is there any possibility for a *historical* consciousness within such a continuous perception of time? Marc Bloch believed there was "a vast indifference to time" in medieval culture.[34] Following in his footsteps, Le Goff adds that "feudal society, in which the church became bogged down between the ninth and the eleventh centuries, froze historical reflection and seemed to arrest historical time or, in any case, to assimilate it to the history of the church."[35] Citing the example of the bishop and historian Otto of Freising, uncle of Frederick Barbarossa, Le Goff shows that medieval thought, though curious about the past, wanted at the same time to ignore time. During the same period, the *chanson de geste* and the epic also contributed to a "negation of history" by means of their timeless ideal, devoid of all historicity.

There is a medieval historiography, however, though the genre does not appear to be central. It seems to have been disqualified, as it were, by the Aristotelian notion that art must be autonomous: "Until the end of the eighteenth century, the subject of history remained to a large degree a sideline, dominated by theology," writes Alain Guerreau.[36] That historiography took an interest in the actions of remarkable or powerful men, in the lives of saints and kings, in memorable and edifying events. It produced monographic histories, of an abbey or a monastery, for example, in order to place these institutions within a legitimate continuity—hence the connections between history and law. It was entirely marked by the idea that all human actions occur by the will of God—hence the domination of theological thought, historians being at first primarily bishops (Gregory of Tours in the sixth century, Otto of Freising) and later monks. If we give credence to the historian Hans-Werner Goetz, the medieval chroniclers, especially from the eleventh and twelfth centuries onward, nevertheless developed a historical consciousness marked by three elements: "a consciousness of a historic nature of the world," which integrates the different moments of history by divine will; "a distinct sense of (and for) the past" within a perspective marked by the quest for origins, the search for genealogies as remote as possible in time, and a mythic vision of the movement of history that made it possible to distinguish the past from the present; and, finally, a representation of the past "strictly oriented towards the present."[37]

No doubt that last point may be of particular interest to the historian of the present time writing today. If there was a *preponderance* of the present in that view of time and not, as there is today, a *domination* of the present, if there was a political or moral purpose for reflecting on the past, it still lay within the tradition of a history that ought to guide the actions of the living. According to that conception, the values cast into relief are immemorial because they conform to an order of things beyond the human will: "Such thinking actually finds its explanation in a belief that historical events were open to interpretation for the present because they did not happen by chance but were inspired by the divine will and thus had a 'sense' for the contemporaries."[38] This is almost the opposite of presentism in our own time, which assesses and judges the past by the measure of the present. Here, on the contrary, it is the past, at least the past of certain remarkable men and actions—all considered marks of the divine nature of the movement of time—that is set up as judge of the present. It is therefore difficult to distinguish a "historiography of the contemporary" in that era, since the past and the present, the noncontemporary and the contemporary, permanently coexist.

The question is not without pertinence, however, from the standpoint of a regressive history of the very notion of the history of the present time. In fact, if we consider not the "paradigms" but the sources and methods of medieval historiography, we find that it too accorded a determining importance to first- or secondhand testimony, to oral transmission, to verbal exchange rather than to the analysis of written texts.

> Two traits characterize medieval historiography: the same authors deal in a single movement with the history of ancient times and with contemporary history; and though historians recounted the events of their own time based exclusively on what they had seen and heard, for the modern age as a whole and even for more ancient times, they still dared make use of oral sources. In the nineteenth century, conversely, the scholars and antiquarians who studied times past on the one hand, and the journalists and memoirists who bore witness to the present time on the other, were far removed from each another, and the oral was greatly devalued in comparison to the written. Nineteenth-century historians, to be sure, had no way to assess their distant predecessors. But now, when the study of the present is being reintroduced into the field of history, and when the worth of oral traditions as fundamental sources—difficult but fundamental— is being restored, we may be in a better position to understand the historians of the Middle Ages.[39]

This remark by the great medievalist Bernard Guenée has an even greater piquancy when we recall that he supposedly once declared, speaking of his own career, "that he chose the medieval period because he was too intelligent to do contemporary history, where the profusion of sources leads one to take the easy way out, and not intelligent enough to do ancient history, where their rarity leads one to a great deal of reflection."[40] And yet, writing in 1980, at a time when a new history of the present time was emerging, he unexpectedly bridged the gap between it and medieval historiography. He did so not to tell us there is nothing new, but because he sensed intuitively that that historiography, still in its infancy and based in part on oral transmission, had driven a wedge into the methodological orthodoxy of the late nineteenth century and begun to attack the fetishism of the written source that marked a portion of historiography beginning at that time. According to him, the practice of contemporary history taking shape did not belong to a tradition that had been perpetuated without change across the ages; rather, it constituted an unexpected return a century after the methodological school (*école méthodique*) had been discredited.[41]

CONTEMPORARY HISTORY AND MEDIATE HISTORY

"The most important result of the Scientific Revolution of the sixteenth and seventeenth centuries is . . . the replacement, as the foundation of science, of immediate knowledge by mediate knowledge," writes Krzystztof Pomian regarding the relation between the development of the sciences and that of historical thought.[42] That major change, which began during the Renaissance, now provided access to the reality of things not only through thought or faith, but also through new methods of observation, especially of time and space, by means of instruments of measurement. That new paradigm made possible the observation and analysis of increasingly distant objects, as indicated by the progress of astronomy. It opened "the way from the closed world to an infinite universe, from the world of rough approximation to that of precision," which had direct consequences for the perception of history.[43] Recent research has even shown that scientific progress was accompanied at the time by a new reflection on the role of fiction, which allowed one to name, to represent, what for lack of adequate instruments was unobservable, such as a journey to the stars. "The inaccessibility of the object being considered required writing techniques for describing the invisible and for expressing the unknown of the new cosmological worlds, [and] in that context, fiction played a central role, since it allowed one to substitute a new image of the cosmos for the old."[44] In a sense, a similar movement was at work in historical writings via the emergence of the notion of traces that have to be observed before a narrative can be produced to fill in the blanks. What is known as the modern era was characterized by a celebration of the present at the expense of the near past and not in osmosis with it, as it once had been. The invention of the Middle Ages played a role in designating a new time, the Renaissance, which distinguished itself from the earlier period and rejected it. Whether it was the idea of the progress of the arts, letters, and sciences professed by humanists or scientists, or of a return to the sources of Christianity by Protestants of the Reformation, "one always reached the point of shattering the continuity between [the present] and the past, which placed the historian in a new situation."[45] Once the present was detached from the past, or in any case distinguished and distanced from it, the means of access to the knowledge of history changed in nature. Testimony and oral transmission, which pertained to "immediate knowledge," were replaced by an interest in material traces, especially the written traces of the past, hence by a "mediate knowledge": texts, especially those of a religious nature, were no longer simply "authorities," aspects of the tradition, but rather "sources," hence modes of access to the past. A historian of a new kind would be able to cast a more critical gaze on mythic or legendary narratives using new disciplines such as epigraphy, numismatics, historical geography, or the diplomatics developed by Mabillon:

> It was therefore in the seventeenth century that the past became the object of a mediate knowledge, which analyzed traces and reconstructed by that means the circumstances that produced them. It was these traces that allowed the historian to gain knowledge of remote events, even in cases where no participant, no eyewitness had left an account of them. It was also these traces that, when such narratives existed, made it possible to critique them. In short, the point of view of the historian who observed the past became altogether independent, at least in theory, from the point of view of those for whom that past was a present. Their accounts no longer offered the historian anything but information, and furthermore, the historian did not take them at their word. Historians were obliged always to verify what the witnesses had said. As for interpretation, it was the historians themselves who provided it.[46]

That modification in the relationship between the past and the present produced a different notion of contemporaneity, a hypothesis that Pomian does not explicitly mention but that follows almost naturally from his analysis. Seventeenth-century literati would not only create a new demarcation of historical time—"antiquity," the "Middle Ages," "modern times"—but would also gradually distinguish *a present time of the past*, whose surviving traces the historian must analyze, from a *present time of the historian*, who is placed in the position of a distant observer of the object, like the astronomer or cartographer. History gradually made the shift to mediate knowledge, based on new methods of analysis and techniques, such as scholarship. The important thing was the theoretical and no longer simply intuitive differentiation between the past and the present, between a time accessible through the mediation of the sources and a time accessible to immediate knowledge by means of testimony, oral transmission, or direct experience. As Jean-Marie Goulemot writes:

> The scholarly history that dominated the seventeenth century was neither a novelty nor a break. Just as absolutism cannot be separated from a slow affir-

mation of historical time, the secularization of the religious, and the experience of civil and religious unrest, scholarly history cannot be conceived outside
the new forms of culture imposed by the triumphant sixteenth century. The
cultural break of the Renaissance has to be conceived first and foremost as a
radical transformation of the medieval relationship to time. The philological
return to the Greek and Latin texts, to the biblical text itself, postulated their
history—lacunae, the addition of commentary and scholia—as increasing distance and loss.[47]

According to Goulemot, two major ideas dominated humanist thought:
the return to the origins, to "antiquity as a fragile time of perfection"; and
history understood as "decay." Once history is perceived as alterity, as
change, there is room for a sharper distinction between a history that is contemporary, written on the spot by observers bearing witness to their own
time and basing their analysis on their own experience, and a history that
would be something else, something other, that would give an account of the
experience of other times and other people. Paradoxically, it is because history ceased to be essentially contemporary that contemporary history, which
had previously constituted only one aspect of what was not yet a discipline,
would gradually be identified as such. In any case, it is not without interest
that the syntagm "contemporary history" seems to have made its appearance at that time.

In the seventeenth century, for example, we find occurrences of the term
Zeitgeschichte in Germany and of *histoire du temps présent* in France.[48] In
French, the term *histoire contemporaine* appears in a passage from Pascal's
Pensées, written from 1657 onward and published after his death, in 1670.
This text, devoted to the place of the Jews in history, is often quoted but
rarely analyzed from the angle of an epistemology of contemporaneity:

> What a difference there is between one book and another! I am not surprised
> that the Greeks composed the *Iliad*, nor the Egyptians and Chinese their histo-
> ries. You have only to see how that came about. These historians of fable were
> not contemporary with the things they wrote about. Homer composed a tale,
> offered and accepted as such: for no one ever doubted that Troy and Agamem-
> non had never really existed any more than the golden apple. He never meant
> to write history about it, but only a diversion; he is the only writer of his times,
> the beauty of the work makes it survive; everyone learns it and talks about it;
> it is something that has to be known and everyone knows it off by heart. Four
> hundred years later the witnesses of these things are no longer alive; no one
> knows any longer from his own knowledge whether the work is fable or his-
> tory; it has simply been learned from earlier generations. It may pass for truth.

Any history that is not contemporary is suspect: thus the Sibylline books and those of Trismegistus, and many others which have enjoyed credit in the world, are false and have been found to be false in the course of time. This is not the case with contemporary authors.

There is a great difference between a book composed by an individual, which he hands over to the people, and a book that a people composes itself. It is beyond doubt that the book is as old as the people.[49]

This passage is inserted into Pascal's celebration of the Jewish people, whom he praises both for their antiquity and for their constant fidelity to the original covenant with God. He returns several times to the force of law in the Jewish tradition, the most ancient law in history and one that has survived almost intact across time, even constituting the basis of Christianity. In this passage, therefore, he contrasts the Old Testament to other traditions and mythologies, especially the Greek. On the one hand, there is fable, diversion, uncertainty, that which is held to be true by virtue of repetition over time, and even the false. On the other, there is history, the true, the authentic. Although the mathematician Pascal belonged to the very era of mediate knowledge to which Pomian refers, he does not seem to have given credence to the historians except with respect to things seen—hence the superiority he grants to contemporary history, understood here as a history written by direct witnesses, themselves mere conveyors of the word of God. His perception of history, which, to be sure, is not central in a work devoted to an apologia of Christianity, seems to place it in opposition to scientific thought. This hypothesis is advanced by Louis Marin in his comment on "the tragedy of the century" and "the perversion of the order of the sciences" that Pascal denounced in his youth: "To cite the authority of Aristotle as proof in matters of physics that are subject only to experiment and argument, and to introduce innovations, to make inventions, to use reasoning in theology *instead of* the authority of scripture and the church fathers, [is] to profane the discourse of God."[50] Criticism, reason, and the rejection of authority were valid for the sciences but not for history, which was still entirely dependent on theology.

And yet, at least as far as my argument is concerned, it is not so much the opposition between "scholarly" history and "literary" history—one of the great debates of the time[51]—that needs to be emphasized as the implicit definition that emerges of contemporary history, an expression that was still rarely used. Pascal evokes the relation of a people to a sacred text, the question of its transmission, its translation, and thus its "contemporaneity," even though the term does not appear in that form. In another passage, for example, he underscores the fundamental role of Moses, whom he sees as, yes, a historian of the present time: "When the creation of the world began to recede into the past, God provided a single contemporary historian, and charged an entire people with the custody of this book, so that this should be the most authentic history in the world and all men could learn from it something which it was so necessary for them to know and which could only be known from it."[52]

The use of the term "contemporary" is particularly interesting here in that it appears paradoxical, at least with regard to the meaning it later acquired. What makes the history related in the Book "authentic" is not only that it was written by contemporaries, hence by witnesses (the Greek historiographical tradition makes another reappearance here). Rather, the very permanence of its message across the ages "even makes us contemporaries of the events recounted by the Bible," as Pierre Force writes.[53] The power of the sacred text lies in its resistance to all historicity, its transmission intact with the force of the original message of the covenant. The characteristic of the Jewish people is thus to be "the perpetual enunciator of the Old Testament," which, moreover, confers on them an almost supernatural and anachronistic character. The expression "contemporary history" does not refer here to the history of one's own time or to a break between the past and the present, or even to a distinction between a direct knowledge of a history seen and experienced in opposition to a history that is studied and recounted. It refers to a past that has itself remained contemporary and has survived in the form of an eternal present, an intact presence of the past, so to speak, an unaltered past. If contemporary history is the only history that is not suspect in Pascal's eyes, it is because it is a memory, to use a term from our own time. When he evokes a book "that a people composes itself," one as old as that people, it is possible to detect an idea similar to that developed by the historian of Judaism Yosef Yerushalmi: the ancestral relation of the Jewish people to the past, before the upheavals of the twentieth century, belonged to the register of memory and not to that of history, not even to the register of a tradition of practices perpetuated precisely to maintain the present of an original past, thus remaining unchanged, immutable.[54]

Despite almost identical formulations, then, there is a great distance between Pascal's assertion and that made two centuries later by Croce, who calls contemporary history "the only history worthy of the name," even though both authors refer to the ancient principle of history guiding the present. For Pascal, that contemporary history, by means of its reference to the Bible, is synonymous with an absence of historicity, while for Croce it is the inscription in the present of any approach to the past, near or remote, a tradition closer to Thucydides. Pascal situates contemporaneity in the past, whereas Croce situates it in the present. That difference in the meaning of what would become a term of art is not trivial, since it underscores the fact that the notion of contemporaneity can designate very different temporal regimes.

The advent of a historiography founded on mediate knowledge also exacerbated certain structural problems in the practice of history itself, particularly with respect to the objectivity of knowledge and the historian's independence. The development of methods and techniques that allowed an objective apprehension of the traces of the past was based on reason, hence on the affirmation of a necessary independence from the passions, from faith, the church, and royal power: a "utopian doctrine," Pomian tells us.[55] That doctrine directly raised the question of the legitimacy of contemporary history, since it was not clear whether it lay on the side of immediate knowledge, as Pascal's theological approach would have it, or on the side of mediate knowledge, hence still within the field of history, a rapidly evolving art. The new questions about scholarly contemporary history were all the more pointed in that they belonged to a particular context: that of the traumatic memory of the wars of religion in the second half of the sixteenth century and the first half of the seventeenth. The intensity and violence of these wars obsessed contemporaries and led to a general aspiration for civil peace, which in the seventeenth century found expression in an extensive output of historiography marked by that event, by the impact of an unrealized but retrospectively frightening revolution, written in part by the victors, that is, by the Catholics. It vindicated monarchy, even absolute monarchy, considered the only one capable of guaranteeing peace and order.

Historiography, and quite specifically the historiography of the present time, also played a role in the emergence of the modern state, which set in place new mechanisms for knowing and making oneself known on the one hand, for surveillance and concealment on the other, and used literature as an instrument of seduction and domination: "Throughout the seventeenth century, monarchical power [in France] encouraged the writing of a contemporary history that would satisfy the monarchy and with which it could identify. Various methods were used, different projects were established and began to be realized; large books were even written. But the result never seemed to meet expectations. The rulers' determination and the writers' declared zeal were not sufficient: it was as if an evil genie of misunderstanding ran interference every time, making the force and clarity of intentions collapse in the impotence of the results."[56]

In the Middle Ages, the content of history was divine will. In the modern age, it was the sovereign. The history of the present time thus acquired an important place at that moment, but not for the same reasons as in previous eras. The present now belonged to a conjuncture, a particular historical sequence, and not to an eternal present. The king, to be sure, remained divine in his essence, but the history of the present time was enlisted in the service of his temporal power. Although the aim of historical writing was still to present exemplary deeds and to guide the present, its production now belonged to the logic of mediate knowledge based on documents. But though the demands of monarchical power and the exigencies of scholarship seemed compatible in theory—or at least, official historiographers wanted to believe they were—in the end they turned out very difficult to reconcile: "History is an inevitable and inconvenient challenge to authority," writes Christian Jouhaud.[57] Repeating the observation of Scipion Dupleix, Louis XIII's historiographer, he shows that three constraints were brought to bear on that task: the decision to undertake a historical study, which fell not to the man of letters but to the sovereign; the question of censorship and, more generally, of freedom of expression; and the sources the historian would or would not be able to use.

The seventeenth-century historian of the present time thus clashed head-on with the logic of the modern state and its need to preserve the secrecy of its actions. François Charpentier was assigned by Louis XIV to write a history of his reign, but Colbert denied the historian access to the royal cabinet's records and did not allow himself to be questioned on a regular basis. That situation is somewhat suggestive of the dilemma raised in our own time by public archives, which impose on the state and citizen alike the dual constraint of transparency in public actions and the preservation of secrets of state and of private life. History and power must tell and not tell at the same time. Conversely, the question of censorship was not a new problem. If a historian criticized the sovereign too much, he obviously ran the risk of incurring the ruler's displeasure or of deviating from reality. Too much deference, by contrast, could damage the historian's credibility, hence that of the historical subject, and could impel the historian to take risks by way of compensation. The historian Charles Sorel, author, notably, of *Avertissement sur l'histoire de la monarchie française* (1629; *Notice on the History of the French Monarchy*), reports an anecdote in which Alexander the Great threatened with death a historian "who was reading before him what he had already composed of his history, in which he recounted fabulous and incredible things."[58] What level of praise, what degree of criticism is acceptable to the forces in power? All the historian's responsibility lies in that question. And that responsibility changed in nature once the knowledge the historian produced no longer had its source solely in experience, which by definition is shared with others, but in a mediate knowledge entailing a more or less solitary relationship to traces and writings, which made sense only if the historian was reliable, albeit compliant. A century earlier, Machiavelli had articulated the pitfalls arising from the writing of a history both contemporary and mediate. In his *Florentine Histories* (1521–25), commissioned by Pope Clement VII, he writes:

> Because I was particularly charged and commanded by your Holy Blessedness that I write about the things done by your ancestors in such a mode that it might be seen I was far from all flattery ... I very much fear that in describing the goodness of Giovanni, the wisdom of Cosimo, the humanity of Piero, and the magnificence and prudence of Lorenzo, it may appear to Your Holiness that I have transgressed your commands ... for in all my narrations I have never wished to conceal an indecent deed with a decent cause, or to obscure a praiseworthy deed as if it were done for a contrary end.
>
> But how far I am from flattery may be known from all parts of my history, and especially in speeches and in private reasonings, direct as well as indirect, which with their judgments and their order preserve the proper humor of the person speaking without any reservations. I shun hateful words in all places as of little need to the dignity and truthfulness of the history. ... I have striven, meanwhile, Most Holy and Blessed Father, in this description of mine, while not staining the truth, to satisfy everyone; and perhaps I will not have satisfied anyone; nor would I wonder if this were to be the case, because I judge it impossible without offending many to describe things in their times. Nonetheless, I come happily to the task.[59]

Civic pride, sincerity, courage, distance, lucidity, impartiality, and temperance: Machiavelli is painting the portrait of the ideal historian of the present time, the very one whom the court of the king of France would fail to promote. Machiavelli articulates a truth that seems to pervade the modern age: the writing of a "history of our time," whose particularity—if not singularity—is increasingly apparent, is as necessary to the exercise of power as it is difficult, indeed impossible, to undertake, precisely because of its proximity to the sovereign. The more such historiography distinguishes itself, the more it raises questions. The more it seems to mark a break in the linearity or continuity of time, especially divine time, the more disturbing it is. The more history becomes a measure of alterity, the more the question of distance from the passions arises.

THE BIRTH OF CONTEMPORARY HISTORY IN THE MODERN AGE

In *Les mots et les choses* (*The Order of Things*) Michel Foucault, in his quest for a modern *episteme*, evokes the break that occurred in Western societies at the turn of the nineteenth century. The "human sciences," a recent body of knowledge that took man as its subject, shifted from a regime of intelligibility founded on Order—that is, on taxonomy, the classification of beings and things within a relatively stable space—to one founded on History, understood here not as the narration of events that have occurred but as the movement of time itself and as a principle of organization. "History, as we know, is certainly the most erudite, the most aware, the most conscious, and possibly the most cluttered area of our memory; but it is equally the depths from which all beings emerge into their precarious, glittering existence. Since it is the mode of being of all that is given us in experience, History has become the unavoidable element in our thought."[60] Foucault is pointing to the very birth of historicity, understood as a characteristic of modern societies, which think of themselves no longer in terms of the continuity of an immutable tradition (or as a protest against it) but as being in motion, in a state of constant, sometimes brutal change, open to all the promises of Progress but also weighed down by all the uncertainties of a henceforth indecipherable future. From that standpoint, the French Revolution was a major turning point, whose effects were still being felt in the last third of the twentieth century. Reinhart Koselleck, developing the same intuition as Foucault but by different means, demonstrates that, between the beginning and the end of the Revolution, the very concept of history changed in meaning. It expanded to make room for a new "metaconcept": that of a History (from the German *Geschichte*) that can no longer be reduced to the sum of particular histories or stories (*Geschichten*) or to the juxtaposition of facts and their narration (*Historie*)—that is, to "histories of . . . ," which describe the life of a sovereign, a reign, a country, or a religious institution, whether these belonged to the near or the more distant past. Henceforth, the culture of the Enlightenment, then postrevolutionary culture, would seek to grasp history "as such," history "in general," located above the developments in any particular historical subject or another. "Over all these and such histories is *History*" (Über den Geschichten ist die Geschichte), wrote Droysen, one of the founders of the German historical school in 1858.[61] It was a history now detached from providence and divine will, one that "gave birth to itself" and found it was the source of its own movement. It thus played the role of last instance, indistinguishable from the principle of advancing reason, and "became an agent of human destiny or of the progress of society."[62] As a result, the function of history as a discipline also changed: it consisted no longer of relating "the truthful account of things past," the time-honored formula since antiquity, but rather of grasping the very movement of human destiny. History now became an autonomous discipline that could and even should allow us to conceive of "world history" (*Weltgeschichte*) within a universalist perspective.

> That is an achievement of Enlightenment philosophy, by means of which history (*Historie*) as a science detaches itself from the adjoining fields of rhetoric and moral philosophy, even as it frees itself from theology and jurisprudence, which stand above it in the academic hierarchy. It made no sense to say that history (*Historie*), which had previously dealt only with the singular, the particular, and the accidental, might be capable of "Philosophy." Although historico-philosophical methods and the auxiliary sciences had, with humanism, already achieved their autonomy, history (*Historie*) as such became an independent science only when—in "history in general"—it acquired a space of experience. At that time, it was able to distinguish its specific "field of objects." The constitution of the philosophy of history is an indicator of that process.[63]

The philosophy of history thus became a separate genre, and though it helped the discipline of history to acquire its autonomy, it also raised new challenges. "It found itself provoked," writes Koselleck, "since, once the divine became null and void, history was constrained to elaborate coherencies, supposing there were any, on the basis of components stemming from history itself."[64] That new history had to bring about a metamorphosis both theoretical and empirical, in order to move beyond the positive analysis of the actual traces of the past and undertake the reconstitution of a coherent whole, in great part hypothetical and deductive, hence closer to a philosophical posture. The competition between history and philosophy became more heated, inasmuch as history consequently shed its status, inherited from Aristotelian thought, as a minor art. It would even become the reigning discipline of the nineteenth century, at least in France and Germany.

The Enlightenment played a role in the outbreak of the 1789 Revolution and therefore configured that event to a certain degree; the French Revolution, in turn, reverberated like the spectacular transposition into the material world of the birth of history "as such" in the world of ideas. Through the fracture it produced within a millennial order believed to be immutable, the Revolution profoundly modified the relation to the past, the present, and the future, which consciousness no longer perceived as a continuity. It gave birth to a perception of history on the march founded entirely on the acceleration of the present time, now perceived as an unstable, uncertain transition from what Koselleck calls "the space of experience" to the "horizon of expectation." These two notions, which have become popular within the rhetoric of historical writing and are often used as mere decorative metaphors, do not designate simply the past and the future as perceived by contemporaries at a given moment. They underscore the discontinuity and difference in *nature* between the past and the future, as they emerged with the revolutionary fracture and to which we are still largely beholden. They mark the change in perspective on the part of historians, who would henceforth have to write the history of the present time and rewrite that of the most remote times in light of that discontinuity. And it was not only history as it was being practiced whose foundations changed: the history that had already been written had to change as well, since the ancien régime, an order declared and considered immutable, had proved mortal and had collapsed within only a few years—rather like Soviet Communism in our own time. If the end of history changes, if there even is an end of history, then everything that comes before has to be conceived differently. That state of affairs ratified the break between the past and the future. The past was proclaimed over and done with (a relatively unknown notion until that time) and no longer dictated its law to present actions, since it was necessary in fact to break away from it. Conversely, the future was entirely open, and the anticipation of that future had to dictate present behaviors—the invention of a new society—at a time when divine providence could no longer serve as a foundation. The problem thus lay in creating new paths of communication between acquired experience and a horizon that was no longer predictable. That accounts for the emergence of a new reflection on contemporary history, one that constituted a way of conceptualizing those paths and responding both to the rejection of history as a repository of experience and to the instability created by the disappearance of a now-unpredictable future for which new interpretive keys had to be found.

Historians thus found themselves vested with largely unprecedented responsibilities. That new conception of a dynamic history driving humanity allotted a significant place to the way posterity would view the present. History became a supreme court of appeal: it was given the last word. D'Alembert therefore speaks of an "upstanding and terrible tribunal," while Schiller declares that "world history is the tribunal of the world," a famous formulation repeated and further developed by Hegel.[65] Chateaubriand assigns the historian a heavy responsibility: "In the silence of abjection, when nothing can be heard but the clanking of the slave's chains and the voice of the informer; when everything trembles before the tyrant and it is as dangerous to incur his favor as to merit his disgrace, the historian appears, charged with avenging the people. In vain does Nero prosper, Tacitus has already been born in the empire; he grows up anonymous amid the ashes of Germanicus, and already upstanding providence has delivered to an obscure child the glory of master of the world."[66]

This famous passage merits a moment's reflection, since it has been cited often in recent historiography of the present time. It constituted a key moment, for example, in Pierre Vidal-Naquet's choice of a vocation. It was "a reason to live," writes that historian of antiquity, the son of deportees and a man engaged in the battles of his time—against colonialism especially—who, beginning in the 1980s, militated in favor of constituting a memory and a history of the Holocaust.[67] In that view, what counts is not so much vengeance, in the sense of a response to a criminal or tyrant, but rather the hope of seeing truth prevail over time—with, incidentally, the historian's assistance. Here the function of the tribunal of history is not to punish, even less to take the place of a real court of justice—Vidal-Naquet always rejected "judicial" history—but to allow truth the time it needs to emerge from the bottom of the well. This is a Dreyfusard tradition, which Vidal-Naquet embodied in postcolonial France.[68]

That approach is very remote from the idea that historians, through their writings, must compensate for the absence of a tribunal and themselves constitute a court of appeal, by using the vocabulary of criminal offenses and even by pronouncing verdicts. That tendency came into being after the fall of the Berlin Wall with regard to the crimes of the Communist system. "The idea of establishing ourselves as champions of an enigmatic 'revenge of the people' is alien to us," writes Stéphane Courtois in his preface to *Le livre noir du communisme* (1997; *The Black Book of Communism*), an important book that gave rise to many controversies both because of its content and because of the posture adopted.[69] For in fact, that is the attitude his text takes. In an essential passage, he situates the in-depth research on the crimes of Communism conducted by his historians' collective within the grid of criminal offenses developed at Nuremberg, particularly war crimes and crimes against humanity, even genocide.[70] What is problematic about that approach is not the stigmatization of mass crimes that have gone unpunished and were long denied, even less the fact that the historian expresses his subjectivity. Rather, it is the misuse of the legal and judicial method. The historian has personally taken on the case, standing in for the police and the examining magistrate, the prosecutor and the judge. He pronounces judgments not subject to a review process that would determine their compliance to the "law" he is using and often grants only a minor place to the objections and arguments of the defense. Such procedures are the exact opposite of those used during a legitimate trial. In that sense, the use made of legal and judicial categories does lie within the register of "revenge," which seeks to compensate for the failure—often real, in fact—of temporal justice.

That attitude, which has become widespread in recent historical writing on the present time, shows that historians of the contemporary, in the face of the short- or medium-term legacy of a great catastrophe or major upheaval, must confront issues that go far beyond a mere intellectual and academic exercise. At stake is the quest for truth, the taking into account of all the suffering endured, the avid need to distinguish between good and evil, the often urgent and anguished necessity of a narration, even imperfect, that will make sense in the event's aftermath. Such was the case after 1945 and after 1989; such was also the case after 1789, but for very different reasons having to do with the sense given to the event. That is because the Revolution was the advent not only of a new world, but also of a new conception of time and history, one that in the following decades would bestow on the very notion of contemporary history its full modern sense.

The reason I insist—even by means of a digression—on the legal and judicial dimension of historical discourse about the present time, whether in the wake of the French Revolution or at the end of the twentieth century, is that I believe it constitutes the extreme limit for reflection on the historian's practice. Whether in the guise of enforcers of a nondivine providence, "avengers of the people," substitutes for an abortive "Nuremberg of Communism," not to mention "judicial witnesses," historians—whether they adopt the posture consciously or not, assume it freely or against their will—come face to face with the very limits of the practice of history, especially the history of the near past. By virtue of the tensions at work, the most obvious historiographical issues, at least for historians writing today, become incomparably more acute: the search for truth, the question of impartiality, the choice between objectivity and subjectivity, the definition of the proper distance, the style of argument and narration, the suspension of judgment or its opposite. And it is truly because history changed in meaning at the turn of the eighteenth century and was vested with a share of what had previously fallen to divine providence that its importance as a mode of thought would change considerably in the following decades, culminating in the emergence of a discipline that was no longer just autonomous but also claimed to be scientific.

The advent of Enlightenment philosophy, followed by the revolutionary upheavals, resulted in contradictory feelings about the uses and usefulness of the historical gaze. On the one hand, there was a rejection of traditional history, especially history solely in the service of the sovereign, one that lacked a general perspective, a history that usually perpetuated and legitimated the established order by anchoring it in an immemorial past. On the other, a new historical mode of thought emerged, a philosophy of History that made increasingly holistic claims. During and after the Revolution, there was also a penchant for, an expectation of—one could almost say an obsession with—history, which can be explained by two factors: first, the sense that, just as a ship headed for an unknown world loses sight of the familiar shores of the old, the revolutionary break and the acceleration of time were suddenly distancing the past, whose presence was no longer obvious; and second, the need to understand, to give meaning and intelligibility to the outbreak of revolution and the possibilities it opened up. That ambivalence, that rejection and expectation, is primarily a matter of concern for contemporary history.

The rejection of traditional history, for example, played its part in the emergence of the philosophy of History, a term invented by Voltaire in his work by that title, which he published in 1765 under the pseudonym "Abbé Bazin." Later, in 1769, he used it as a "Preliminary Discourse" to introduce his *Essai sur les moeurs (Essay on Morals and Customs).*[71] Although that text is hardly a reflection on history, presenting itself rather as a counterhistory with universal aims, it brings together the two forms of thought, or rather, marks an entry of sorts on the part of philosophy into the field of historical interpretation. At the same time, it provides a radical critique of history as it was practiced at the time, under the control of the theological and the political. "You would like philosophers to have written ancient history, because you want to read it as a philosopher. You seek only useful truths and, you say, you have found little more than useless errors." In these two introductory sentences, Voltaire denounces the meaninglessness of classical historiography and its lack of credibility. D'Alembert is right on his heels:

> History, then, ought not to be disdained by the philosopher: far from it. Rather, history is truly useful only to the philosopher. Nevertheless, there is a class to which it is even more beneficial. That is the *unfortunate* class of princes. I dare use that expression without fearing to offend them, because it is dictated by the interest that the inevitable misfortune to which they are subject must inspire in every citizen, namely, *that of never seeing men except masked*, those same men whom it is so essential that they know. History, at least, shows men to princes in a tableau and in human form: and the portrait of the fathers cries out to them to distrust the children. Therefore, one is the benefactor of princes, and indirectly, of the human race they govern, if, in writing history, one never loses sight of the superstitious respect one owes to the truth. It goes without saying that one must never allow oneself to alter it: let us add that there are very few cases where one is permitted to keep it to oneself.
>
> But how will a historian who wishes neither to debase himself nor to do harm to himself avoid both the peril of telling the truth when it offends and the shame of keeping it to himself when it is useful? Perhaps the only response to that question is that a writer, on penalty of being proved guilty of lying or at the very least suspected of it, ought never to give the public the history of his own time, just as a journalist should never speak of the books of his own country if he does not want to risk dishonoring himself by his praise or mockery. The wise and enlightened man of letters, while respecting as he must those whose power or prestige puts them in a position to do a great deal of good or a great deal of harm to their fellows, judges and assesses them in silence, without bile and without flattery, keeps a ledger, so to speak, of their vices and virtues, and preserves that ledger for posterity, which must deliver the verdict and administer justice. A sovereign who, to shut the mouths of flatterers, would, upon ascending the throne, forbid his history from being published during his lifetime, would by that prohibition cover himself in glory; he would have to fear neither what truth would dare say to him nor what it might say about him; it would praise him after enlightening him, and he would benefit in advance from his history, which he would not wish to read.[72]

That reflection is obviously central to my argument. D'Alembert seems to be proclaiming that the only authentic history is noncontemporary, a rather remarkable reversal of the previous trend. His argument leads to a conclusion that is the opposite of Pascal's and even more of Machiavelli's in *Florentine Histories*, though the premises about the relationship between power and truth are similar. The more one advances through the Age of Reason, which witnessed the victory of philosophical history over scholarly history, the more history, and a fortiori contemporary history—too dependent on the realities of one's own time—becomes suspect. It is now proximity, the absence of distance, that obliterates perspective. That development is noteworthy not only because it argues against the very possibility of writing a history contemporary with the events it claims to describe and analyze, but because, in so doing, that criticism casts into relief the division between the recent past and the bygone past. No doubt it also contributed toward creating that division, even before the social and political break of the Revolution. In my view, the important thing is that contemporary history began to be identified as relatively singular—in any case, as displaying particular characteristics, which would mean that its very emergence within the intellectual field produced most of the arguments for its rejection. As we saw at the beginning of this chapter, that hypothesis was put forward by Pierre Nora, though regarding the end of the nineteenth century. Yet that characteristic of a practice that emerged only to be immediately contested took shape much earlier, especially in Germany. It seems to have been linked both to the emergence of a historical discipline that aspired to be a science and to the early stages of the professionalization of the historian's craft, more or less direct consequences of the change in historicity that occurred between the eighteenth and nineteenth centuries. That rejection is therefore not linked to the history of the Third Republic, much less unique to the French context.

The very advent of history as an autonomous discipline, then, led to suspicions about contemporary history, which until then had been an intrinsic part of the historian's viewpoint and practice. Once the Revolution was over, at least for the time being, what had earlier constituted an uncontroversial aspect of historical reflection—consideration of a present time not separate from the past—became problematic. It was, in the first place, a political problem. In Restoration France, for example, school curricula were indecisive about the place to be granted to the revolutionary period: for tenth grade in 1818 and for ninth grade in 1826, the directives recommended going up to "our own time," a notion that, though not new in practice, had acquired a name only relatively recently. By contrast, in the tenth-grade curriculum of 1828, the history cycle ended in 1715, with the early days of the Regency. These hesitations reflected the disagreements between liberals, such as Adolphe Thiers, who recommended studying the Revolution and analyzing its causes to avoid a possible repetition, and ultras, such as Joseph de Maistre, who saw it as an accident or a divine punishment that had to be considered a deviation. In general, debates about recent history elicited antagonistic and contradictory reactions. The rejection of revolutionary values and the fear that they would be transmitted to future generations were countered by the desire for reconciliation, consistent with the policy of willed amnesia advocated by the constitutional Charter of 1815. In the face of the increasingly obvious impossibility of returning to the status quo ante (or in the desire to turn the page), some argued for granting the revolutionary period, in spite of everything, a proximity that was not yet "historical," so as to make it easier to rewrite the past—for example, by returning confiscated property.[73] Later, especially at the instigation of Victor Duruy, the teaching of the near past would become an essential part of training young *lycéens*, just as history teaching in general became somewhat more autonomous (especially when compared to historiography), because it corresponded to specific civic goals: "[The philosophy curriculum] must run from 1789 to our own time, so that those who will be conducting the country's affairs in a few years will know how this country has lived until now. . . . Our present-day society, its organization and its needs, dates from the Revolution and, in order to understand that society and serve it well, one must know it well."[74]

   That new way of conceiving of contemporaneity within the context of an acceleration of time also raised intellectual problems and made certain historians more circumspect. "They therefore hesitated," writes Koselleck, "to write modern histories, particularly those that, as had been the custom, were supposed to extend to the 'history of the present time' [*Zeitgeschichte*]."[75] The absence of a stable present, a fixed point from which to look back, constituted a first obstacle: historians were beginning to realize that writing a history that extended into what was now an uncertain present could only be conceived as an unfinished history, a history in suspense. Since the present time was provisional, it could not be recorded as history. "Everywhere, in civic, political, religious, and financial life," wrote Gustave Poel, "is not the situation provisional? Yet the aim of history is not the process of becoming but what has become."[76] History cannot and must not be written except by taking into account the time that has elapsed. For an entire historiographical current, therefore, a history of the present time proved to be impossible *from now on,* "since at most it would contribute toward setting off a partisan dispute." As a result, "nothing lasting, no genuine history can be expected from a history written today." And Koselleck points out Friedrich Christoph Dahlmann's "bitter words" in writings from 1847: "history is far too distinguished to go up to our own time."[77]

   It is important to note here that the major objections made to the aspiration to write a contemporary history beginning from the mid-nineteenth century—the absence of distance, the intensity of passions, the unfinished nature of the processes being observed—follow directly from the advent of a scientific practice of history and a professionalized discipline and also from the rejection of classical history. They are a consequence of the shadow cast by a revolution that turned the order of time on its head. That reaction was both intellectual and emotional: the difficulty lay in conceiving of the world after such an upheaval otherwise than by rethinking the entire discipline. That rethinking would in fact occur, but only gradually. The objections raised to the possibility of writing a history of the present time seem all the more remarkable in that this form of skepticism developed concomitantly with a movement in the other direction, which led contemporaries of the Revolution to pay greater attention to history, that is, to a world that had suddenly been engulfed, whether that development was considered an occasion to rejoice or to lament. That is one of the factors that made the postrevolutionary century the century of history, that of the historian-writers (Michelet) and the writer-historians (Dumas), that of historian-politicians (Thiers, von Humboldt) and historian-philosophers (Droysen, Tocqueville). It was also the century that invented the archive, patrimony, and even the first "policies of memory," with the advent of the major archaeological excavation campaigns and the construction of museums and other institutions charged with preserving the past. Although a European phenomenon generally, it was particularly marked in France, where historians were vested with the mission of writing a coherent narrative that would show the connection between the past and the present, between the various components of a fractured society—a narrative that would give meaning to the discontinuity people had experienced and even prepare the way for the judgment of posterity. "As a result, it was an essential task to conceive of a history that explained the revolutionary break and managed to connect the disjointed parts of the history of France. History was expected to make comprehensible the conflicts that divided the French people and also what united them. In the face of the fragility of governments and political institutions, in the face of the compulsive repetition of the revolutionary impulse, which pitted even the heirs of the Revolution against one another, historians were acknowledged to have a formidable authority: to tell the truth about France. In a curious reversal, the specialist on the past was considered a prophet."[78]

Another notable trait would recur many times: not only did history in the broad sense take on greater importance at the time, but the history of the present time also developed everywhere, despite the suspicion and rejection expressed by some. The Revolution obsessed too many people—and would obsess them for a long time—for the most curious or most personally concerned writers to be discouraged. Early on, in the very first years of the nineteenth century, it gave rise to historiographical texts, such as Emmanuel de Toulongeon's *Histoire de France depuis la Révolution de 1789* (*History of France since the Revolution of 1789*), undertaken at the start of the Napoleonic Empire. Toulongeon recommended that the historian relate "not only what he knows, but what he can learn; not only what he has seen from the place where he was, but what he might have been able to see, had he been in all the places at once that the spectators occupied."[79] Here again is an ancestral tradition: the historian as witness, the historian who writes on the basis of his own experience, the contemporary historian who, from Thucydides to Pascal, has felt duty bound to produce a history "worthy of the name." But there is also a trace of the progress of historiography in the use of sources and in a speculative argument that harnesses the imagination: "what he might have been able to see." What was true for the Revolution, the major subject of history throughout the nineteenth century, was equally true for the Restoration: once again, the first histories of that period were produced on the spot. Within a decade, for example, Charles de Lacretelle was able to write his eight-volume *Histoire de la Révolution Française* (1824–26; *History of the French Revolution*) and his *Histoire de France depuis la Restauration* (1829–35; *History of France since the Restoration*), a work that borrowed its form from both historical narrative and personal testimony or journalism. And what was true for the Restoration was also true for later periods. Louis Blanc's famous *Histoire de dix ans* (*History of Ten Years*), for example, was a satirical look at the beginning of Louis Philippe's reign. The proliferation of studies in contemporary history, though partly a result of the persistence of the revolutionary event, also demonstrated that a literary genre that had developed throughout the nineteenth century within the context of a disrupted social and political order had become commonplace. It was often an informed historiography, based on a body of sources and collections of official documents, but it was also almost always committed to one side or another, pervaded by the political passions inherited from the Revolution and its aftereffects, and therefore marked by the tension between the will to understand and the need to take a stand. The originality of the postrevolutionary period, therefore, did not lie solely in the development of a new form of contemporary history; it lay even more in the fact that history had become a weapon of choice in political and ideological battles. The analysis of the present and of the near past, of history being made, from which practical, short-term lessons had to be drawn—so that the world would be transformed and not merely interpreted (Karl Marx)—became essential elements of a political mode of thought and philosophy now profoundly informed by historicity.

PARADOXICAL REJECTION IN THE LATE NINETEENTH CENTURY

The last third of the nineteenth century witnessed the emergence of new historical schools that capitalized on the developments that had occurred before and after the Revolution. Without returning in detail to a well-known story, I would like to point out a few traits of significance for my argument. History in the Western world, having abandoned its status as a minor art and acquired its autonomy, was gradually erected into a scientific discipline. Not all historians shared the radical position of Fustel de Coulanges, who saw it as "a pure science, a science like physics or geology," the science of past events, which nevertheless had to be constituted as such.[80] But many now considered it a true métier requiring professionalization, another major trait of the time, when new university degrees, new academic positions, and new forums for the spread of knowledge (journals, scholarly societies, and so on) were being created in French, German, and American universities. That historical knowledge of a relatively new kind was based on normative methods, in particular, a systematic study of archival sources and texts, which required greater rigor and more technical skill. Rhetoric or eloquence was no longer sufficient. These new generations of historians (in Germany in the first third of the nineteenth century, Wilhelm von Humboldt, Johann Gustav Droysen, and Leopold Ranke; in France during the Third Republic, Charles-Victor Langlois, Charles Seignobos, and Ernest Lavisse) denounced the excessive proximity, embodied by Michelet, of history to literature. At the same time, they distinguished their practice from the philosophy of history under the influence of Kant and Hegel, which they called merely a "secular disguise for the old theological theory of final causes."[81] As a consequence of the revolutionary break between past and present, the historian henceforth had the task, not of providing examples of good conduct through the study of an edifying past ontologically linked to the present, but of bringing to light the traces of a bygone past, which it was imperative to know so as not to cut oneself off entirely from previous generations. The discipline served no longer to maintain continuity but to attenuate the effects of the ruptures in History. Its role was no longer to hold onto a tradition, which had previously belonged to the nature of things, but to anchor the present and the uncertain future in a continuity to be reestablished with a past. That past, having existed prior to the Revolution, was at risk of vanishing from collective memory if it did not become the object of systematic and thorough investigation by a new professional guild. It followed that the historian's first priority had to be "to present what actually happened," to reconstitute it "purely and completely."[82] That credo, which seems to coincide with an ancestral conception of history as a "truthful account of past events," was later denounced as "positivist." Obviously, it now appears dated. But we must not forget its pertinence, less as a timeless and universal canon of the historian's métier—which was being founded at the time—than as an intellectual project within the postrevolutionary context. At the time, when the revolutionary upheaval and the Napoleonic Wars had turned the world these historians were living in upside down, when the traditional interpretive frameworks had become obsolete, and when a number of traces had or seemed to have disappeared, it was no simple matter to aspire to explain what had "actually" happened in earlier days. Consumed by the fear of being cut off from the past, critical of the philosophy of history developing at the same moment, these historians invented the principle of retrospection, that is, distance from the passions, from mythologies, from the acceleration of lived time. Historians of the present time writing today, though informed by structural history and influenced by contemporary hermeneutics—which stands at the opposite extreme of positivism (or of its caricature)—also have to face the primordial task of reconstituting what "actually happened" in the first half of the twentieth century. They must do so in a cognitive universe where passions, the long and painful memory of the major catastrophes, the fear of seeing the traces or recollection of them vanish, and mythologies of all kinds (including the negation of massive historical facts) are especially persistent. And yet, though in both cases the near past constitutes a central issue in the public space—a public space that began to emerge in the wake of the Revolution—it did not play the same role in scientific historiography. In the nineteenth century, the writing of a history of the present time, especially that of the revolutionary conflagration (and even because of it), aroused ambivalent and contradictory feelings. Pierre Nora, in his 1978 article on the present as a singular category for the historian, was among the first to insist on the paradox of a historiography that was being rejected just as it was beginning to exist:

> So long as the only history there is is that of the past, there is no *contemporary* history: it would be a contradiction in terms. Contemporary history in itself has, in fact, never existed. It is merely what follows. According to a French academic demarcation inherited from the early Third Republic, it dates to the French Revolution (and there is an element of truth in that). But who would take a curriculum for scientific truth? . . . The hypothesis we would like to propose here is that contemporary history, that history without object, without status, and with-

out definition, is not merely the temporal addendum to a history sure of itself but an *other* history, and that the exclusion of the contemporary from the field of history is precisely what gives it its specificity. In other words, the split from which it stems, that between present and past, is based on a linear conception of history and itself belongs to the past—to a past that still weighs on the present but that does not suffice to define it. The very arrival of a historical present would thus coincide with its expulsion from the field of history, its exile, its suppression, its repression. And the mark of its exclusion would be the sign of its advent. Between the emergence of a "contemporary" history and its dismissal, there is a historical correlation so close that contemporary history would itself no longer be decipherable except in negative relief, in the movement that denies its threat and erases its novelty.[83]

That observation rests in great part on established facts, though the rejection of—or at least, the ambivalence toward—contemporary history as a genre predates the emergence of the French methodological school by several decades. The suspicion dates to the aftermath of the original event and is therefore more integrally linked to the upheaval itself, to the postrevolutionary period, than to the much later constitution of a scientific and professionalized historiography. It is true, however, that that historiography would bolster and give substance to the arguments about why that part of the discipline had to be kept at a distance. It was precisely because there was a fracture that historians no longer dealt with the most recent history as a matter of course, as they had in the previous century and since the very origins of history. So long as the past and the present (as well as the future) were conceived as a single continuum, whether cyclical, as among the Greeks, or linear, as in the eternal present of the Middle Ages, the notion of contemporary history as such did not make much sense, since there was no reason to single it out. That explains the term's lack of prominence at a time when the near past was in fact being taken into consideration. Conversely, after the revolutionary break, recent history came to be identified with the transitional period between the old world and the new. In research, literature, and education, it took on an unprecedented singularity. And because it was singled out, it elicited forms of rejection in response: one excludes what appears to be different, not what is the same. It was because, after the Revolution, a history with scientific pretensions sought to devote itself first and foremost to the bygone past (but without really managing to do so) that the very possibility of a history of the near past, it too scientific, gave rise to reservations. Only diplomatic history, especially after the War of 1870, escaped that interdiction. For example, in 1875 Albert

Sorel published a history of the Franco-Prussian War, having already written seven volumes on the history of Europe and the Revolution.[84]

The many signs of that early rejection have often been enumerated in historiographical studies on history in general or on the history of the present time. "In 1900," writes Gérard Noiriel, "more than half of all French academic historians were medievalists, and at the École Pratique des Hautes Études (the institution responsible for the most advanced research in the human sciences at the time), of some fifty seminars, only two were devoted to the period after 1500."[85] In Germany too, the best-known and most influential historians were specialists in antiquity or the Middle Ages. The prominent *English Historical Review*, between its founding in 1886 and the aftermath of World War I, published no articles on British history after 1852 or on European history after 1870. The courses taught at the Modern History School at Oxford University in 1914 left out English political history after 1837 and world history after 1878, a temporal exclusion that went hand in hand with a reduction in the geographical area studied. For example, the study of India was confined to the India of the English colonials, that of China to Western trade: "The exclusion of contemporary history from the subjects of academic study had serious practical consequences. The English governing class ... went into politics or the civil service or the professions knowing less about the state of the contemporary world than they knew about ancient Greece and Rome. Ten or twelve newspaper correspondents in the late nineteenth or early twentieth centuries had a better understanding of the dangers which threatened the peace of Europe than most of the leading members of British Cabinets."[86]

The situation was different in the United States, in that the practice of contemporary history appeared to be neither as problematic nor as differentiated as in Europe. This is, in fact, an interesting counterexample regarding the questions raised here. In his major book on the evolution of American historiography, Peter Novick shows that there too history became a profession in the late nineteenth century, with its methods of validation, its career paths, its particular organizations (the American Historical Association was founded in 1884) and especially its dominant ideology: the passion for objectivity. "Objectivity" must be understood here as the belief that the historical facts preexist interpretations and that interpretations must be tested against the facts; that there is only one truth; that history is a discovery and not a construction; and that, finally, despite the differences in assessment of generations of historians, the meaning of the events remains unchanged.[87] That historiography was greatly influenced by the German model and by the French methodological school. Novick tells us that Langlois and Seignobos's *Introduction aux études historiques* (*Introduction to the Study of History*) was translated into English in 1898, a year after its publication in France, and remained a classic in the United States until World War II. The epistemological frame of reference was somewhat different there, however, and the belief in history as an objectifiable science tended to follow the precepts of Francis Bacon: the primacy of empiricism, distrust of hypotheses, and the search for taxonomies (naming, classifying, describing).[88] Nevertheless, despite that passion, one finds neither suspicion nor any particular rejection of contemporary history in the United States. On the contrary, that branch of history was particularly dynamic in the late nineteenth century, when one of the issues at stake was national reconciliation after the Civil War and the problems raised by Reconstruction. Novick shows that historians of the North ultimately reached a kind of "consenus" with those of the South with, according to him, a predominantly racist and nationalist component.[89] The important thing to note here is that Novick does not even raise the question of the legitimacy of contemporary history, despite the fact that his book is a remarkable and almost exhaustive study of the history of American historiography. That tallies with an easily observable fact in our own time: the theoretical debates on the definition or parameters of contemporary history past and present, which have engaged European historians, at least in France, Germany, Italy, and the countries of Eastern Europe, and also Latin Americans, appear to have gained no foothold in the United States, where contemporary history seems to be practiced "naturally," without any particular epistemological inquiry. Are we to attribute that to an apparently more "empirical" historiographical tradition, or one oriented toward different structural questions (ethnicity, gender, the global)? Is it the consequence of a national history that has unfolded for the most part in the "contemporary era," in the European sense of the term, hence on the far side of the revolution? That is possible. But these characteristics have not prevented American historiography from producing generations of medievalists and modernists of great international renown. Furthermore, American national history acquired greater temporal depth once interest began to be directed toward the history of the Native American communities, which predated the arrival of the Europeans. There is thus no causal link between the fact that the United States was still a young country in the late nineteenth century and the absence of any rejection of contemporary history. It is all the more noteworthy that American historians of the time passionately adopted positivist European principles. But they did not import all the attendant prejudices, which shows that the methodological principles could easily accommodate a practice of contemporary history.

One of the reasons for the rejection of contemporary history in France and Germany in the late nineteenth century was the effort on the part of historians to distinguish themselves, a commonplace mechanism in any activity undergoing professionalization. The more one moves away from the present, the more difficult historical investigation seems—or the more difficult it is declared to be—because of the scarcity of traces. And the farther back in time one goes, the more that investigation requires a knowledge of classical texts and languages, in which academics, unlike "amateur" or nonprofessional historians, are trained. That makes it easier to exclude the nonprofessionals and protect a scientific milieu in the process of formation. This is one of the arguments Louis Halphen advances. He thinks that contemporary history had a disadvantage in the eyes of methodologists, that of being "too easily accessible" and hence open to the "legion of browsers attracted by the lure of anything unpublished, with which the most insignificant archives are overflowing."[90] In order to constitute a true body of professional historians, a line must be drawn between what pertains to the "scientific," to an academic elite, and what belongs to "literature" or "politics," open to all comers. That is a situation familiar to professional historians of the present time working today: the competition, whether conscious or not, with journalists, bloggers, amateur or militant historians, and, in fact, any citizen interested in the past. That competition is considerably more limited in the case of medieval or even modern history, a subject matter less easily accessible than recent history. I should also mention here the division of labor established in the late nineteenth century between that new historical discipline, oriented toward the distant past, and sociology, by definition directed more toward the contemporary. The division was not only practical but also theoretical and would challenge the assumptions of the methodological school and the demarcation it made between the past and the present. The opposition between a historical method oriented toward the bygone past, based on the division between past and present, and an emergent "social science" that considered time a social construct and one variable among others for understanding societies, made the historiographical study of the contemporary world even more difficult. Granted, the Annales

School of the 1920s would play a role in making the discipline of history a human science as much as a social science and in rejecting a large share of these prejudices. In the editorial comment of the very first issue of *Annales*, dated January 15, 1929, Marc Bloch and Lucien Febvre denounced the implicit division of labor that left the past to the historians and the study of contemporary societies and economies to others. Yet that division would persist until the last third of the twentieth century and would break down only with the emergence of a new history of the present time.

The rejection of contemporary history is further explained by the advent of a new intellectual and cognitive framework that demonstrated the limits and difficulties specific to a history of the present time. These difficulties were not, strictly speaking, new, but they took on a particular configuration within the postrevolutionary context. Because the mission of historians was to understand a bygone past, they increasingly had to confront the question of alterity: to write the history of the past was no longer to retrace a genealogy culminating in the present or to write the history of the same. It was rather to immerse oneself in a different world, a world that was sometimes completely alien to the historian's. This does not mean, however, that there is a difference in nature between ancient facts and recent facts, as Seignobos points out in a text considered one of the manifestoes of the methodological school:

> But as soon as one seeks to delimit the field of history in practical terms, as soon as one attempts to draw the boundary between a historical science of human facts in the past and a current science of human facts in the present, one realizes that that boundary cannot be established, because in reality there are no facts that are historical by nature, in the sense that there are physiological or biological facts. In common usage the word "historic" is still taken in the sense it had in antiquity: worthy of being told. People speak in this sense of a "historic day," a "historic remark." But that notion of history has been abandoned: every past incident is a part of history—both the costume worn by a peasant in the eighteenth century and the storming of the Bastille—and the grounds that make a fact appear worthy of mention are infinitely variable. History encompasses the study of all past facts—political, intellectual, and economic—most of which have gone unnoticed. It would therefore seem that historical facts can be defined as "past facts," in opposition to current facts, which are the object of the descriptive human sciences. It is precisely that opposition that is impossible to maintain in practice. To be present or past is not an intrinsic difference, one having to do with the nature of a fact: it is only a difference in position in relation to a given observer. The Revolution of 1830 is a past fact for us, but a present one for the people who made it. So too, yesterday's session in the Chamber is already a past fact. There are therefore no facts that are historical by nature; they are historical

facts only by virtue of their position. A historical fact is anything that can no longer be observed directly because it has ceased to exist. There is no historical character inherent in the facts; only the way of knowing them is historical. History is not a science, it is only a process of cognition.[91]

There is no question, then, of rejecting contemporary history on the basis of its nature. To consider "yesterday's" debates in the Chamber as already past, for example, is a way of supposing that they can enter the historian's field of observation. But insofar as that new history is defined as a "knowledge by means of traces," it becomes an indirect knowledge—here again is the mediate knowledge of the Renaissance—elaborated on the basis of written sources that are not immediately accessible to the historian. The historian can apprehend a reality that is a priori alien only through an effort of abstraction and imagination, the foundations of the new textual criticism. That perspective makes method, more than the objects studied, the basis for the historian's new métier (though the methodologists had a preference for political history). From that standpoint, the near past cannot enter the historian's area of investigation, because the task officially assigned to the historian is to study what is no longer: "A historical fact is anything that can no longer be observed directly because it has ceased to exist." Granted, Seignobos does not say that a present fact, nonhistorical according to his definition, cannot also be studied, but that is not the primary task of the historian, at least in the scientific aspect of historical activity. Nor is it a matter of blindly embracing a principle of objectivity. The methodologists were perfectly well aware that history was in part a "construction," to use a current term, a deliberate form of "problematization," though the word would not be used in that sense for a long time yet. The new German historiography underscores that point early on: "All empirical investigation governs itself according to the data to which it is directed, and it can only direct itself to such data as are immediately present to it and susceptible of being cognized through the senses. The data for historical investigation are not past things, for these have disappeared, but things which are still present here and now, whether recollections of what was done, or remnants of things that have existed and of events that have occurred."[92]

But if, in the great Augustinian tradition, the historian must adopt an anachronistic position in relation to the objects studied and thus measure the difference between things past and their trace or imprint, the historian's own present and own experience can become obstacles to be overcome in order to write history. After all, the first priority is to place oneself within the perspective of men and women of the past in order to understand their world, their way of thinking, acting, and feeling. That is the principle of historical empathy theorized by German historiography. The historian will have to make an effort of the imagination and of distanciation to restore to the present trace its original past form. Historians therefore had to detach themselves from their own contemporaneity, and hence from all or part of their own subjectivity. That explains the importance of the principle of historical objectivity in the historiography of the era. That posture, taken to its extreme, can lead to a form of scientism—to which the methodologists did not subscribe, since the separation between past and present was for them relative rather than absolute, stemming as it did from the historian's position first and foremost and not from an ontological conception of time. As Fustel de Coulanges wrote: "When I read the works of the moderns on antiquity, my first impulse, I confess, is to doubt, because I too often recognize altogether modern thoughts. But when I read the ancients, my first impulse is to believe, and I believe them all the more the farther their ideas are from my own."[93] The historian's anachronistic position, like the need to consider the past as an alterity, can thus lead not merely to suspicion with respect to contemporary history, but even to the assertion of a radical impossibility:

The way we look at present things is always clouded by some personal interest, some prejudice, or some passion. It is almost always impossible to see properly. In the case of the past, conversely, our view is calmer and more reliable. We better understand events *and revolutions* [my emphasis] from which we have nothing to fear and nothing to hope for. Acts that have already been completed [*faits accomplis*] appear to us with a great deal more clarity than acts in the process of being completed. We see the beginning and the end of them, the cause and the effects, the whys and the wherefores. We distinguish the essential from the incidental in them. We grasp their forward movement, their direction, and their true sense. While they were being completed, men did not understand them; they were clouded, mixed together with foreign elements, obscured by ephemeral accidents. There is always in human events a part that is only external and apparent; ordinarily, it is that part that strikes the eyes of contemporaries the most. It is therefore very rare for a great event to have been understood by those who worked to produce it. Almost always, every generation has been wrong about its achievements. It acted without knowing clearly what it was doing. It believed it had one goal before it, and its efforts led to a completely different goal. It seems that it is beyond the powers of the human mind to have a clear intuition of the present. The study of history must have at least the advantage of accustoming us to distinguish, in the facts and in the progress of societies, what is apparent from what is real, what is the illusion of contemporaries from what is truth.[94]

Not all historians of the time shared that idea of a history that human beings made without realizing it, a history driven by deep and invisible forces that could only be apprehended with temporal and psychological distance. But many embraced the conviction, all in all modern in its time, that history could be written only after a waiting period: the time to establish and organize the archives, the historian's raw material; the time to let passions die down, especially political passions arising from the revolutionary conflagration and its consequences, an obstacle to any impartial and objective history; the time for forgetting to do its work and thus allow the historian to escape the effects of memory, believed to be sharper the closer one is to the events; the time for the historical processes to reach their completion.

That perspective was in line with another major idea of the time, perceptible in history and literature, in the arts and philosophy, and which viewed the present as an ephemeral illusion. "There is no Present, no—a present does not exist," wrote Mallarmé, adding: "He is ill informed who would cry out that he is his own contemporary, deserting, usurping, with equal impudence, when a past ended and a future is long in coming, or when the two once more mingle together perplexedly in the aim of masking the gap."[95] The possibility of rationally grasping one's own time would in that sense be a kind of intellectual chimera. Nietzsche expressed that idea with a certain virulence in 1874, in the second of his *Untimely Meditations*: "This meditation too is untimely, because I am here attempting to look afresh at something of which our time is rightly proud—its cultivation of history—as being injurious to it, a defect and deficiency in it; because I believe, indeed, that we are all suffering from a consuming fever of history and ought at least to recognize that we are suffering from it. . . . That much, however, I must concede to myself on account of my profession as a classicist: for I do not know what meaning classical studies could have for our time if they were not untimely— that is to say, acting counter to our time and thereby acting on our time and, let us hope, for the benefit of a time to come."[96]

Nietzsche may have denounced historicism in this text, but in fact he is in agreement with the critique formulated, explicitly or not, by a large swath of the historiography of the time, concerning the illusion of wanting to understand one's own time, at least with the historian's tools. He does so with a completely different objective, that of a "history for life," for action, hence turned toward the future. But one consequence is to make the present, the present-day, an unstable, uncertain, volatile moment with respect to the movement of History.

That need to apprehend a "completed" history, to take an interest in an "untimely" history, to stand back from the contemporary world, can be explained not only by the scientistic and positivistic postures, but also by a form of intellectual weariness. The political debates in Europe at the time were still profoundly marked by the original tumult of a revolution whose effects seemed to be interminable. That absence of closure gave many historians the sense that an objective and consensual interpretation of the facts was impossible for that event, still fresh in the collective memory, even though these principles appeared indispensable for establishing a different way of apprehending history—hence the need for a waiting period before one can understand the forward march of societies. That stance is dually historicist: it assumes, first, that the temporal factor remains the essential element of explanation, a view that was being contested by sociology at the same moment; and, secondly, that temporal distance offers the guarantee of a greater detachment and a wider viewpoint. That idea is now known to be erroneous in part, since distance in time from the great historical upheavals in no way attenuates the passions they can arouse. The French Revolution, in fact, provided a stunning counterexample. That quest for a distant, if not serene, historiography was certainly marked by a new scientific ethos. It may also have expressed a need for repression, a hypothesis that has rarely been advanced. After all, to take one's distance from the catastrophe, to stop talking about it, or to make it a central object of investigation, going farther back in time to reconnect with a long-term identity and thereby participate in a form of relative forgetting, is a *nontraumatized* response to the ordeal suffered. It signals that the shock of the Revolution had in part been dulled or was in the process of being dulled, since in spite of everything, the Revolution was coming to an end, to paraphrase François Furet. Here again, that is the opposite of what we have experienced for the last thirty years or so, given that the response to the catastrophes of the last century—which are, to be sure, of a completely different nature—has taken the form of an obsessive presence of the past and of a compulsive appeal to a memory that is duty bound to be omnipresent. Historians, especially those of the present time, are called on to maintain that memory. That is a *traumatized* response to the original shocks; the past turns out to be inescapable, insurmountable.

The principles recommended by the methodological school therefore rest in part on a need, to be expected all in all, for a repression of the political passions in which their predecessors were caught up. In spite of everything, however, these principles were expressed in the form of a blatant contradiction, itself the consequence of the ambiguous effects of the shadow cast by the event. Although contemporary history seems to have been rejected even as it was beginning to exist, it was not condemned by all historians, nor was it systematically denounced by its principal detractors. That is a second paradox. In fact, despite the suspicion, contemporary history, that of a near past that began with the Revolution itself, did indeed develop throughout the nineteenth century. The first histories of the event appeared very early on, and what was at stake was as moral and political as it was scientific. Throughout the nineteenth century, important authors, writers, journalists, and politicians produced major essays (Tocqueville) or general histories on the subject, the best known of which are clearly those of Michelet (1847), Quinet (1865), and Jaurès (1900). With the approach of the centennial in 1889, an actual policy of memory was set in place, with the launching of a journal (*La Révolution française*) that welcomed only original articles based on sources, even while defending the ideological line of the Radicals regarding the unicity of the event ("the Revolution is all of a piece"). In addition, a commission was created to collect and publish documents, including the Proceedings of the Committee of Public Safety.[97] In 1891 Alphonse Aulard, the expert accredited and appointed by the government, occupied the Sorbonne's first chair in the History of the Revolution. Even as contemporary history was increasingly giving rise to reservations, the history of the Revolution, an event now a century old, entered a scientific phase. More generally, many indicators show the relative vitality of contemporary history in France, despite the ostracism from which it suffered. Although a minority phenomenon in academia, it was far from absent, as attested, for example, by the creation of chairs in modern and contemporary history at the Sorbonne (1884 and 1888), the advent of the *Revue d'histoire moderne et contemporaine* (1899), the creation of the Société d'Histoire de la Révolution de 1848 (1904), and the publication of *Répertoire méthodique de l'histoire moderne et contemporaine* (*Methodological Repertoire for Modern and Contemporary History*) by the Société d'Histoire Moderne (1901), which listed books and articles on the history of France "from 1789 to our time." That expression, which became widespread in historiographical works, demonstrates that a form of integration of the very near past into history in general had occurred.

That apparent paradox can be explained by what is now a well-known factor. The proponents of the methodological school, who dominated the discipline at the time, found themselves caught up in a real contradiction: excluding recent history from the scientific field meant denying oneself the possibility of integrating the decisive event that had founded both a new political and a new intellectual and scientific order. The contradiction was all the more untenable in that their conservative and reactionary enemies, often outside academia, had taken over the place left vacant and had successfully occupied the field of the history of the Revolution and of recent history. Taine, for example, published his *Origines de la France contemporaine* in 1875; and the Société d'Histoire Contemporaine, created in 1890, was conservative Catholic in its inspiration.[98] To keep from abandoning the field to their enemies, the methodological historians thus added recent periods to university curricula and dealt with them in their textbooks and popular works. In France, one of the architects of that development was Victor Duruy, minister of public education under the Second Empire (1863–69), who understood how important it was that knowledge of one's own time be part of the young citizen's education:

> [Secondary school students], saturated with the past, want something of the present and take it wherever they find it, in lampoons and in partial and truncated compositions, none of which, moreover, presents in its entirety, and as a result in its truth, the new character of contemporary civilization. If history is truly the depository of universal experience, if there is no administrator who, to resolve a question great or small, does not judge it necessary to study how it was resolved before him, why do we prohibit those who will be running the country's affairs in a few years from knowing in what manner this country lived in the period immediately preceding that in which they will be called upon to act? Some fear an invasion of politics. But, in the first place, if we owe the dead the truth, we owe the "living" respect; and these lessons in contemporary history, which our neighbors on the other side of the Rhine and on the other side of the Channel do not fear as we do, should never deal with people or with anecdotal facts in the manner of Suetonius or Saint-Simon. We should look from high above and far away, which is a good way to see properly. Do they engage less in politics in the taverns of army barracks or in the Latin Quarter because they are ignorant of the things being discussed there? No, certainly not, but they definitely engage in poor politics. To thrust a man into the commonwealth without having told him anything about the organization of the necessities amid which he will have to live and fight is like throwing a foot soldier into battle with the weaponry of Charles VII's *francs-archers*.[99]

The historian Ernest Lavisse, singled out by Duruy, would later put into practice the idea that contemporary history is a civic and political necessity, whatever the scientific objections that can be raised against it, by overseeing the publication of *Histoire de France, depuis les origines jusqu'à la Révolution*

(1903–11; *History of France from the Origins to the Revolution*) and then *Histoire de la France contemporaine depuis la Révolution jusqu'à la paix de 1919* (1920–22; *History of Contemporary France from the Revolution to the Peace of 1919*). These twenty-eight volumes are a veritable national monument beyond compare. It is in fact difficult to imagine how that work—a true "theory of France," in the words of the man who conceived it, written at the dawn of the twentieth century before and after World War I—could possibly have excluded the storming of the Bastille and the conflict (victorious, moreover) that in part shaped national sentiment in the second half of the Third Republic.[100] We therefore find once again the paradoxical dimension of a contemporary history that is declared both scientifically impossible and civically necessary.

CHAPTER TWO

War and the Time After

History is the sewer of humankind's evil deeds, it emits a cadaverous odor, and the massiveness of past calamities, in appearing to weaken present calamities, even seems to require—by virtue of a link assumed to be physical—future calamities. If history, that is, the example of so many political crimes committed and justified with impunity, could be annihilated, who can doubt that the tyrants of the earth would lose their awful rights and that humankind, no longer seeing anything but the present and not the past, would return reasonably to its ancient privileges?

LOUIS-SÉBASTIEN MERCIER,
Du théâtre ou Nouvel essai sur l'art dramatique (1773), 47–48

THE HORIZON OF CATASTROPHE

The hopes and illusions of the methodological school and its emulators of a history perceived as an objective science of social time, as a cumulative knowledge and a rational understanding of the past, would be shattered, at least in part, in the trenches of World War I. Yet historians of every nationality, often mobilized as combatants, were not immediately aware of that fact. In its violence and suddenness, that event, in the very midst of the conflagration and then immediately afterward, produced the sense that a new fracture in historical continuity had occurred. The term "catastrophe" is not a metaphor here; it actually falls short of describing the material, physical, and psychological upheavals brought about by a conflict unprecedented in nature. The thresholds of violence reached, the unheard-of scope of the human losses, the magnitude of the material destruction, and the expanse of the territories affected marked several generations in a lasting way and left enduring scars. The French Revolution, despite its intrinsic violence (to which it cannot be reduced), bore within itself the promise of progress in the near future, which may have rendered acceptable the suddenness of a break in History between an evolving present and a now bygone past. World War I, for its part, brought only destruction. Its only promise was the hope, almost immediately dashed, that it would be—that it must be—the first and last of its kind. The belief in a rational, continuous, and contained progress gave way within a few years to the almost universal sense of a world in the grip of chaos, a time marked by discontinuity, a history suddenly and once again torn off its hinges. Nevertheless, though World War I shattered the dream of continuous progress, of a historical time that was masterable through reason and knowledge, it also inaugurated new revolutionary sequences with eschatological overtones. The Bolshevik Revolution on the one hand, Fascism and Nazism on the other, though opposites and even mortal enemies, had at least one thing in common: they conveyed a vision of History marked both by a radical revision of the past and by the expression of new forms of millenarism that purported to accelerate the advent of a new man through extreme violence and absolute control over bodies, space, and time. Yet most of these systems were also aware of their own historical precariousness, which only accentuated the intensity of the violence wielded against their enemies or their own people: when, under Allied bombs, the eschatological realization of a thousand-year Reich turned out to be a utopian dream, the regime preferred to take the path of chaos and self-destruction rather than give up its mastery of the course of History.

In that context, the very notion of contemporaneity would change in meaning. So too, the function of history, its place in society, the role of historians, their way of conceiving of a discipline traversed by strong tensions. Initially history, like the scientific and intellectual world as a whole, was enlisted everywhere in Europe in the service of the war, a well-known process in our own time.[1] In France, the sociologist Émile Durkheim denounced the "morbid" character of the German mentality and detected in it a "social pathology," which would constitute a theme of reflection for future historians and sociologists. The philosopher Henri Bergson defended the idea that "the struggle against Germany is nothing less than the struggle of civilization against barbarism." The historian Ernest Babelon, a specialist in antiquity and a professor at the Collège de France, followed close behind, attempting to demonstrate that the Rhine represented the natural border between the two forces. And the geographer Paul Vidal de La Blache sought to prove "scientifically" that the Sarre belonged to France, in support of future claims to the left bank of that river.[2] Comparable statements were made on the German side. For example, the famous Manifesto of the Ninety-three was signed by (among other scholars) half a dozen historians, including Karl Lamprecht, one of the most famous of his generation. Published in 1914, that text, which supported the German government and denied the accusations of atrocities, constitutes one example among others of the war being waged by petition on the part of intellectuals in the belligerent countries.[3] In the United States, the situation was complicated by the fact that the country entered the war belatedly and that, before 1917, historians were divided between a current that favored the British and the French and another, smaller one favoring the Germans. The underlying question was whether military intervention in Europe was necessary. That changed in 1917: historians, having condemned the nationalism of their French or German colleagues, which according to them had led to the war, now explicitly reproached themselves for having "insufficiently promoted American patriotism."[4] Even more interesting, and though their commitment turned out to be in complete contradiction with their ideal of objectivity and impartiality, academics became engaged in their turn. They sought to show the relevance of their discipline and the social role they could play in the conflict. The task at hand was to demolish the image of a historian "occupied solely with the dates and details of remote transactions having no relation to the fateful exigencies of the present day."[5]

During and after the conflict, the configuration of World War I, especially its national component, would cast into relief the question of borders, languages, peoples, ethnic groups, and migrations, all subjects that appealed to the authority of geography and history, sometimes the most remote in time. As a result, the war turned on its head the relationship between practitioners of these disciplines and their own time. Throughout the nineteenth century, historians had been encouraged to detach themselves from the present; to increase their credibility by setting aside the field of the contemporary, at least in their scientific works; to be wary of long-lasting passions; and to be parsimonious in their political engagements, at least in the possible connection between science and politics. Certain events came to contradict these recommendations, however. During the Dreyfus affair, for example, the "neutrality" of knowledge collided head-on with the need to defend the values underlying that same knowledge and thus obliged historians to take sides. In any case, total war and the general mobilization of minds and bodies toppled that world of objectivity. Engagement became the norm, neutrality unthinkable, the scientific ivory tower a reprehensible chimera. Historians had to be "useful" as both combatants and experts, and like everyone else had to place their art in the service of the nation at war—even a little more than everyone else, since a good share of the war objectives depended on antagonistic readings of the past.

The present time was therefore in command, because of the needs of the moment but also because the simultaneity of the experience of war on a continental scale and across all social classes would give new substance and significance to the notion of contemporary history. As had been the case after the Revolution, the writing of a history of the present time was once again confronted with opposing currents and imperatives. On the one hand, there was the need to produce narratives about the conflict that had just ended. National opinion in each of the belligerent countries was waiting for the incomprehensible character of the war—its violence, both extraordinary and unprecedented in History—to be explained and for the responsible and guilty parties to be designated. History was once more urged to confer meaning after the fact, to help nations recover from the trauma, and sometimes to set up a court of judgment for posterity. The Treaty of Versailles stipulated that war criminals, or those denounced as such, would be brought to justice, which would lead in particular to the project, eventually aborted, to try the kaiser and also to the Leipzig war crime trials of 1921. For the first time a tribunal was vested with the responsibility of giving a normative interpretation of the history of the near past. That dimension, however, did not appear in all its originality at the time, as it would after 1945.

On the other hand, there were the usual obstacles: insufficient temporal distance, passions at least as heated as they had been after 1789 and on a vaster scale. To what extent was it possible to write a noncontentious history of the war, produce a narrative that could be generally agreed upon, at a time when radically antagonistic conceptions of the event were clashing in the political and intellectual field: the view of the victors versus the view of the vanquished, universalists versus nationalists, doves versus hawks, heroic narratives versus critical narratives? It was not only that written histories of the present time risked remaining captive to the passions of the moment; they themselves became among the most passionate aspects of the postwar period at the national and international level.

Although studies of the conflict began to multiply even before the ink on the armistice agreement had dried, they continued a tradition that had arisen in the early stages of the conflict. In 1911 the new Carnegie Endowment for International Peace had begun to publish regularly a large number of documents on international relations and on the conflicts under way. Beginning in 1914, the belligerent countries had also published many collections of documents to justify their positions: the French Yellow Book, the British Blue Book, the German White Book. These constituted major sources for analyzing the conflict. Likewise, most of the military general staffs had set up "historical services" or had reinstated agencies that in some cases dated far back. In France, the Dépôt de la Guerre, established in the late seventeenth century to collect military archival materials and reorganized after the defeat of 1870 with the creation, notably, of a historical section and a geographical service, was overhauled in 1919. It now comprised army and navy historical services, to which an army air force historical service would be added in 1934. The objective of these services was to "draw the lessons of the past by scientific and critical methods" and "to undertake a history of the French armies during the Great War."[6] It was not of course a new idea in the military world to collect on-the-spot experiences of a conflict still under way or only recently ended: war strategy had always been based on a form of historical analysis. But it now took on a memorial dimension, as homage was paid to the combatants, and made use of the most recent historiographical techniques.

That history of the near past, then, developed in the heat of the action, without a well-defined program or epistemological postulates. "It is striking how soon it appeared," Antoine Prost and Jay Winter write. "The Battle of the Marne, only just won, became a historical subject" in a book published in 1915.[7] In academia, suspicions seem to have been partly dispelled, though contemporary history had not yet acquired a legitimacy equivalent to that of other historiographical periods. In any case, the entire historical discipline was an object of suspicion, as the French historian and former infantryman Jules Isaac would later point out: "For the war veteran historian, there was no duty more urgent, more imperious, than to tackle head-on the imposing, complacent official history that was already working hard to mask too many sickening truths. There was no enterprise more necessary and more salubrious than to expose to the light of day the realities of the war and, beyond an illusory victory, the precariousness of peace. Was not the future itself, national and human, at stake in that debate?"[8]

Then there was Lucien Febvre's famous challenge during his inaugural lecture at the Université de Strasbourg, French once more, where he had just been appointed. He too painted a portrait of a discipline morally in ruins:

> A history that is of service is a servile history. As professors of the French University of Strasbourg, we are not the newly arrived missionaries of an official national gospel, however beautiful, however grand, however well-intentioned it may appear. We do not bring to Strasbourg, in the folds of our academic robes, stocks of antidotes skillfully concocted to destroy the last effects of the historico-providential pharmacopeia of our predecessors; nor do we bring counterevidence, dressed up and decked out in French disguise, of that hel-

meted and armor-plated truth with the phony airs of Bellona or Germania, the one true goddess of what was in times past an official temple and is at present a free center for research. As for Truth, we do not bring it back a captive in our baggage train. We seek it, we will seek it to our dying day.[9]

The loss of credibility of a discipline enlisted to wage war, one that played an important role in defining the war objectives and constructing the enemy for the principal belligerents, was thus universal. The historians most attached to objectivity and impartiality had showed they could put their craft in the service of the most negative passions of the present. The objections against contemporary history, supposedly impossible because too deeply marked by high stakes, therefore lost a large share of their relevance. The bygone past, which scholarly history was supposed to look back on objectively, had been instrumentalized to the point of caricature; knowledge of the very near past, now the object of everyone's attention, required rigorous study. It no longer made any sense to argue for a necessary and orthodox temporal distance. Could anyone imagine waiting half a century to publish the first reliable histories of the war that had just ended? On the contrary, almost everywhere in the historiography of the 1920s, the need took hold to invent a new form of epistemological distance, a new way of doing history that broke its ties to objectivism. The Comité International des Sciences Historiques (CISH; International Committee of the Historical Sciences) was created in Geneva in 1926 with the mission of forming a transnational community of historians, in response to the desire of Marc Bloch and the Belgian historian Henri Pirenne for a comparative history, a factor of mutual understanding among nations.[10]

In that context, a new space opened for the history of the present time, marked by the memory and aftermath of the catastrophe. Mobilization had dispelled the illusion of objectivity among historians; demobilization posed unexpected challenges. As soon as the conflict ended, in both Europe and North America historians began to publish abundantly on the "Great War." That event had not yet entered the lexicon as "World War I," though the Germans spoke of *Weltkrieg* in the same way they spoke of *Weltmacht* (world power). Woodrow Wilson used the term "world war" for diametrically opposed reasons, viewing the conflict as a confrontation between universal values that went well beyond the territories concerned—one of the arguments he invoked to involve his country in the war.[11] The first books, predominantly diplomatic and military in their focus, disagreed on the causes of and responsibilities for the war, the theme to which they returned obsessively. For some, the Central Powers alone had triggered the conflict, a view that in part reflected the official French position. For others, especially American revisionists such as Harry Elmer Barnes and some pacifist and Germanophile French intellectuals such as Alfred Fabre-Luce, the Entente Powers bore the responsibility. For a third group, including French historians such as Jules Isaac and Pierre Renouvin, Germany was largely but not unilaterally responsible. Others condemned all the belligerent parties. Then there were the Marxists, for whom the war was merely the foreseeable consequence of imperialism.[12]

It is clear, therefore, that the history of the present time remained actively engaged after 1918. It was at that time, in fact, that what would become a fairly widespread figure emerged: the historian as expert. Unlike historians in the service of the Prince, experts occupied a place within a field of knowledge and power where their scientific credibility was their chief asset. They were no longer simply isolated literati but scholars operating within an organized, recognized, and autonomous discipline who placed their skills, rigor, and pursuit of truth in the service of a public cause. Like psychiatric expertise, which emerged in the nineteenth century, that kind of attention generally contributed toward accelerating the professionalization of the discipline, giving it new horizons, new parameters, new responsibilities. In that sense, there could be no "experts" in the field of history unless there was in the first place a somewhat organized profession regulated by internal procedures, a movement that, precisely, came to fruition before 1914 in both Europe and North America. The advent of expertise required, in the second place, a field of action where the techniques for investigating the past could serve concrete and immediate political or legal ends. Apart from the limited precedent of the expert historians during the Dreyfus affair, the end of World War I served as a large-scale experiment in that new function of history. After producing propaganda in the service of the nation at war, many historians collaborated on drafting treaties and helped to define the new European borders in 1918. That was the case for Robert William Seton-Watson, a British historian specializing in Slavonic studies and a friend of Masaryk and of Beneš. A militant for the Czech cause and a war veteran, he defended the idea that historians ought to play a political role in the reconfiguration of Central Europe.[13] That was the case as well for the French historian Ernest Denis, a specialist in Bohemia and Germany, who assisted in the creation of the future Czechoslovakian state, even becoming a mythical figure in its national narrative.[14] Ernest Denis was also on the Comité d'Études, created in 1917 by the French prime minister Aristide Briand and de facto dissolved in 1919; it included about thirty academics and was headed by Ernest Lavisse and Paul Vidal de La Blache. The committee was formed to help the French government define the country's war objectives and territorial aims, but, despite having drafted some sixty memoranda, it would have little influence on the definitive wording of the treaties. It wasted the time of the scholars solicited and produced bitterness, especially among historians and geographers: they had responded to the government's entreaties in a way that profoundly altered their usual academic practices and yet produced no tangible effects.[15] Woodrow Wilson, himself a historian by profession who was rejected by some of his colleagues, also enlisted a team of historians to assist him during negotiations on the peace treaties. This was a first in the governmental practices of the United States, justified by the fact that the country was for the first time exerting a notable influence on the conduct of other countries' affairs.[16]

The postwar period therefore saw the birth of a new history of the present time, spurred on by the urgent issues of the moment, especially diplomatic issues. France, in the wake of the Senate Investigation Commission on the Events of the War, created the Société d'Histoire de la Guerre (Society for the History of the War), aimed at collecting documents and publishing works that conformed to the research criteria, with the aid, notably, of a new journal: the *Revue d'histoire de la guerre mondiale*, launched in 1923 and published regularly until July 1939. In 1922 the Sorbonne introduced a course of study devoted to the conflict. It was initially assigned to the journal's secretary, Pierre Renouvin, a twenty-nine-year-old historian and war veteran who had lost his left arm and right thumb in the conflict. Renouvin, who began his career at the crossroads of several initiatives, all oriented toward writing a history still in progress, was also tasked by the minister of public education, André Honnorat, with conducting a large-scale investigation on the causes of the conflict, based on the documents available. His research would lead to a fundamental work: *Les origines immédiates de la guerre: 28 juin–4 août 1914* (1925; *The Immediate Origins of the War, June 28–August 4, 1914*). Renouvin was named professor at the Sorbonne in 1931, a post he would hold until 1964. His first book and those that followed would contribute toward founding a new history of international relations. Having arisen from an evolution in classic diplomatic history, that history was more attentive to the "deep forces" of societies in contact with one another than to the behavior of the political and diplomatic elites alone.[17] It would ultimately constitute one of the branches of the historiography of the contemporary more or less tolerated within the university.

More significantly, no doubt, in addition to the production of scholarship, the Great War and its legacy over the medium term also fostered the development of new political and social practices relating to the past—new not in their essence, but in their uses, and in the scope of their field of application. The mobilization of the masses on a continental scale gave rise to the formation of a collective memory of the war, structured by practices of mourning, national or local public commemorations, and testimony that took on a massive and unprecedented dimension, no longer concerning elites but rather the deepest strata of European societies.[18] The very concept of "collective memory" in its sociological sense, which would be rediscovered and exploited in the 1980s, was invented by Maurice Halbwachs in the 1920s and 1930s. It arose within a space of experience dominated by the Great War and the horizon of expectation of the war to follow, though Halbwachs almost never mentions the conflict directly.[19] Whether enlisted men or officers, established or first-time writers, illustrious scholars or anonymous souls, many told of the war through the prism of their personal experience, giving a strong subjective dimension to that recent history—a history that remained fresh in the memory, at least until the outbreak of World War II. This phenomenon, unprecedented in its diversity, scope, and impact, created new social figures destined to endure, or at least to reappear regularly throughout the century. That was the case, for example, with "moral witnesses," survivors who speak in the name of their dead comrades and maintain a relation to the past marked by the obligation to remember and the refusal to forget.[20] Such a witness was a subject, an "I" speaking in the first person, with the idea that those who did not live through the experience of battle could not grasp the meaning of the war that had just ended. But that witness was also a "we" who spoke in the name of a collective that included both those who had died and those who still lived—or rather, who survived. In some cases, privileged witnesses would portray themselves as rivaling the historian—or at least the historian "who wasn't part of it," who did not experience directly the shock of the trenches (in this case) and later that of deportation. That witness of a new kind forcefully asserted the authenticity and primacy of lived experience. The best-known, most controversial, and most emblematic example is Jean Norton Cru. Having enlisted in August 1914, he spent two years at the front, notably at Verdun. In 1929 he published a resoundingly successful book titled *Témoins* (*Witnesses*), in which he collected and critiqued testimonies of the war that had appeared in the previous decade, especially by such important names as Henri Barbusse and Roland Dorgelès. Tracking down factual errors, implausibilities, and boasts, he was obsessed with bringing to light a single, indivisible historical truth. He fashioned himself into a veritable judge of the proper way to bear witness to the war, not without a few scientistic excesses and a certain anti-intellectual populism—even though he taught literature at Williams College in Massachusetts. His book represented an important moment in the emergence of a real ideology of testimony. In it the author defended a position that was destined to endure: for a catastrophe such as the Great War, the witnesses who had lived through the events amid the muck and corpses had an almost exclusive right to write about it first, on the spot. Only that direct, physical experience was in touch with the facts before any mediate knowledge, which Cru did not reject as an eventuality but whose application in the immediate present he denied. He thus explicitly turned to his own account the methodological school's objections to contemporary history, especially regarding the necessity of temporal distance. His position on this question is in my view altogether significant: "Those who anticipate by writing histories right now are condemned to produce the provisional, and a provisional of very short duration. They are wasting their time and their knowledge."[21] Because a rigorous history of the war is impossible on the spot, only the authentic and sincere writings of genuine witnesses must prevail, all of whom will constitute sources for historians— but only for historians of the future. In reaction to that positivism, which the war had in great part rendered obsolete, Jules Isaac would reply:

> It is an assertion consistent with popular opinion and generally undisputed, but it does not seem indisputable to me. I myself am a little wary about that "distance necessary to the historian." It may be practically necessary (because of the materials the historian must gather together). In theoretical terms, I wonder whether the disadvantages of distance do not outweigh the advantages. The greater the distance, the more the event is seen "from the outside": the superficial outlines are no doubt easier to make out, but it is more difficult to break through the hard crust of legend that has attached itself to the event. To know it in all its reality, to perceive its true substance, one must, as Péguy said, have seen it from the inside, especially in the case of an event as complex and shattering as war. "Only war speaks well of war" is a valid axiom for the historian as well. . . . History knows of no masterpiece that equals *The Peloponnesian War*. Yet it is the work not of a historian who waited until he had "the necessary distance," but of a witness who had a sense for history, a historical genius to the highest degree. I conclude therefore that it is better not to build an impenetrable barrier between the witness and the historian and that, to begin historical work proper, there is no need to wait for "the necessary distance."[22]

It is striking to observe that World War I introduced, or reintroduced, into the public space both the figure of the historian of the present time, called upon by circumstance to give meaning to the catastrophe that had occurred, and that of the witness, who sought by other means and other venues the words to tell of it. Throughout the twentieth century, their partnership, their rivalry, and their antagonism would constitute a central element in the act of writing about the tragic history of the present time.

Everywhere, at least in the territories affected by the war, the history of the latest catastrophe (which was also the first of its kind) occupied a significant place in the social field. It was omnipresent in the visible traces of the conflict, in war wounds, in literary writings, in the press, in popular publications, in film, in political debates. It was truly a "public history," which often emerged spontaneously. For example, the new Bibliothèque-Musée de la Guerre (BMG; Library-Museum of the War) was founded in France in 1918, run at the time by Camille Bloch, with Pierre Renouvin as head of the department of documentation. That institution arose from a collection, unique of its kind, belonging to Louis and Henri Leblanc, a pair of Paris industrialists who beginning in 1914 had assembled tens of thousands of documents of every kind about the war: books, newspapers, archives, paintings, posters, photos, toys, and other small items that attest to the patriotic culture and to an entire country's involvement in the conflict. In 1917, the war having lasted longer than expected, they donated the collection to the state, which created a true "laboratory of history" open to the general public.[23] That institution was original in two ways: it opened in the heat of the event, and its initial impetus came from civil society. It is not a *lieu de mémoire*, a site of memory, oriented toward the celebration of the past, but rather a place that envisions the horizon of a memory to come. Its task was in fact to constitute that memory: it is a singular example of a perception of the present, of a form of contemporaneity experienced as ephemeral, of which the largest number of traces possible must be retained. World War II would provide many other examples of sites of memory *for the future* constituted during the event itself.

That "public history," that general need to seize the "present" in every sense of the term, was an integral part of a new popular "historical consciousness," a major cultural fact and an essential element in the evolution of contemporary historicity. It contributed, on the one hand, toward homogenizing the societies that emerged from the conflict, since it expressed a contemporaneity inflected in the form of a *simultaneity* of lived experiences, starting with the combat experience of tens of millions of men in Europe, even throughout the world when the troops from the colonies are included. But it also developed a *desynchronized* form of contemporaneity, because of the lags and discontinuities between experiences and perceptions of time. These experiences and perceptions varied greatly, depending on whether one was a war veteran or a civilian; whether one belonged to the generation under fire or the generations that followed; whether one was among the victors, who experienced a sort of "end of history" (national independence, the return of lost provinces), or the vanquished, for whom history was not over and who projected themselves into a more or less imminent future that bore the name "Revanche." A widely shared and overwhelming feeling predominated, that of having lived through a major rupture in History. At the same time, there was an awareness, just as acute, that these events had profoundly antagonistic meanings, which would be difficult to reconcile without a new catastrophe. The French Revolution, despite the conflicts and movements of resistance, had generated a "positive" memory, embodied in the invention of new political traditions that proudly embraced that past and gradually integrated its most ferocious adversaries, beginning with the Catholic church. By contrast, World War I gave rise to the first forms of "negative" memory, the perpetuation of mourning and the haunting sense that the past would be repeated. That feeling may have been attenuated by the hope (rather quickly dashed) raised by the Bolshevik Revolution, but the fear of a return to wartime violence, the war veterans' "never again!," occupied a large place in postwar societies. That watchword had no borders and introduced a particular kind of relationship between the present and the past. The near past was rejected as a recollection of terror, but at the same time it haunted consciousness to an unprecedented degree. It did not pass away, it would not pass away (that is the traumatic aspect), it must not pass away (that is its moral and political expression). Indeed, the memory of it, whether masterable or not, now served, like Walter Benjamin's angel of history, as a warning, an alert to the possibility of a recurrence:

> A Klee painting named "Angelus Novus" shows an angel looking as though he is about to move away from something he is fixedly contemplating. His eyes are staring, his mouth is open, his wings are spread. This is how one pictures the angel of history. His face is turned toward the past. Where we perceive a chain of events, he sees one single catastrophe which keeps piling wreckage upon wreckage and hurls it in front of his feet. The angel would like to stay, awaken the dead, and make whole what has been smashed. But a storm is blowing from Paradise, it has got caught in his wings with such violence that the angel can no longer close them. This storm irresistibly propels him into the future to which his back is turned, while the pile of debris before him grows skyward. This storm is what we call progress.[24]

This is one of the best known and most widely discussed passages from the "Theses on the Philosophy of History," written in 1940 and not intended for publication, at a time when the next catastrophe had in fact arrived. For

Benjamin, of course, that catastrophe was not the war but a certain conception of progress, propelled in particular by a social democracy for which he does not have words harsh enough. But in these lines, interpreted in a nonpolitical manner, Benjamin expresses in a few words of prophetic density the change in historicity of the previous two decades. History is a gaze cast on the catastrophe, a debt to the dead, the victims, the vanquished. History is an education in radical alterity, which must however reestablish the connections between the time bursting forth and the time of ruins, but without losing sight in that acceleration of the need to understand, though that is not Benjamin's first concern. Paul Ricoeur would later write of that text: "For the professional historian, what remains on the near side of that vanishing horizon is the uncanniness of history, the interminable competition between the vow to be faithful to memory and the search for the truth in history."[25]

THE TRANSITION FROM WARTIME AND CONTEMPORANEITY

In many respects, then, World War I rendered somewhat obsolete the radical demarcation between past and present, a cultural inheritance of the French Revolution. Methodological historiography had turned that demarcation to its own account, in the name of a necessary distinction, if not a separation, between science and politics, observation and engagement. Memories of the most recent history now invaded the social and political field, a social fact that professional historians cannot ignore. The evolution in cultural and scientific paradigms (including the theory of relativity) declared null and void the linear views of time, on which that demarcation rested. After all, the division was itself only a scientific fiction, as its promoters were in great part aware. By definition, the deployment of a more conceptual history based on the importance of preliminary frames of reference, of a "problematic," of an inquiry unique to the historian, gave a greater place to contemporaneity in Croce's sense, since the historian/actor and the context in which the history was elaborated became essential elements for understanding the most remote past. Subjectivity (or rather, the subjective stance), previously heretical, became widespread among postwar historians in Europe and the United States:

> The historian can free himself from some of the unnecessary difficulties raised by Ranke's formula, *as it really happened*. That formula is in many ways still use-

ful. . . . But the famous formula contained certain metaphysical overtones we are well rid of. As interpreted by many of the older historians it implied that a historian could somehow get at a reality that lay altogether outside his thinking—that "what really happened" was in itself a fact awaiting discovery. We can now admit that the past in this sense is forever lost to us, that the historian must relate his facts to a pattern, a conceptual scheme of which he can require only that it prove useful; that, like the physicist's conceptual scheme for the electron, it proves a convenient way of accounting for known facts and for leading to the discovery of hitherto unknown facts. The historian can get rid of the incubus of absolutism implied in "as it really happened" and accept all the advantages of a frankly relativistic position.[26]

The decline, relative and temporary, of the paradigm of objectivity among professional historians and the growing connection—still marked by mutual distrust, however—to the other social sciences led to a greater attention to the contemporary and encouraged historians to consider more dialectically the relation between the past and the present. In a famous lecture delivered at the University of London on December 13, 1928, the British historian Robert William Seton-Watson, who had taken part in the Peace Conference, articulated a vibrant "plea for the study of contemporary history."[27] This text is essential for understanding how that form of history emerged from its purgatory after World War I. Often quoted in Anglophone historiography, it is almost unknown in the French branch, no doubt because, at that time, the French were utterly dazzled by the rise of the Annales School. The first issue of *Annales* appeared in January 1929, and that school ultimately eclipsed all other similar innovations or anticipations originating outside France. In his article Seton-Watson denounces the incongruity of a field that had been neglected even as the discipline as a whole had for three decades been experiencing an unprecedented expansion: "I am not attacking other branches of history—either modern, medieval or ancient. I am merely advancing on behalf of their younger sister, who has just attained to years of discretion, a plea for recognition and equality of treatment. In effect, I am suggesting that all of us, whether we be students, teachers, or men of action, should not, in our researches, in our interests, or in our demands upon our pupils' interest, stop just at the point where historical studies acquire their most practical value, namely, at the very threshold of our own age."[28]

He predicted the growth of contemporary history in the near future and easily swept aside the objections being raised against it. Did it risk becoming quickly obsolete? That was the fate of any historiographical proposition, in that every era revises its entire history, not just its most recent part. Was it too dependent on contemporary sources and hobbled by their rarity, given the obligatory waiting period to gaining access to the archives? It was in the very nature of the historian's task to rely on such sources, even long afterward, while considering them from a different viewpoint. As for the risk of a scarcity of archives, that was absurd: it was the opposite risk, that of an overabundance, that the historian would have to face. More important, the very nature of the Great War, the publication of numerous diplomatic documents and memoirs written by politicians, the partial breach in the traditional principle of secrecy protecting the actions of nation-states meant that no comparable crisis in the entire history of humanity had so quickly made available so many sources essential for writing the history of a present-day event. "It is surely superfluous to insist that the general process thus briefly indicated received a gigantic impetus from the great war and the series of revolutions in which it culminated. Joseph de Maistre, writing to a friend at the height of the French Revolution, argued that 'the project of putting the Lake of Geneva into bottles is much less mad than that of re-establishing matters on the same footing as before the Revolution'; and it may be contended that the great war has had the same revolutionary effect upon historical studies, and, above all, the study of contemporary history."[29]

As for the question of objectivity and whether one must abjure all political positions or religious beliefs in order to write history, contemporary or not, Seton-Watson, himself an active supporter of the Czech cause, wondered whether we must "fill our veins with milk instead of blood" and thus repudiate our human condition. He even pleaded for increased engagement on the part of historians of the present time in the urgent affairs of the postwar period: "A close study of recent history is an essential corollary of the new international peace movement which centres round the League of Nations, and on which the avoidance of fresh upheavals must so largely depend. I am not so foolish as to plead for the enlistment of historians as mere propagandists of this or that campaign of pacifism or disarmament; but it is self-evident that they have a very special function to perform in promoting that scientific study of recent times which is one of the essential foundations on which a new world and a new mentality must be constructed."[30]

By contrast, at no moment in this article, or indeed in similar texts that at the time defended the scientific practice of a contemporary history, was the idea of the singularity of that historiographical period put forward. On the contrary, these pleas insist that it is a history "like any other." That is not at all surprising, since the matter at hand was precisely to promote *integra-*

tion after a period of exclusion and thus to show that that history was identical in its methods and paradigms to the other, more "noble" branches of historiography. It was only much later, once that historiography had been acknowledged and had even acquired a form of hegemony within academia and among the general public, that the question would arise, not in an effort to distinguish contemporary history but because, having reached its maturity, it now had to refine its epistemological assumptions.

Beyond the necessary development of a contemporary history for which recognition and legitimacy were being demanded, it was truly the respective place of the past and the present that changed in the historiographical approach, itself a reflection of a profound cultural evolution. Seton-Watson perceives it intuitively at the end of his remarks: "I contend that a close study of (supplemented if possible by personal acquaintance with) the political, intellectual and industrial leaders of to-day is one of the most effective means of testing theories evolved from a documentary study of the age of Metternich and Franz-Joseph, of Kossuth and Déak. I am not, of course, advocating the dire heresy of judging the present by the past or the past by the present: I am only suggesting that the method of constant comparison between the two, of frequent but vigilant reference from one to the other, is likely to sharpen and humanise the historian's judgments upon men and affairs. It is one very practical side of the comparative method, which to my mind is one of the most profitable of all historical methods, when kept within due limits."[31]

That call to consider the relation between past and present differently, no longer in terms of division but in terms of comparison and dialectics, was a logical result of the plea for full inclusion of contemporary history in historical studies. Once a reunification of the discipline of history, all periods combined, was being defended, the separation between the bygone past and recent history—history still being made—by definition no longer had any pertinence: it was almost a tautology. Even if that was merely an intuition, it was rather remarkable, in that it anticipated one of the major paradigms of the Annales movement, namely, the need to redefine the link between the past and the present in the work of historians and social scientists generally. It did so not by beginning with the idea that the historical method as a whole had to be rethought but by asking, more modestly, that contemporary history be taken seriously by virtue of that same method.

At the same moment, the Annales project, a much better-known process that has been analyzed and tirelessly self-celebrated, set out to establish anew all

the foundations of historiography. From the outset, it granted a large place
to the "present" and condemned the artificial separation between it and
the past. In fact, Andre Burguière identifies a form of "presentism" in the
milieu associated with *Annales* during the founding period of the 1930s.[32]
"Presentism" is in the first place a scientific posture that grants a determining place to the historian's point of view and to the construction of the historical object, which by definition means putting the present, the historian's
own time, first in historical writing. That primacy of the observer's present
over the past of the object studied can be illustrated by the development
of what is known as the "regressive" method, which begins with a question embedded in the present and then moves back in time. For example,
Henri Hauser's inquiry on "the historical problem of prices" was solicited
in February 1929 and launched in 1930 within the context of the start of the
Great Depression.[33] That concern with the present also found expression
in a greater attention to contemporary history and current events. Between
1929 and 1945 the review devoted 16.4 percent of its total pages to nine-
teenth- and twentieth-century history and 21.7 percent to current events or
subjects from the recent past. That means that more than a third of the review was dedicated to "contemporary" history in the institutional sense of
the term; many articles from other disciplines, such as sociology and economics, were included. In the same period, the *Revue historique* and the *Revue
d'histoire moderne et contemporaine*, which displayed a greater disciplinary orthodoxy, devoted, respectively, 23.7 percent and 57.9 percent of their pages
to the nineteenth and twentieth centuries (this is in itself noteworthy and
shows that contemporary history had emerged from its purgatory), but almost nothing to very recent history or subjects of topical interest.[34] That evolution, however, owed as much to the personality of the *Annales'* founders,
Lucien Febvre and Marc Bloch, as to the scientific climate and to changes in
the general context of the time. The medievalist Bloch has in fact often been
portrayed as a "historian of the present time."[35] Not only did he take the risk
of writing about his own time on many occasions; under the Occupation, he
also formalized his idea of the relation a historian of one's own time ought
to maintain with the past and the present. Most of Bloch's texts on recent
history, whether scientific, political, or autobiographical, deal with the world
wars. He writes of rumors, photography, and his own memories of the Great
War (*Souvenirs*). And his most famous text, *L'étrange défaite* (*The Strange Defeat*), was written after the debacle of 1940, before he joined the Resistance,
where he would meet his death. The war experience was thus decisive in his
way of thinking about the historian's craft.[36]

Bloch's contribution was obviously also decisive in the emergence of a new perception of contemporaneity. Although he was not the first to do so, he formalized the place that the past and the present ought to have in the historian's work. In his *Apologie pour l'histoire* (*The Historian's Craft*), he developed an idea that is still pertinent: "understanding the present through the past" is just as important as "understanding the past through the present."[37] The project of understanding the present through the past seems to be a return to the very long tradition in Western historiography of history as life guide—if the tradition ever really disappeared. In reality, that approach combated the modernist illusion of his time and of the previous decades, which sought to make the contemporary a time outside time. That accounts for the methodological school's exclusion of the contemporary, with the result that the study of the present became the prerogative, not to say the exclusive privilege, of the other social sciences: "In the vast flow of times, it is believed that a phase of brief expanse can be set apart. Relatively near to us at its starting point, it covers at its endpoint the very days we are now living. Nothing in it, it seems—not the most outstanding characteristics of the social or political condition, not the material tool kit, not the general tone of the civilization—displays profound differences from the world in which we have our habits. In a word, it appears to be marked, in relation to ourselves, by a very strong coefficient of 'contemporaneity.' Hence the honor, or the defect, of not being confused with the rest of the past."[38]

Bloch is criticizing a purely "biological" conception of contemporaneity that would rest simply on the degree of temporal proximity to individuals and generations. That critique comes as a result of his rejection of objectivity: on the one hand, present-day time is in great part only a fleeting moment in a longer evolution; on the other, lived or perceived time is just as important as so-called real time, if not more so. A historical approach to contemporaneity can prove more difficult, because it brings in elements that allow one to identify close relationships between the past and the present other than the fact of belonging to the same time. Nonetheless, nothing justifies their being separated:

> One of our *lycée* teachers, who was very old when I was very young, told us, "After 1830, it's not history any longer, it's politics." We would no longer say "after 1830"—the *Trois Glorieuses* have aged in their turn—or "it's politics." Rather, in a respectful tone we would say, "sociology," or, with less deference, "journalism." Many would readily concur, however, that since 1914 or 1940, it is no longer history, but without really agreeing on the reasons for that ostracism.
>
> Some, believing that the facts nearest to us are for that very reason unamenable to truly dispassionate study, simply wish to spare chaste Clio overly ardent contacts. This, I imagine, is what my old teacher thought. That view most cer-

tainly attributes to us a poor mastery of our nerves. And it also forgets that, once feelings come into play, the line between current and not current can hardly be regulated of necessity by the mathematical measure of an interval of time.[39]

The suspicion that contemporaneists (a rather recent coinage) are doing "political science" at best, "journalism" at worst, still had some currency in the 1980s: resistance to the history of the present time persisted for a long time. Nevertheless, Bloch is quite explicit—that is the novelty of his argument—about how the present too can explain the past. He shows that knowledge of one's own time offers the historian essential resources for understanding the past. That idea rests, first, on the observation of continuities, the permanence of certain structures, both material (for example, the design of campaigns) and cultural (the modalities for passing on inheritances). When observed in their present state, these allow us to grasp what they may have been in the past. Despite the disagreements between him and the methodologists, he is not far from the logic of traces that school defended. His view rests, second, on the hypothesis that major historical convulsions (the Reformation) can continue to produce their effects over the very *longue durée*, sometimes in a more lasting manner than convulsions closer in time (he may be alluding to Nazism). Once again, by observing them in the present, we gain access to a certain intelligibility of the past. His argument rests, finally, on the fact that historians' direct experience can lead them to understand by analogy—or by virtue of an anthropological permanence—gestures from the past by observing their own gestures in the present. That register is not made explicit in the *Apologie*, but it comes through in his works after World War I. From that standpoint, Bloch would undoubtedly have been a great historian of both world wars, not merely because of his talent as a scholar but also because of his direct experience in the field, first in combat and then in the Resistance. That was a trait he shared with many historians of his generation everywhere in Europe. The link between the past and the present then becomes self-evident: "That solidarity among different ages has so much force that, between one and another, the links of intelligibility truly move in both directions. Incomprehension of the present inevitably has its source in ignorance of the past. But it may be just as futile to exhaust oneself understanding the past if one knows nothing of the present."[40]

Did these reflections play a role in establishing contemporary history in the field of historiographical studies in a lasting manner, and ought Bloch to be considered a precursor in that respect as well? Nothing is less certain, though Bloch, Febvre, and that first current of the Annales School no doubt contributed toward undermining a form of orthodoxy on the subject. Bloch's *Apologie* defends a certain ethic of history in general, recent history included, but without setting up a particular program or explaining how the discipline ought to integrate contemporary history not as a heuristic approach but as a specific field of study. That was, quite simply, not the author's intent. And it is one thing to invite medievalists to be attentive to their own time so as to understand feudalism, quite another to purport to write, with the same degree of rigor and credibility, a history of Nazism on the spot. Granted, *L'étrange défaite* can be seen as an emblematic history of the present time, inasmuch as its author demonstrates great lucidity. That pleased historians, since Bloch appears to have seen the 1940 defeat as they themselves would later see it. But they were forgetting that the book was first and foremost testimony about its time—Bloch presents his remarks as "a witness's deposition"—and not the work of a historian. It is also interesting to note that such a view, which makes contemporary testimony, explicitly embraced as such by its author, a history of the present time, has become particularly widespread in the last twenty years in the context of an increasingly uncertain borderline between the witness and the historian. And yet, as Gérard Noiriel recalls, Bloch never confused the two: "The harsh judgment he makes of French society in *L'étrange défaite* is only the point of view of an actor, a point of view that the historian of the future will compare to other testimonies and other sources."[41] Here Bloch embraces the tradition of an academic who speaks out as an intellectual engaged in his age, rather than taking the stance of a historian of his own time, as he had done in his analysis of rumors during World War I. It was only much later, in the 1970s, for reasons both strategic and intellectual, that Bloch would be deemed—not without a certain manipulation—one of the founding fathers of the new history of the present time. This was an effort to demonstrate clearly to its detractors that this history too was linked to the dominant current of French historiography.

Furthermore, within the logic of the historiographical revolution that has occurred in the previous decade, Bloch's way of imagining in 1940 the link between past and present is often described as an innovation. Yet Bloch was the first to remind us that the act of establishing such a connection belongs to a very long tradition. In denouncing the division between the study of the past and the study of the present, he comments as if in passing: "The odd thing is that the idea of such a schism arose very recently. The old Greek historians, Herodotus, Thucydides, are closer to us. They are the true masters of our studies, ancestors whose images would deserve to be included for all time in the cella of the guild. They never dreamed that, in order to explain the afternoon, it could be sufficient to know, at most, the morning."[42]

Granted, he goes on to cite Michelet and the need to understand the actual by means of the nonactual. But he may also be reviving a prerevolutionary historiographical mode of thought, in which there was neither discontinuity in the approach to historical time nor any contemporary history proper, since there was no difference between the near and the remote, between history and the present. Was this an indirect consequence of his criticism of the methodological school, which had formalized that demarcation and which therefore led him to reestablish a connection with what had preceded? Did he feel a need at the time to envisage a long history in order to reopen his own horizon of expectation and to believe that the triumph of barbarism (of which he would be one of the victims) may be among those "fleeting" phenomena he speaks of several times in *Apologie*? Perhaps he wanted thereby to escape the deadly present and to reopen possible futures by immersing himself in a remote past and finding hope there. Bloch may thus have been behaving both like a man of his time and like his father's son, reestablishing connections, despite his secularism, with a Jewish tradition that had its roots in the immemorial, hence in a time when past and present were in permanent coexistence.

THE AFTERMATH OF NAZISM

Humankind now stands in "the gap between past and future," wrote Hannah Arendt in 1954.[43] It finds itself in an unstable and uncertain place, between a past that has become distant and now demands to be deciphered (hence the new importance of history as an intellectual activity and of memory as a social and political practice) and a future that has become unreadable for several generations (hence the importance of the moment of transition between the past and the present that characterized the writing of history of the present time in the twentieth century). Between the two wars, Franz Kafka, Walter Benjamin, and many other intellectuals expressed the same sentiment in the face of the fracture in historical continuity. René Char, another sentinel summoned forth by Arendt, also expressed it during his time in the underground in 1943 and 1944: "Our inheritance was left to us by no testament." Arendt repeatedly quotes that famous aphorism, which expresses the idea that the generations following those of the war will have to

deal with a legacy whose meaning is unreadable.[44] After the French Revolution, humankind in the modern age had found itself detached from its past
but projected into the future. After the two world wars, it once again found
itself in the solitude of the present, confronted by a near past whose burden,
paradoxically, would grow heavier the further humanity moved from the
caesura of 1945.

During and after World War I, a form of rootless historicity developed, one
that had broken away from the historicity of the nineteenth century, which
had been grounded in the idea of a continuous and cumulative progress, in
the belief in a mastery of the world by scientific knowledge. The memory of
the conflict, the persistence and even weight of recent history, greatly influenced political, social, and scientific life in the decade of the 1920s, giving
a new importance and a new dimension to the notion of contemporaneity.
After 1945, the combined aftereffects of the war, Nazism, and the Holocaust led to an even more marked interest in the history of the present time
throughout the Western world. That history would develop decisively in attempting to confront the inheritance of the latest catastrophe. The strong
connection between politics, memory, and history that arose in 1918 within
the context of the first total war was perceived even more clearly after 1945:
it was once again urgent to understand the present time. But there were
also major differences, almost all of them having to do with the nature of
the wartime violence, which had been combined with a political and ideological violence of an intensity rarely before equaled.

In 1914–18, it was really only the war fronts that were physically devastated,
only combatants who suffered massive losses, with the notable exception
of the organized genocide of the Armenians by the Turks. By contrast, the
1939–45 conflict in Europe, and to a lesser degree in Asia and the Pacific,
led to physical and human destruction beyond compare. The target of that
destruction was first and foremost the civilian populations or disarmed combatants, and it took the form of an intentional elimination of entire swaths
of the conquered populations, huge massacres of prisoners of war, the intentional demolition of large nonstrategic urban areas, and forced movements
of populations; tens of millions sought refuge or were displaced, deported,
held captive, or enslaved. As it had twenty years earlier, the terrible question
had to be confronted: how to preserve the memory of the dead and disap-

peared without sepulchers, how to come to terms with the collective losses, give meaning to events that seemed beyond the reach of reason? One of the oldest cultural and religious traditions in humanity's history had partly disappeared through the systematic elimination of its people, places of worship, schools, and cemeteries. The genocide of the Jews, which extended over the entire continent, was certainly not the first or the last, but it was unprecedented in its scope, nature, and modalities.

Almost everywhere in occupied Europe, underground actions took shape to safeguard the threatened cultural heritage of Judaism and to constitute, on the spot and with the means at hand, traces of the crime still being perpetrated. The objective was also to gather testimony about something likely to produce incredulity, even denial. The work of the historian Emmanuel Ringelblum and his group Oneg Shabbat (Joy of the Sabbath) comes to mind: beginning in Warsaw in October 1939, then inside the ghetto, the group collected an impressive quantity of information on the daily life and fate of the Jews during that period.[45] In the same vein, on April 28, 1943, Isaac Schneersohn created the Centre de Documentation Juive Contemporaine (Contemporary Jewish Documentation Center) in Grenoble. Initially tasked with collecting the traces of the persecution of the Jews of France, after the war it would play a decisive role in the construction of a memory of the Holocaust in that country.[46] Finally, in a different register, Mordechai Shenhavi, a former delegate to the Zionist Congresses, took an unbelievable initiative in Jerusalem on September 30, 1942, proposing that the Jewish National Fund erect a memorial in Palestine in tribute to the "dead and heroes of Israel," victims of the Nazis, at a time when the Final Solution was still being carried out. The plan and its formulation would be taken up again in May 1953, after the creation of the state of Israel, giving rise to Yad Vashem, a memorial charged with commemorating the "heroes and martyrs" of the persecution. For the historian Tom Segev, who uncovered the first, unfinished project, "there was no clearer, more grotesque, even macabre expression of the tendency to think of the Holocaust in the past tense: while the yishuv discussed the most appropriate way to memorialize them, most of the victims were still alive."[47] In reality, by that date nearly 4 million people had died, and a great deal of information had filtered out of Europe. Nevertheless, the initiative bore the mark of a desire to escape the reality of the present, a desire that was itself the consequence of a form of powerlessness. It also shows that the extermination of the Jews was beginning to turn on its head the relation to time and to memory, but without completely abolishing every vision of the future—very much to the contrary. Most of these initiatives indicate that, in the very midst of the genocide process, there were voices and pens that were deliberately preserving past and present traces of an unfolding event, to hold onto the possibility of a future history and a future memory. Could these historians, these scholars, these rabbis, have imagined that the genocide of the Jews, which was about to sweep away almost all of them, would decades after the end of the conflict end up forming a nexus of Western culture? Whether under the name "Shoah" or "Holocaust" (both terms were used in Israel beginning in 1948), it remains in our memory even now, nearly four generations after the events, the central element of a culture of memory that profoundly marks our regime of historicity. It is especially interesting to note that it was precisely the Holocaust that turned the Jewish perception of time upside down, making history, here understood as contingency, rupture, uncertainty, an essential element of Jewish culture, which had previously been based on memory, understood as the permanence of a tradition supposedly impervious to passing time.[48]

In the months immediately following the liberation of the occupied countries, that will to write an early memory of the war also became manifest at a different level. It developed in a general manner in the 1950s and 1960s, reproducing on a large scale the situation after 1918. Everywhere in Europe, often at the impetus of the state and on the margins of the academic world, history institutes and committees were created with the mission of collecting documents and testimony and of producing the first histories of an event that had only just ended.[49] The phenomenon is particularly noteworthy in that, initially, these structures were spontaneously national in character, though the desire for international coordination quickly surfaced. The Netherlands was the first, chronologically, to take action. There, too, the desire to preserve the traces of the event manifested itself during the German occupation itself. A first initiative was undertaken by the economic historian Nicolaas Wilhelmus Posthumus, who in 1935 founded the International Institute of Social History in Amsterdam, itself conceived as a center for documentation and reflection on the European workers' movement after the Nazis came to power. With other academics, he envisioned the creation of a documentation center on the Netherlands at war. A second initiative came from the Dutch government in exile, in particular from Gerrit Bolkestein, minister of education, the arts, and the sciences. Speaking from London on Radio Oranje, he addressed his compatriots on March 28, 1944: "History cannot be written on the basis of official decisions and documents alone. If our descendants are to understand fully what we as a nation have had to endure and overcome during these years, then what we really need are ordinary documents—a diary, letters from a worker in Germany, a collection of sermons given by a parson or a priest. Not until we succeed in bringing together vast quantities of this simple, everyday material will the picture of our struggle for freedom be painted in its full depth and glory."[50]

That appeal shows the extent to which the desire to constitute an alternative history and memory of that colossal conflict was an essential element of wartime culture itself. Is it necessary to insist on that extraordinary situation, in which a representative of a government in exile, a few months before the establishment of a new front destined to liberate Western Europe, was concerned with how the history of that war would be written? The appeal was heard by Anne Frank, who mentions it in her diary:

> Dear Kitty,
>
> Bolkesteyn, an M.P., was speaking in the Dutch News from London, and he said that they ought to make a collection of diaries and letters after the war. Of course they all made a rush at my diary immediately.
>
> Just imagine how interesting it would be if I were to publish a romance of the "Secret Annexe," the title alone would be enough to make people think it was a detective story. But, seriously, it would be quite funny 10 years after the war if people were told how we Jews lived and what we ate and talked about here. Although I tell you a lot, still, even so, you only know very little of our lives.[51]

In the early days of the country's liberation in April 1945, the government of the Netherlands created a National Bureau of War Documentation, which in October 1945 became the Rijksinstituut voor Oorlogsdocumentatie (RIOD; National Institute for War Documentation), headed by the historian Louis de Jong, who would become a dominant figure in Dutch postwar historiography.[52]

The same type of initiative had appeared in France a few months earlier with the creation, by the decision of the Gouvernement Provisoire de la République Française (Provisional Government of the French Republic), of two institutions: the Commission d'Histoire de l'Occupation et de la Libération de la France (CHOLF; Commission on the History of the Occupation and Liberation of France), formed on October 20, 1944, which succeeded a short-lived Comité d'Histoire de la Libération de Paris (Committee on the History of the Liberation of Paris), created within the Bibliothèque de l'Arsenal in late August 1944; and the Comité d'Histoire de la Guerre (Committee on the History of the War), created on June 6, 1945. By a decree of December 17, 1951, the two merged into the Comité d'Histoire de la Deuxième Guerre

Mondiale (CHGM; Committee on the History of World War II), which would be part of the Office of the President of the Council of Ministers, and then, after 1958, the Office of the Prime Minister.[53] In 1949 Italian anti-Fascist resisters and militants created in turn the Istituto Nazionale per la Storia del Movimento di Liberazione in Italia (INSMLI; National Institute for the History of the Liberation Movement in Italy), which became an official institution in 1967, with nearly seventy associated regional institutes throughout the country.[54] In Austria, it was former resisters as well who in 1963 founded the Documentationsarchiv des Österreichischen Widerstandes (DöW; Documentary Archives of the Austrian Resistance) in Vienna; it became a state-financed center in 1983. In Belgium, because of internal political divisions, especially regarding the "Royal Question," that is, Leopold III's attitude during the war, the Centre de Recherches et d'Études Historiques de la Seconde Guerre Mondiale (CREHSGM; Center for Research and Historical Studies of World War II), under the authority of the Ministry of National Education, was not created until 1967. It was linked to the national archives and had the aim of "documenting the heroism" of resistance fighters and war victims.[55] The examples could be multiplied for formerly occupied Europe, including behind the Iron Curtain, where archival and documentation centers dedicated exclusively to the history of World War II were also created—especially in Poland and the USSR, where that war was a founding moment for a new national and political identity.

The importance of that phenomenon, which has prompted several works on a national scale but few studies covering Europe as a whole (with the exception of Lagrou's book, mentioned above), lies in the intellectual convergence of these initiatives, despite the cultural and historical differences among the countries concerned and even more their respective situations during the war. These ad hoc organizations played a decisive role not only in the emergence of a European historiography of the present time, which had had a scattered existence since the end of World War I, but even more in its institutionalization. Thanks to their official aspect, which rather quickly made them the beneficiaries of staff and resources, and moreover of a certain social visibility, these organizations found a place in the academic landscape. Most of them were automatically consulted whenever expertise on the war was needed. Granted, until the 1970s or 1980s these institutes thrived outside the control of universities and major research institutions, though these contributed toward their operation: in France, for example, the Comité d'Histoire de la Deuxième Guerre Mondiale was financed in great part by the Centre National de la Recherche Scientifique (CNRS). That accounts for the term, "official history," that has sometimes been attached to them, though that label obscures the fact that the general history practiced during the same period in European academic institutions was not a model of ideological impartiality. On the contrary, the discipline was everywhere preoccupied with mobilization for the Cold War. After the end of Fascism and Nazism, and in the face of the dominant Soviet model on the other side of the continent, the misgivings in Western Europe about a politically controlled and tendentious history were for good reason set aside. Nevertheless, as Lagrou writes, "if an exception was made for recent history, it was only because the circumstances were perceived as unusual: the urgency of collecting the documents and of preserving national honor, and the need for a shared narrative of the traumatic events of the occupation for both internal and external use. Academic historiography was averse to producing that narrative out of methodological conservatism and contempt for 'journalism.'"[56]

Academics' mistrust, though it did not disappear completely, was obliged to recede in the face of what appeared at the time to be a form of patriotic and even universalist civic-mindedness. The most prominent representatives of the discipline, who were not "contemporaneists," understood the need to promote contemporary history in general and the history of the latest war in particular. In the first issue of *Cahiers d'histoire de la guerre* (1949), published by the committee of the same name, Lucien Febvre, chair of its scientific board, wrote in his foreword:

> I would have misgivings about tracing an ambitious program at the beginning of this first issue. This is not a time for anticipating on a vast scale, for making presumptuous promises. It is a time for energetically taking stock of oneself. The Comité Français d'Histoire de la Guerre does not seek glory. A historian does not seek glory through the study of such bloody and disturbing tragedies. The Comité Français d'Histoire de la Guerre wants to serve the truth modestly, patiently, painstakingly, while assisting the workers to establish, and thereby knock down, the Babel of lies, inventions, double or triple truths that keep everyone from seeing the events clearly. To do its work, it also does not intend to stay safe at home, to insulate itself in good old France: it extends a brotherly hand to the workers of the world as a whole, provided their own hands are loyal. By that I mean the hands of men who do not plead but who demonstrate. Calmly. With evidence, properly critiqued evidence. It intends to serve no thesis, but also, it must be said, no politics. Nevertheless, it does not deny itself a keen desire: that, by dismantling the complicated workings of a thousand deadly and secret machinations, it will advance the education of our contemporaries' critical faculties. In France in the first place. The critical faculties and something more, if it is true, as Marc Bloch wrote at the beginning of one of the two or three most profound, most thoughtful books we possess about those pain-

ful years—his *Étrange défaite*, to cite it by name—that this defeat was first and foremost a defeat of French intelligence. It is possible to do one's job in good conscience as professional historians and not abstain, in one's proper place and with the resources available, from providing a remedy to such great ills. So then, good luck, long live the *Cahiers d'histoire!*[57]

The leader of the Annales movement is thus defending a historiographical posture advocating humility, the search for truth (including the most factual truths), and impartiality, qualities placed in the service of a better critical and civic education. He even declares straight out the thaumaturgical vocation of that historiography still in its earliest stages. Once again, the history of the present time was enlisted to respond to the effects of the trauma suffered, on the condition that it look at events from a distance, though those events were very near in time and all the historians had themselves lived through them. We are once more in the presence, this time on a grand scale, of a form of nontraumatized response to the trauma suffered. And Febvre supported such a project without reservation precisely because it seemed to respond to the very mission of history as a discipline, all periods combined, as it was now being constituted almost everywhere in Western democracies. The next year, in the preface to an issue of that same review devoted to the European resistance, he went a step further:

> Some will not fail to tell us, either kindly or pointedly, that it is too early to write something truly valid about the resistance to oppression by the European countries invaded by Germany. We thank our informants in advance, but they would not be telling us anything. We are not so naïve as to believe in the "definitive" in History, since we know that History, the science of changes, is itself in a perpetual state of change, and therefore that it can proceed only by a series of successive approximations, the first very crude, the following ones increasingly precise. We have, moreover, the strong feeling that, on pain of suicide, honest historians cannot, must not, leave in ignorance a wide audience about what can already be known, an audience who asks that we not wait until they have died to bring them—what?—something provisional, hardly less provisional than what we can give them today. We have therefore decided to disregard scruples about playing a waiting game and devote this journal, as of now, to a rapid overview of the Resistance as it spontaneously manifested itself almost everywhere in Europe in the countries occupied by the Germans and as early as 1941.[58]

At issue here is no longer the civic urgency of an on-the-spot history of the catastrophe and a response to a legitimate social demand—which Febvre invokes in spite of everything—but rather a statement of the epistemological foundations of the history of the present time as such. Yes, that history belongs to the provisional, the unfinished: but, Febvre tells us, that is characteristic of the discipline as a whole, since any historical writing is provisional, or at least, it can claim to express only postulates or truths that are subject to revision over time. Therefore, the early state of the event can in no way constitute a valid objection. He goes even further, affirming that to neglect that branch of history would be a form of "suicide" for the discipline, since (this claim is implicit) if professional historians do not fill the demand, others with no doubt less laudable intentions will take over the field, are in fact already taking it over. It is true, however, that a good part of the committee's work consisted initially of collecting primary sources, "documentation for the historians of the next generation," as Henri Michel said in 1949. But they did so under working conditions often typical of any very early history: the constitution of an ad hoc corpus of testimony, the confidentiality of certain remarks collected, self-censorship, and a practice of silence on the part of the historians.[59]

That first wave of historiography, official or not, was thus deeply marked by what was at stake at the time and by the first social and political interpretations of the conflict. Its purpose was to produce first and foremost a national narrative that could contribute to the moral and intellectual recovery of the countries emerging from war and restore to them a dignity that had sometimes been greatly compromised by the Nazi occupation. At the time, that program did not seem incompatible with a history of scientific dimensions. That historiography also had to confront the enormous difficulty of reporting the crimes of Nazism and the violence of the war. Many of these institutions, in fact, served directly in the proceedings under way against Nazi criminals and their collaborators. But not all subjects were given equal attention. The collaboration remained a subject that, if not taboo, was at least secondary to the study of all forms of resistance and opposition to the occupier and various assessments of the war's physical and material toll. That observation was made not only by later generations, but by contemporaries. For example, René Rémond formulated a criticism of Michel's CHGM, which he reproached for not yet (in 1967) taking an interest "in the other side," that is, in Vichy and the collaboration, which led to an unbalanced view of the period.[60] Documenting the extermination of the Jews also did not appear among the foremost objectives. To be more precise, there was a sort of division of labor between these official institutes, which were in charge of a history with a national dimension, and specifically Jewish institutions (declared to be such), which took on the history of the genocide. From the perspective and in the vocabulary of our own time, that can be seen as an opposition between a history with a common purpose and a history with a "community" dimension, and there has been no dearth of controversies on this point over the last twenty years (like many others, I have participated in them). But that was how things were perceived by participants at the time. By way of example, consider the case of Léon Poliakov, one of the first historians of the Final Solution, who collaborated with the Centre de Documentation Juive Contemporaine but remained somewhat marginalized. When he commented on the newly created Comité d'Histoire de la Deuxième Guerre Mondiale—which, by contrast, was quite prominent—not only did it not occur to him to criticize the committee for its lack of studies on the persecution of the Jews, not only did he emphasize "the solid friendship fostered by the parallel interests and tasks" of the two organizations, but he also praised the historiographical institution for being fully engaged with its time, not without an implicit allusion to his own situation and to that of his colleagues at the CDJC:

> Not long ago, Clio was supposed to be an impassive and indifferent Muse: it was incumbent upon her to reconstruct a Babylonian palace or an Etruscan era without displaying passion, without pronouncing any judgment. History is a science, they used to tell us; it must stand above the fray, and the problems of Good and Evil do not interest it. And yet, men selected from among the most prestigious French historians are now becoming chroniclers of events in which they took part—and with what passion, what self-sacrifice!—barely a decade ago. Whatever their detachment and professional integrity, these qualities will be accompanied by a vigorous ethical stance. It is fortunate that this is so. For history is not only truth, it also acts on reality. From that standpoint, it is fortunate that the heads of the committee are for the most part men on whom the last war made an indelible mark in the deepest recesses of their being.[61]

It is obvious, however, that these official organizations did not approach head-on, at least not immediately, all the questions that in retrospect ought to or might have been raised at the time; that is a constitutive trait of all historiography. In spite of everything, they were constrained to respect certain domestic sensitivities: the history of Vichy in France, the Royal Question in Belgium, anti-Semitism in Poland. The list of thorny subjects related to that conflict is particularly long, and it is not certain that the following generations of historians have tackled or resolved them all. They also had to respect external sensitivities. International cooperation, which existed despite the Iron Curtain, required compromises and even the setting in place of actual taboos (in the sense of an imposed silence), particularly about certain crimes committed by the Allies: mass rapes, massacres of civilians or combatants, the treatment of German prisoners of war, the bombing of cities, the expulsion of the Germanic populations from Eastern Europe. These subjects, highly charged polemically and ideologically, gave rise to violent political controversies and would not truly be dealt with scientifically for decades, notably after the fall of the Berlin Wall. Writing the history of the present time does not mean writing the entire history right away. But that did not prevent this historiography from laying solid foundations for a narrative of World War II that, if not generally shared, was at least cross-disciplinary and pluralistic. In May 1967, upon the initiative of the French historian Henri Michel, secretary-general of the CHGM, most of these institutions joined together to form the International Committee for the History of the Second World War, which at first comprised a dozen members (The Federal Republic of Germany, Belgium, Bulgaria, Denmark, the United States, France, Israel, the Netherlands, Romania, the United Kingdom, the USSR, and Yugoslavia). Later affiliated with the International Committee of Historical Sciences (ICHS), the organization grew, incorporating committees created within countries that had been neutral during the war (Switzerland, the Vatican) and Asian countries (China, Japan, South Korea).[62] From its origin, fifty years after Bloch's and Pirenne's exhortations and nearly half a century before discussions of "global history" and recent invocations of the need to abandon the national paradigm, that history of the worldwide conflict took on a dimension that was in fact global. It emphasized that the history of the present time as it was developing in the second half of the twentieth century had no choice but to depart from the national domain, though that excellent idea had its vicissitudes before coming to be more or less widely accepted—if not actually implemented.

Another difference between the two wars deserves mention, since it has played an essential role in the assessment of a new form of contemporaneity. The need to confront the magnitude of the crimes committed by the Nazis, the Fascists, and their collaborators was an essential issue from the era of the conflict onward, since punishment of war criminals was one of the war objectives declared by the Allies. That distinctive situation led to the first major international tribunals in history, those of Nuremberg and Tokyo, decisive moments not only in the emergence of a supranational justice system but also in the writing of history. The proceedings set in place to judge Nazi crimes and, to a lesser degree, the crimes of the Japanese army, and the field research aimed at collecting the largest quantity of reliable information—documents, narratives, material and human traces, public court hearings—made it possible to assemble a considerable number of archives and testimonies. They were accessible almost immediately not only to magistrates, lawyers, and victims, but also to journalists from throughout the world and to historians, political scientists, and psychologists. Whether intentionally or not, the work by these courts of justice of a new kind produced the first historical narrations of the catastrophe: the first coherent analyses of the event based on conclusive evidence subject to open debate and intended to make sense of the past. The Nuremberg trials, by virtue of their reach, their rigor, the resources invested, and the publicity given them, were a starting point for the elaboration of a very early historiography of Nazism and World War II. To a lesser measure but following the same logic, the trials of Nazis and collaborators had similar effects everywhere in a Europe just emerging from war. They set in motion a first historiography of the event, also very early, thanks especially to the publication of a great deal of testimony, whether arguments for the defense or the prosecution's case, collections of documents, or analyses of political or military history, all of which found a fairly wide audience. Contrary to a recent belief that that history was "concealed," rarely have events been analyzed, documented, dissected, and recounted so soon after they occurred—although, to be sure, with blanks, lacunae, denials, and sometimes lies. It is their early disclosure that merits attention, though we must keep in mind that these first historical narrations were marked throughout by a normative dimension: the historical analysis was in this case secondary to the legal analysis, inasmuch as the most urgent task was to describe the crimes committed before judging them. That original characteristic would for decades, even down to our own time, influence the writing of the history of the major catastrophes of the twentieth century. It explains why the historiography of the present time still maintains connections both close and conflictual to the law and the justice system.[63]

IDEOLOGICAL MOBILIZATION AND DEMOBILIZATION

Another difference between the two wars was that in 1939 there was not a collective mobilization everywhere of intellectuals, scientists, and historians defending, within the context of national unity, the war objectives of each of the belligerent parties. In the new conflict, the political dimension became crucial. It led to a confrontation not only between rival powers, but also between ideological systems whose influence transcended borders. Scientists, like everyone else, were split between resisters and supporters of collaboration with the Nazis, between those who agreed to ally themselves with Stalin to fight Hitler and those whose anti-Communism prevailed over everything else. In France, historians joined the Resistance or faithfully served Vichy, but they did so as individuals, not in the name of a professional guild. There were exceptions, however. The most notable of these for understanding the evolution of contemporary history as a discipline after 1945 were West German historiography and North American historiography. Moreover, the two maintained close ties to each other during the Cold War, given the number of German intellectuals welcomed to the United States in the 1930s and 1940s.

Within Nazi Germany, history and historians, like jurists and physicists, played a large role in legitimating the regime. The magnitude of that ideological support continues to be an object of disagreement and one of the recurrent controversies about the interpretation of the Nazi past. In general, the strong development of contemporary history in the Federal Republic of Germany after 1945 was the almost obvious consequence of the considerable weight of Nazism's aftereffects. "In the late 1940s and the 1950s the academic study of *Zeitgeschichte* was primarily perceived as a consequence of Germany's Nazi experience. In historical research as in many other academic fields, the Third Reich disrupted lines of continuity. A consensus arose among historians that they should assist any attempts to investigate and interpret National Socialist rule."[64]

That apparent consensus stemmed from a form of guilt, more or less conflicted or accepted depending on the case, which had to do with the personal situation of many of the most renowned historians during the Nazi period. It also rested on the situation of the profession as a whole after 1945, which was called on to draw up a critical assessment of Nazism before the world's eyes but felt pressure from within to reestablish the foundations of a German identity, especially after the country was split into two nations. The dilemma crystallized in 1946 with the publication of two emblematic, if not entirely representative, texts of that period: *Die Schuldfrage (The Question of German Guilt)* by the philosopher Karl Jaspers, and *Die deutsche Katastrophe (The German Catastrophe)* by the venerable conservative historian Friedrich Meinecke, who lamented the disappearance, because of Nazism, of a united and sovereign Germany.[65] These tensions would condition in a lasting way historiography and public debate about the past, at least until the 1980s. At the same moment, on a global scale, a large portion of the new historiography of the present time also focused on the history of the two world wars, on Nazism and Fascism. The history of the other great totalitarian system, Communism and its variants, also began to be the object of systematic studies within the context of a bipolar world. As a result, the contemporary history of Germany became an emblematic case of twentieth-century history generally. It was an obligatory stopping point for all historians of the present time, especially in the English-speaking world, whatever the subject being discussed. After 1945, (West) German historiography once again held an important place in epistemological reflections, less by the originality of its paradigms, as in the nineteenth century, than by the urgency of the ethical and moral questions it was facing. Some of these were not new, such as differences in the interpretation of national history, but they acquired an unprecedented intensity whose ramifications extended far beyond the borders of the country. To cite only the best-known debates, they included both the controversy Fritz Fischer launched in 1961 about German responsibility for the outbreak of World War I and the *Historikerstreit* (historians' dispute) of 1986-87 on the "proper" place of the years 1933-45 within the overall history of Germany. Other issues, by contrast, were largely new, so much so that some have spoken in this context of "the invention of contemporary history": "It was an invention, indeed, as most historians perceived the institutionalization of contemporary history as an outright departure from standard practice, as something decidedly new. Martin Broszat, for example, who would subsequently rise to become one of the Federal Republic's most prominent contemporary historians, emphasized the novelty of the new subdiscipline: 'The term contemporary history and the praxis of contemporary historical research and teaching have been established in Germany only after 1945.'"[66]

In reality, the use of the term *Zeitgeschichte*, as we have seen, dates back to the eighteenth century,[67] a genealogy deliberately ignored at the time, like the longer genealogy of contemporary history I am trying to retrace here. In the postwar period, however, it acquired a very special meaning, which may not always have been taken into account when that notion was exported, notably to France thirty years later in a completely different context. At least at first, the history of the concept was confused with the history of the research center that more or less directly trained most of the historians of Nazism: the Institut für Zeitgeschichte (IfZ). The plan for an institution that would take exclusive charge of the history of National Socialism appeared in the immediate aftermath of the surrender, with the creation in Munich (in the American zone, therefore) of an Institut zur Erforschung der Nationalsozialistischen Politik (Research Institute on National Socialist Policy). In 1949, upon the creation of the two sovereign nations, it became the Deutsches Institut für die Geschichte der Nationalsozialistischen Zeit (German Institute for the History of the National Socialist Period). It acquired its definitive name in 1952, becoming a de jure autonomous private institution, outside the university system. It was financed at first by the federal government and the Free State of Bavaria, which later assumed oversight of it, and then, beginning in 1961, by the other *Länder* as well. "As a result, its diverse activities, which, within the framework of the de-Nazification measures implemented by the Allies, planned to undertake a political education of the population, were dictated by 'strictly scientific principles.'"[68] The IfZ became the premier institution of the time, holding, if not a monopoly on the history of the Nazi period, then at least a dominant position, and possessing in addition an extensive archival center, though access to a large portion of Nazi documents in the German Democratic Republic was very difficult before 1989.

At first glance, the IfZ's situation resembles that of the other institutions created in Europe at the same time to write the history of the war. Furthermore, when the International Committee for the History of the Second World War was founded in 1967, it automatically called on the IfZ to represent West Germany, a task taken on by the historian Helmut Krausnick.[69] Like the French CHGM and the Dutch RIOD, the IfZ works outside the national university system, with earmarked funds and an almost exclusive object of study: the history of the period between 1933 and 1945. Like the others, it is a leading center of expertise, especially in judicial matters. For example, it issued as many as six hundred reports or opinions a year within the framework of the proceedings initiated by West Germany against Nazi war criminals after the creation of the special prosecutor's office in Ludwigsburg in 1958.[70] Without it, the historiography of Nazism would never have become so highly developed. Yet that unique, almost "extraterritorial" position did not have the same significance for its European counterparts: writing the history of Nazism in the "victim" countries, or those that considered themselves victims first and foremost, did not have the same implications as writing that history from within. Contemporaneity did not have the same feel there: although the historical time at issue was obviously the same, neither the space covered nor the experiences the historians had to report were comparable—and that is an understatement. The historian Sebastian Conrad would go even further. According to him, though that institutional singularity allowed for a privileged treatment of the Nazi period and thus made that history possible very early on, it also participated, consciously or not, in an "immunization strategy": "The call for the privileged treatment of the history of National Socialism, however, may very well have also formed part of an immunization strategy. The demand for a special institute, that is, the administrative segregation of the history of the Third Reich—which would then be researched with specially devised methods—could also be understood as a detachment of National Socialism itself from the continuum of German history. What is more, the call for special research institutes implied that National Socialism could not be understood on the basis of knowledge of German history and its traditions but only as a phenomenon sui generis."[71]

The hypothesis is appealing, albeit paradoxical. In the first place, the objection could be made that there is no mechanical link between the two attitudes: the development of the history of Nazism at a specialized site ultimately made it possible to raise most of the questions that deserved to be raised, even if they were raised both within and without. Second, it can be noted that all the European institutes working on the war benefited from similar privileged treatment, and they too had a tendency to isolate the period of the war from the rest of national or European history. Granted, they may have adopted a similar immunization strategy in doing so, for example, by underestimating indigenous collaboration and its roots in the specific history of the country, privileging only the circumstances of the Nazi occupation, as in the case of the French CHGM and its superficial treatment of the Vichy regime. And they were sometimes inclined to produce a customized history that preserved national honor by giving priority to forms of resistance and victimization. Nevertheless, these more or less conscious choices were the result not so much of the institutional novelty of these places as of the sense characteristic of a whole generation that the war had been like no other and that it—like Nazism, its principal cause—had to be studied as truly a phenomenon sui generis. Finally, that way of conceiving of the event as exceptional only increased over time, on the basis of moral and political assumptions completely at odds with those suggested by Conrad for the immediate postwar period. As the historiography of the Holocaust experienced an exponential development in the 1980s and 1990s, many argued for that subject as well to be treated in specific places, with special methods and particular objectives, this time in the name of the radical singularity of the event. That tendency ran the risk—denounced many times—of isolating the genocide of the Jews from any comprehensive historical vision.

Conrad's hypothesis, however, has the merit of showing that the proclaimed singularity of *Zeitgeschichte*, though resting in large part on tangible scientific data, was the result of a very particular political and cultural context, as indicated by the now-classic definition given by Hans Rothfels, the first director of the journal *Vierteljahrshefte für Zeitgeschichte*:

> The concept of *Zeitgeschichte* rests on the idea that, in about 1917-18, a new era of universal history began to take shape. Its roots lay in the heavy-handedness of imperialist policy and industrial society, which must not be excluded from treatment ... through the choice of an automatic time limit. Even World War I, however, as revolutionary as its outbreak and as strong as its impact on security were, could justifiably be said to have been only a conflict of nation-states expanded to the global scale. It was only with two remarkably congruent events—the United States' entry into the war and the outbreak of the Russian Revolution—that the constellation really became universal and that a conflict between peoples and states became at the same time a conflict marked through and through by deep social contradictions. Fundamentally, the antithesis between Washington and Moscow was already a reality in 1918. It was followed by decades during which democracy, Fascism, and Communism coexisted in a sort of "triangular" relationship, in a play of variable oppositions and alliances until, in 1945, the bipolar partition began to operate anew.[72]

Rothfels, a conservative historian who converted to Protestantism at a very young age, had to immigrate to the United States in 1939 because he was born of Jewish parents. Having returned to Germany to teach in the early 1950s, he relentlessly defended a profession marked by its submission to Nazism.[73] His role in establishing contemporary history in the international scientific landscape was essential, but he has also been criticized, especially in recent decades, by those who see that history of the present time after 1945—not without a certain generational excess—as a disguised effort at justification.[74] In fact, the definition Rothfels gave of the present time rested not on a reflection about the historian's degree of temporal or cultural proximity to the events recounted, but rather on a subjective division of historical time that arbitrarily had the contemporary era begin with the United States' entry into World War I and the Bolshevik Revolution, thus eliminating the intrinsic unity of the Great War. The contemporary world in this case was thus defined by the emergence of a revolutionary dynamic, a form of globalization, the birth of a mass society, or even the confrontation between systems—democracy, fascism, and communism—that extended beyond the national framework. Granted, that reading of the first half of the twentieth century does contain real interpretive value. But it also seems to bow to other considerations, since, in a way, it amounts to diluting the unique responsibility of Germany for the outbreak of the two world wars and the advent of Nazism. It has, in any case, been criticized for doing so.

Once the singularity of the period 1917–45 had been proclaimed, the question arose of how to study the later period, that of the postwar era and the Cold War, and even the long-term aftereffects of Nazism. Surprisingly, however—though not incoherently, in view of what had gone before—a number of figures of that German history of the present time believed that the concept no longer had any validity *after* 1945, that the "present time" was the time that gave rise to Nazism, witnessed its development and then its collapse, but was not the time after or the history of the near past in the structural sense. That accounts for the appearance in the 1970s of a new historical division: the *neuere Zeitgeschichte*, or "history of the most recent present time," a notion almost as vague as the "history of the very contemporary," which once again reduces contemporaneity to a question of temporal proximity. "'Contemporary history,' as it was conceived following the Second World War, did not merely denote the confrontation with one's respective recent past but also implied the preoccupation with a very particular period of (primarily German) history."[75] It may be noted, however, that that history, so singular, so apparently irreducible to the Nazi period alone, actually led—twenty or thirty years later, in Munich and in almost all the European institutes that had taken on the history of the war—to a history of the long-term aftereffects of the event and to a practice of contemporary history partly emancipated from the original catastrophe, though it remains a founding paradigm for understanding the second half of the twentieth century. Whatever the inadequacies or ambiguities of that historiography, whatever its original narcissistic introversion, it has raised an impressive number of ethical and theoretical problems that have enduringly structured the writing of the history of the present time, which this book is attempting to describe: the dialectic between history and memory; the question of "historicization" (*Historiesierung*), or what place to grant morality in the approach to a phenomenon such as Nazism and what choice to make between a history that privileges the viewpoint of the victims and one that takes an interest in the criminals or in decision-making processes; the opposition between an empathetic stance and a detached stance, important in and of itself in the practice of any contemporary history but particularly thorny once an understanding of mass crimes is at stake; the problems raised by the emergence of a judicial historical writing; and the sometimes excessive focus on the catastrophic dimension of twentieth-century history.

In the end, the importance of that historiographical turn lies in its very instability, in the absence of a lasting consensus on how to define its principal object of study, in its profound ideological ambiguities, in the forced transition between the old historicist tradition and the obligation to think about history in a different way. That obligation must henceforth take into account the necessity not of inserting the present into the continuity of a positive history (the source of national pride), but of writing about a near past that ended in humiliation, loss, and guilt. The writing of history is no longer merely an exercise in understanding and reflection; it is a *confrontation*, a battle with a still-present past, which for decades will be a source of problems more than a guide from which lessons must be drawn. Hence the notion, both central and ambiguous, of the necessity of "coming to terms with the past" (*Vergangenheitsbewältigung*), which since the 1950s and 1960s has profoundly marked Germans' relation to their history. Ultimately, in the 1980s and 1990s, it spread—with variants, such as the "duty of memory"— almost across Europe.[76] The need for such mastery is felt precisely because that history is beyond anyone's control.

The United States is another special case with respect to the situation of history and historians in World War II and during the postwar era. Even more than in 1917, the need to justify a massive engagement in the conflict mobilized all sectors of society, from Hollywood studios to the major universities. Like those in other professions, historians found themselves in the position of defending the values of Western culture, and the most conservative circles claimed that these values were being "undermined" by the advance of relativism and subjectivism, theories denounced as having paved the way for Fascism. This was not an incidental matter, since that mobilization, as ideological as it was patriotic, continued during the early years of the Cold War in the 1950s and 1960s, with two consequences. First, the notion of "objective historical truth" returned to favor, and it was the task of historians to exhume that truth, an essential weapon first against Nazism and then against Communism: "The really frightening thing about totalitarianism is not that it commits 'atrocities' but that it attacks the concept of objective truth: it claims to control the past as well as the future," wrote George Orwell in February 1944.[77] Secondly, the war, the postwar era, and then the Cold War would bring significant growth to the history of the present time. Now, however, respect for objectivity did not stand in the way of the study of the present, as it had in the nineteenth century. On the contrary, it was in the name of a necessary objectivity that the contemporary became a major object of investigation, both in universities and in some government institutions. For example, the Office of Strategic Services (OSS), the first major U.S. intelligence service (established in June 1942), recruited many anti-Fascist intellectuals, including preeminent members of the Frankfurt School: Herbert Marcuse, for instance, and Franz Neumann, who in 1942 published *Behemoth*, one of the first in-depth analyses of Nazi polycracy.[78] These individuals played an important role in fostering an understanding of the enemy. The Office of War Information (OWI), created the same year to oversee domestic propaganda, also used the services of many academics, including the anthropologist Ruth Benedict. Her studies of Japanese culture, based especially on the personal diaries of captured soldiers, led in 1946 to another major publication: *The Crysanthemum and the Sword*. In like manner, the Department of War created a "historical branch" in August 1943 within the military intelligence division of the general staff to take on a true "history" function within the U.S. army, different from the merely didactic use traditionally made of history in military schools since time immemorial. That branch sent nearly three hundred historians into the field, enlisted in the service of a new concept: "Military History Operations." The objective was to collect on the spot the testimony of combatants, in order, on the one hand, to use it as a kind of "feedback," and, on the other, to maintain the internal cohesiveness of the engaged units by distributing the interviews thus collected, especially among wounded soldiers isolated from their comrades. The originality of the method, developed by the head of that service, the former journalist Samuel L. A. Marshall, consisted of following a unit into combat and having conversations with the protagonists in the hours following a confrontation, using two innovations that would have a great impact: "The first was to conduct a group interview at the very site of engagement, to guarantee both the authenticity and the pertinence of the facts but also to favor a certain vividness of the account; the second was to combine the account with an analysis of different tactical situations, so as to allow the reader to draw lessons from the operation taken as a whole."[79] Several thousand testimonies by World War II combatants were collected in this manner, opening the way for a very active branch of the history of the present time in the United States: an oral history of the war, which stood at the crossroads between two great historiographical traditions anchored in the present time, oral history and military history.[80] In fact, it was within the context of the postwar era that the first large oral archives were constituted, in particular the Oral History Research Office, established at Columbia University in 1948-49 by the historian Alan Nevins. It followed a tradition begun in the 1930s during the large-scale social history surveys conducted within the context of the New Deal and the pioneering studies in urban sociology by the Chicago School.[81] Thus the two major events that marked the history of the United States in less than a generation (the Greatest Generation, as it was later called)—the Great Depression, experienced as an unprecedented economic and social catastrophe, and World War II—favored the emergence of a historiography of the near past marked through and through by the idea that the actor's direct experience should constitute both a principal source and an essential object of historical analysis. That gave a new dimension to the notion of contemporaneity that had emerged after 1918. Thus, contrary to the received notion, the development of oral history began well before the 1960s and 1970s and the large protest movements, which sought to give a voice to the voiceless and the anonymous of History. That approach, linked directly to the consolidation of the present time as a historiographical category, was originally just as concerned with the economic and political elites as with the combatants in the Pacific theater and in the Korean War, then later with workers, women, and immigrants. It was Franklin Roosevelt who inaugurated the first presidential library, collecting archives and testimonies on his term in office, a tradition formalized in 1955 by the Presidential Libraries Act. Oral history, like the history of the present time in general, was thus undertaken by means of (and in the aftermath of) the major historical cataclysms of the first half of the twentieth century, before becoming thirty years later an alternative and antiestablishment historiographical program.

During the Cold War, the historiography of the contemporary would continue to develop. The context provided opportunities for historians and political scientists involved in the study of international relations, the analysis of totalitarianism (a concept that took shape at the same moment), or the history of the USSR and the Soviet system, almost virgin territory before the war and a field that would experience spectacular growth.[82] That massive investment, motivated by the circumstances and financed by foundations or organizations enlisted in the fight against Communism, no doubt explains why the development of the history of the present time in the United States does not seem to have sparked debates about its feasibility or legitimacy comparable to those in Europe. That way of doing history proved to be unproblematic almost from the outset and since that time does not seem to have led to epistemological disputes on the same scale as those that shook the German, French, and Italian historians in the 1970s and 1980s, a debate reactivated in post-Communist Europe and in the democracies of Latin America in the 1990s and 2000s. Let me add, only too briefly, that the dependence of historians on the political context was greatly exacerbated behind the Iron Curtain, where contemporary history became an instrument in the service of the Communist regimes. In particular, contemporary history was enlisted in the defense of the system and in the production of a customized history. It included the elaboration of major state lies: the denial, for example, of the existence of the secret protocols of the German-Soviet pact of 1939 and the attribution of the Katyn massacre of 1940 to the Nazis. Within the Communist sphere, therefore, contemporary history became the branch of the discipline most servile to the government. There are certain similarities in that respect to Western Communist circles, though that historiography likely deserves to be approached from a more nuanced viewpoint.[83] After the fall of the Berlin Wall, contemporaneist historians (Soviet, East German, Polish, and others) would in fact have much greater difficulty holding onto their posts or positions than their medievalist or modernist colleagues.

DESYNCHRONIZED TIME

If one had to point out one last difference between the respective historicity of the two world wars, it would be the heterogeneity, even irreducibility, of the lived experience of each. That was only somewhat the case in the United States, where battles unfolded far away and the home front was not subject to wartime violence. It was especially true in Europe: there, contemporaneity consisted less of a simultaneity of experiences than of a radical desynchronization of the times people had lived through. World War I, despite the disparities between the experiences of men and women, civilians and combatants, residents of the combat zones and those in the rear, and, even more, between the experiences of victors and vanquished, gave rise after the fact to a more or less dominant narrative among the former belligerents: that of a mass experience shared by virtue of the intensity of the violence on the battlefield and its repercussions at home. That experience transcended former front lines and created the beginnings of a common memory within the world of war veterans, despite resentments. Post-1918 contemporaneity, therefore, was steeped in the idea—in large part constructed—of a shared experience: that of the "generation under fire," who were joined together by a sort of unity of time, place, and action. After 1945, despite the emphasis on a common destiny, now based not on the experience at the front but on the fact of having been victims of the same barbarism from one end of Europe to the other, of having resisted it and finally overcome it, it was ultimately the radical difference of situations that would prevail in perceptions of the event. And for good reason: there was nothing in common between the experience of the western front and that of the eastern front; between the French unoccupied zone, which saw practically no Germans until 1944, and occupied France; between the fate of France as a whole and that of Poland; between the fate of the French, Belgian, Dutch, and English prisoners of war and that of Soviet prisoners of war, who were victims of targeted and systematic massacres; or in the treatment reserved for these captives after the war, since the Soviets, instead of returning home like the others, were sent to the gulag. There is no comparison, despite the horror of the situations experienced, between deportees to the concentration camps and those sent to the death camps. These differences were not always acknowledged or understood immediately, nor did they all find in the immediate postwar period specific political or cultural spaces in which to express themselves and to exert an equal influence on collective perceptions of the event. There were hierarchies in the celebration of heroes and martyrs, with resistance fighters—or rather, resistant behavior—naturally occupying a preeminent place in the official memory of most of the countries occupied by the Nazis. The idea of a silence on the part of Jewish survivors of the Holocaust after the war is no doubt a recent construction, inscribed within the context of the 1970s and 1980s, when it was claimed, rightly or wrongly, that taboos were being lifted. In addition, in many European countries, sensibilities of the time were not as indifferent to the genocide committed against the Jews as has been said in recent decades.[84] It is nonetheless true that there is no comparison possible between the place occupied by the memory of the Holocaust in the collective European consciousness since the 1990s and that which it occupied in the 1950s. It is that difference that interests me here, since it is the result of what is once again a phenomenon nearly unprecedented in history: a delayed effect in the representation of a catastrophe. Generations born three or four decades after the events have decided to completely reconstruct a system of representation that first arose during the events and immediately thereafter. They have done so in order to "make amends for history" on a grand scale, a true retroactive intervention in the past (belated trials, financial compensation, national apologies, new monuments, new commemorations) directed exclusively, or almost exclusively, at the innocent victims supposedly forgotten after the war: Jewish victims of the Holocaust in the first place, and then, in the interest of equality, the Roma, forced laborers, homosexuals, prisoners of war, and so on. Between the memory of the event as it developed in the postwar period and then half a century later, there is a difference not only in content but also in nature. In the first case, the representations of the past were produced by and addressed to the generation that lived through the tragedy; in the second, they are being produced in part by the actors who have survived and are addressed to generations very remote from the event. The temporal distance from the event is reduced through a whole series of mechanisms, particularly the inapplicability of the statute of limitations, which makes all the participants in a trial, apart from the accused and the victims, "contemporaries" of the crime committed half a century ago, even if they were not yet born when it occurred. That represents a change in the very definition of contemporaneity, which, of course, belongs to the context of recent decades but can be explained in part by the historicity peculiar to World War II and its posterity in both the short and long term.

The two situations, that of the postwar era and that of our own time, harbor a similar misunderstanding. In the first case, the representation of the wartime past rested implicitly on the idea of a supposed shared contemporaneity that was in reality only *relative*, since the experiences lived through cannot be reduced to their simultaneity. In commemorating the martyrdom of resistance deportees in the first place, the official celebrations of the postwar era believed they were commemorating the memory of the deported Jews as well. In the context of the time, there was no reason to give particular emphasis to the singular fate of the Jews. No one imagined that these celebrations would one day be denounced retrospectively as unjust toward forgotten victims. In the same way, the considerable national and international investment over the last three decades in the commemoration of the Holocaust, which has given that event a centrality it did not have in the representations of 1945, rests on the idea that contemporaneity can be created not by ignoring differences of situation—on the contrary, the task at hand is to emphasize them—but rather by *now ignoring the time that has elapsed*. Generations born several decades after the events are asked to consider the memory of that catastrophe as if it had happened yesterday, to feel a share of the emotional impact in the present, to bear moral responsibility for it, and to take on a portion of its material cost. In 1945 efforts were made to abolish the space between the differentiated experiences of the war; in recent years there has been an attempt to abolish their horizon of expectation. Our generations no longer represent the future of the war generations, the hope for a better world for their children; rather, they are thrust headlong into the transmitted and sustained trauma of a catastrophe they did not live through.

CHAPTER THREE

Contemporaneity at the Heart of Historicity

The situation of the second great postwar era in twentieth-century history might have remained unusual, an effect circumscribed by the singularity of World War II. Interest in the history of the present time might have declined the further one moved from the event. But exactly the opposite occurred. Within academia and the public space, the memory of that latest catastrophe resulted in a growing preoccupation with the history of the war in particular and the history of the near past in general. Since the 1980s, the "present" has been the dominant regime of historicity. To speak of history in literature or film, at cultural events or national heritage sites, and even more in political debates is very often to speak first and foremost, if not exclusively, of the near past. The aim is to mark oneself off from that past, to judge it, to atone for it. Images of the catastrophes that have followed in succession since 1914 run in a continuous loop on our screens and constitute a determining element of the contemporary imaginary. Conversely, images from the more remote past seem to be fading, or in any case losing their vividness and the power to structure a collective identity. Even worse (so to speak), the "present"—which in reality covers the span of the last century—has acquired the status of a standard of measure for comprehending other historical periods, to which contemporary categories are now applied. In France, for example, a 2001 law retroactively designated slavery and the Western slave trade "crimes against humanity." In that context, a profound shift has taken place in the balance of the discipline: the history of the present time, whatever name is given to it, now occupies a significantly larger place than modern, medieval, or ancient history, as measured by the number of students and thesis topics and by the institutions, publications, and media space devoted to it. What are the connections between these two phenomena? How are we to explain that reversal, which varies by place and modality? In this chapter, I give a certain precedence to the situation in France. It is true that German *Zeitgeschichte*, despite its ambiguities, played an essential role in the emergence of a contemporary history after 1945; but the French history of the present time, though not the same kind of model, illustrates quite well how the last epistemological doubts about that practice evaporated in the 1970s and 1980s.

THE *LONGUE DURÉE*, OR RESISTANCE TO THE PRESENT

The institutionalization of that history began in 1945, first at special and specialized sites, and developed nearly everywhere in the 1960s and 1970s. In Germany, the work of the Institut für Zeitgeschichte was accompanied in the late 1950s by new courses of study on recent history in some fifteen universities, though the history of Nazism held a relatively minor place compared to the more general history of Germany and Europe.[1] In France, contemporary history increased in influence but still encountered strong, sometimes unexpected resistance. Pierre Renouvin's presence at the Sorbonne, then at the Fondation Nationale des Sciences Politiques (FNSP), which he headed from 1959 to 1971, marked a form of recognition, inasmuch as, after 1918, he had been an emblematic figure for a new approach to contemporaneity. After World War II, however, Renouvin adopted much more conservative positions, if we are to believe René Girault, one of the young historians of the time who took his courses.

> Rather quickly, Pierre Renouvin became extremely cautious about the history of the present time. In 1925, which is to say, barely ten years after World War I, he wrote a first book on the direct origins of that conflict, but he came to be convinced of something that he would erect into a law for historians: Do not do history of the present time. We are faced with the paradox that, in the immediate post–World War II era, it was he who had the scientific board at the Sorbonne decide to prohibit theses dealing with very contemporary history. To be precise, he established a linkage between the opening of the archives and the possibility of writing a thesis on a given subject. At the time, that meant you could not write a thesis on the history of the period after 1914. There were two exceptions in the 1950s; in both cases, the future author of the thesis for personal reasons had access to records unavailable to others. . . . For a very long

time, Pierre Renouvin thus rejected theses that went beyond 1914. It was too "immediate" a history at the time.[2]

Distrust therefore persisted in traditional academic circles toward a practice that was all the more questionable in that many themes could give rise to polemics in an intellectual world split by the Cold War. From that point of view, the situation in France and Italy, where the political and intellectual weight of the Communist Party and the influence of Marxism were unmatched elsewhere in Western Europe, differed from that in English, American, and German historiography. No field of knowledge avoided the rift between Marxists and anti-Marxists of every stripe. Among French historians, the debates about feudalism, the ancien régime, and the Revolution were no less heated than controversies about Fascism or World War II, both within academia and without. But did that politicization from the 1950s to the 1970s discourage the choice of a specialization and slow the development of the history of the present time? "The majority of the young Communist historians of my generation became 'contemporaneists,'" writes Maurice Agulhon, referring to institutional contemporaneity, which begins in 1789.[3] Raoul Girardet, a conservative who came out of Action Française, responded in kind. This historian of French nationalism wrote: "It was by means of an initiation into political militantism that so many members of my generation reached manhood" and entered the profession.[4] By contrast, the Communist militant Madeleine Rebérioux often expressed her hesitancy as an academic about writing on too recent a history. Rebérioux, who was very involved in the anticolonial struggle and served as president of the Ligue des Droits de l'Homme (Human Rights League) between 1991 and 1995, was a specialist in the nineteenth and early twentieth centuries. Her reticence pertained precisely to the history of her own engagement as a citizen and no doubt stemmed from a "refusal to confront the history of the Communist Party."[5]

In reality, France's relative delay can be explained by factors other than the politicization of the environment. Somewhat more in that country than elsewhere, historians focused on a structural approach that seemed at odds with the study of the recent past. Special initiatives such as the CHGM and the CDJC were certainly encouraged by established historians: we have seen that Lucien Febvre supported *Cahiers d'histoire de la guerre*, though it did not provide the model of history-as-problem that he desired. But there was still a sense that a division of labor existed between very specialized sites, whose existence was justified by a moral and ethical urgency, and the university in the broad sense of the word. The task of academia was to develop the canons of the discipline, which had little to do with the most recent history. According to the Dutch historian Henk Wesseling, before the war *Annales* had granted great attention to that history and had set out to find a new dynamic between past and present; but after 1945 it seems to have abandoned the field. Until 1977, the history of the nineteenth and twentieth centuries consistently filled about 16 percent of the review's pages, whereas the history then called "immediate," which represented about 22 percent of printed space before the war, steadily decreased, finally representing only 6 percent.[6] Wesseling finds fault on both sides, arguing that because the historiography of the contemporary had not managed to dissociate itself from the most traditional political history and demonstrated a lack of interest in the advances of the Annales School, the movement gave up on it. The argument is only half convincing: it does not explain why, within the Annales movement and at a time when French historiography was highly influential, no one developed a program that would have allowed historians to write about the near past in a mode other than political history or the history of events. Indeed, the first credible scientific arguments in favor of contemporary history appeared in the late 1930s, around the same time as the first publication of *Annales* in 1929. Yet is was not until half a century later, in the 1970s, that that concern found a place within the École des Hautes Études en Sciences Sociales (EHESS), successor to the sixth section of the École Pratique des Hautes Études (EPHE), created and directed by Lucien Febvre, then by Fernand Braudel. By that time, the entire discipline was taking an interest in the question. In the 1950s and 1960s, there was in effect a rift between a recognized medieval and modern historiography—the French Revolution included—which was creating new paradigms (the *longue durée*, motionless history, mentalities) and new objects (climate, the everyday), and a still poorly established historiography of the present time, prisoner to subjects characterized as "traditional" (wars, revolutions, Fascism) and apparently outmoded paradigms (the event). That situation looked very much like a repetition of the late nineteenth century, when the successes of the methodological school had blocked the development of a scientific historiography of the contemporary. The comparison may appear heretical a priori, since the Annales movement was constructed specifically in opposition to the methodological school. Moreover, it continued to thrive after the war, pretending to believe that the enemy "event," though largely subdued, still threatened the EHESS. In my view, however, the two situations do have something in common: the refusal—perhaps the inability—by both Seigno-bos and Braudel to accept the uncertainty and incompleteness of any history of the present time, which were at odds with their fundamentally scientistic perspective. Added to that was the more precise question of the basic in-compatibility between the concept of the *longue durée* defended by Braudel, a dominant figure in the historiography of the time, and the study of the present time as it was then being practiced, that is, the study of the first half of the twentieth century.

Not only did Fernand Braudel, held captive for the duration of the war first in Mainz, then in Lübeck, conceive his thesis for *La Méditerranée et le monde méditerranéen à l'époque de Philippe II* (*The Mediterranean and the Mediter-ranean World in the Age of Philip II*) in the Oflag; it was there as well that he articulated for the first time his concept of the *longue durée*, which he would formalize in 1958.[7] In doing so, he approached current events and the event in general in a very personal manner: "The proper policy, the manly attitude, is to react against [the events], to bear them patiently at first, and especially to judge them at their sometimes derisory value, since great events vanish quickly, without always leaving behind the major consequences anticipated. Just think of the fate of so many brilliant victories or great political speeches! What remained of them two or three months later? And what, all in all, will history remember in fifty years about our time, so troubled, so monstrously preoccupied with itself?"[8]

Braudel is alluding here to the German propaganda in which prisoners of war were awash and to his way of resisting it. At a deeper level, the text har-bors a desire to escape the weight of his own present, an idea he expressed many times: "All these events that the radio and newspapers dumped on us . . . I had to move beyond them, reject them, deny them . . . believe that history, fate, were written at a much greater depth, take the long view."[9] So it was that his regular companions at the lectures given at Oflag XIIb in Mainz in 1941-42 adopted the habit of reacting to depressing announcements of German victories on the eastern front by shouting: "That's event, nothing but event!" as if to ward off fate.[10] That brings to mind the situation of bril-liant minds such as Norbert Elias, who in their writings after World War I were able to partially deny or repress the violence they had directly suf-fered, observed, or inflicted in combat.[11] In the same way Braudel, one of the greatest historians of the following generation, invented the *longue durée* and rejected the event as "the froth of history," even though he was living in the midst of the greatest cataclysm in the history of humanity—though, to be sure, in relative isolation. Far from being overwhelmed by the urgency of the catastrophe, which would lead Walter Benjamin to commit suicide, Braudel here denied the tragic character of his time, in order to survive and to continue to act creatively in a world where the lethal present had effaced the past and obscured the future. In 1958 he himself would write in his famous article on the *longue durée*: "In the course of a rather gloomy captivity, I personally struggled a great deal to escape the news of the difficult years (1940–1945). To reject the events and the time of events was to place oneself in the margins, out of the way, in order to look at them from a little distance, the better to judge them and not believe too much in them. To move from the short term to the less short term and then to the very long term (if it exists, that long term can only be the time of the sages); then, having arrived at that end, to stop, to consider everything anew and rebuild, even make everything revolve around oneself: that operation is tempting to a historian."[12]

Once again, we have the example of a nontraumatized response to the effects of a historical catastrophe. Nevertheless, that conception of time, forged very early on in the midst of the Third Reich, was not merely a psychological response. It founded an epistemology where the place of the present time and of the event was problematic: "What, in fact, is a great event? Not the one that makes the most noise at the moment . . . but the one that leads to the most numerous and most important consequences. The consequences do not occur at once, they are the progeny of time. Hence the many advantages of observing an age with a great deal of hindsight. It is all the same an advantage to thus grasp alignments of facts, not points of light but lines of light. It is something, when studying a tragedy, to know its last word."[13]

And Braudel cites two examples that demonstrate the pitfalls of not maintaining the sacrosanct distance. The first is Henri Pirenne, who, upon finishing his *Histoire de Belgique* (*History of Belgium*), complained to Braudel "about having to work on a history too close to himself, not yet settled, about drowning in a dust storm of facts where nothing could be made out with certainty." The second is Émile Bourgeois, who, to write the last volume of his *Manuel historique de politique étrangère* (*Historical Manual on Foreign Policy*), had to wait until the end of the Great War, so as to better understand the Congress of Berlin of 1878. Hence the only possible conclusion: "No doubt an era, in order to reveal its deep structure, must have become sufficiently detached from us and from the bonds of living actuality, must, like certain anatomical preparations, have gone into the retting tank and remained there for the time required."[14] Braudel turns to his own account the idea of the nineteenth-century scientist and methodological historians, and certain of his expressions recall those of Fustel de Coulanges—with, however, two major differences. First, the matter at hand is not to understand an event or a process once it has "cooled off," but rather to better observe, thanks to a distant or elevated vantage point (as in an aerial photo), the deep structures of societies. Second, far from believing that the passage of time is a handicap to be overcome through empathy or the objective method, Braudel sees it as "a privilege of the historian," thus assuming the subjectivist position that lies at the heart of the Annales project. In the end, however, the result will be the same: contemporary history is once again reduced to politics and the short term—precisely what has to be gotten rid of. That accounts for the later divorce. At no time, however, does Braudel explain how the long term provides greater intelligibility than the short term, once the historian is no longer looking solely at structures with a slow rate of evolution, or how that method can be applied to understand a century—his own—marked by the acceleration of a particularly mobile time. In reality, though the concept of the *longue durée* makes it possible to understand the temporality specific to the medieval or modern West and even the beginnings of the French Revolution, it is hardly pertinent for analyzing contemporary mass societies, which are notable for the speed and succession of events, constructed or perceived as breaks in a historical continuity that has become unreadable. Hence the rarity of studies based on the concept of the *longue durée* that might have allowed a better intelligibility of the twentieth century, even though the term itself tends to be bandied about at times. The *longue durée* is less a heuristic concept than the interpretation of a conjuncture that, though millennial, is neither eternal nor universal.

There is in fact reason to doubt whether Braudel understood the concept intimately, beyond polemical postures and efforts to distinguish himself. In January 1957 the *Revue d'histoire de la Deuxième Guerre mondiale* devoted a first special issue to captivity. Braudel agreed to write the introduction in commemoration of his own experience. This was another bridge between the historians of the CHGM, a place dedicated to the event if ever there was one, and the aristocracy of the discipline. Paying tribute to Henri Michel's team, Braudel wrote: "As Lucien Febvre said so often and as I will repeat, now that he is no longer with us: history is the study of the past, true, but it is also an explanation of the very present we are living in. Proponents of the need for distance on the historian's part are somewhat mistaken about the essence of our profession. In any case, they allow most of the raw material of history to deteriorate, material that belongs to a time from which we are barely emerging and which continues to weigh upon us."[15]

Braudel is not wrong to recall that he is borrowing the words Febvre used in a review a few years earlier. Printed on the opposite page from that introduction was a brief tribute to the cofounder of the *Annales*, who had died the previous year, and who for ten years had been head of the CHGM's steering committee.

> He liked to joke that he was not a specialist in contemporary history. But no field of research remained foreign to him for long; and his lofty vision, his vast experience of men and things, his great intellectual integrity quickly led him to discover and widen the avenues to be taken. It appeared self-evident to him that contemporaries must be the first, when passions have only just cooled, to give their version of the events in which they were actors or simply witnesses, for the greatest benefit of the generations to come. In that way, the past nearest to them in time would not also be the one they knew least, would not be alien to them. The most pressing issues of World War II have sometimes been tackled in this review; the most rugged human landscapes of our time are sometimes laid out here, clarified by the historian, and we are beholden to Lucien Febvre for that state of affairs.[16]

That steadfast respect for a contemporary history that was nevertheless fairly close in its methods to what they relentlessly denounced might look like nothing more than professional courtesy or a friendly opportunism with respect to a period in which they were actors. At least in the case of Braudel, however, the contradiction between his position on historical distance in 1943 and the one he defended in 1957 is too glaring not to denote an uncertainty, even a tension between two contrary epistemological necessities: the expectation of detachment and the urgency of understanding. That tension structures all writings about the history of the present time, as has been pointed out several times. True, Braudel's position is not identical to Febvre's: Braudel seems to believe that contemporary history consists of gathering primary sources and testimony, a sort of preliminary phase for a future historiography. Michel's committee, by contrast, had moved beyond that stage several years earlier and was now producing its own detailed and well-developed knowledge about the war years, no longer confining itself to collecting materials. But Braudel's position is all the more astonishing in that it coincided in time to his founding article on the *longue durée*, published in 1958.

I do not wish to reopen a debate over which a great deal of ink has been spilled and which now seems somewhat outdated, but it is worth noting that, again and again, the article berates the same intimate enemy—"traditional history, otherwise known as the history of events, that label being indistinguishable from political history."[17] This political history, something of a fantasy, became a reassuring scapegoat because it always appeared to show the same face, a trait typical of any construction of a hereditary enemy or adversary. That condemnation, in fact, applies to history in general, not only to contemporary history, which is not dealt with directly in that article. There is another nuance as well: the author notes that "political history is not necessarily the history of events, nor is it condemned to be so"—an incidental remark whose import can now be measured by the revival of a social or cultural history of the political in France in the last twenty years, set in motion by René Rémond and continued by Jean-François Sirinelli and others. In spite of everything, the ambivalence Braudel displays toward the study of the present remains.

> But what would the voyager of the actual not give to have that distance (or to jump forward in time) so as to unmask and simplify present life, confused and unreadable because too cluttered with minor gestures and signs? Claude Lévi-Strauss claims that an hour of conversation with a contemporary of Plato would teach him more about the coherence or incoherence of ancient Greece than our classical discourses. I heartily agree. But that is because, for years, he heard a hundred Greek voices rescued from silence. The historian paved the way for the journey. An hour in present-day Greece would not teach him anything about current coherencies or incoherencies.
>
> Furthermore, the investigator of the present time does not arrive at the "fine-grained" structures unless he too *reconstructs*, advances hypotheses and explanations, rejects the real as it is perceived, truncates it, moves beyond it, all operations that allow one to escape the given so as to better master it, but which are all reconstructions.[18]

On the one hand, Braudel's criticism is directed at those social sciences that know nothing of history and the work of time over the *longue durée*— economics, for example, which is incapable of reaching back "before 1945." He takes the opportunity to recall the superiority of history, a superiority founded on hindsight. History is once again the discipline that allows access to the truth of an age by means of temporal distance, which alone can identify the essential lines of force. By contrast, contemporaries are blind: they flail about in their own time without understanding anything. And since, by definition, social sciences other than history have to do with the study of the present, one must assert the historian's superiority. On the other hand, Braudel seems to want to rid himself of that question, by recalling that the quarrel between the remote and the current is in fact pointless if, following Bloch and Febvre, one subscribes to the idea that there is a dialectic between past and present. Believing he is driving the point home, he proposes a program that is a priori impossible: to understand the real, one would have to reject the real in order to reconstruct it, a project that in his view is obviously beyond the capacities of specialists in the present, that is, sociologists or economists ignorant of history. In that way, he incidentally opens another avenue, where the distance between past and present is no longer merely temporal and therefore passive (the historian must wait for time to do its work, a notion that is not particularly new) but is rather an intellectual operation, a construction that seeks to break free from its own era by means of a certain viewpoint, method, and posture. In fact, the creation of distance from the very near would be the direction taken by the European history of the present time twenty years later, which would give the notion of contemporaneity a sense other than that of temporal dimension alone.

CAPTURING HISTORY IN MOTION

A year before Braudel's article on the *longue durée* appeared in 1958, another historian, René Rémond, who belonged to a younger generation (he was born in 1918), published a less momentous but not unimportant piece: "Plea for an Abandoned History: The End of the Third Republic." It appeared in a political science review, a choice that is fairly significant in itself. Rémond, riding a wave of acclaim produced by his *La Droite en France de 1815 à nos jours* (1954; *The Right in France from 1815 to Our Own Time*), which quickly became a classic of French political history, lamented that "the last ten years of the Third Republic constitute one of the best examples of an apparently inexplicable disgrace."[19] The article focused on the silence surrounding the history of France during the 1930s. In the lore of the discipline, Rémond's essay later became one of the founding acts of the contemporary historiography of the French Hexagon. The author himself contributed in great part to that legend. In 1987, after he had become one of France's most renowned historians, he wrote: "The article caused something of a stir, and not all the reactions were positive. To argue in 1957 that historians ought to start taking an interest in the Chamber of the Bloc National or in the elections of the Cartel des Gauches still appeared a risky venture and even a provocation to some historians."[20] Which is true, except that Rémond says not a word about the situation outside France, especially in the United States and Germany, where that history was already well established. Nor does he take into account the fact that one of the dominant currents of historiography at the time saw it not as intellectual audacity but as the manifestation of a political history of events held in contempt. In fact, Rémond's plea does not distinguish between contemporary history and political history. It thus unintentionally confirms the consubstantiality that supposedly exists between the two and seems to defend the very thing that Braudel and the Annales current continually berated.

In essence, Rémond criticizes scientific journals and textbooks for ending just after World War I or for treating the years following it in a perfunctory manner. "The proximity of the period easily explains it: it may be too soon for comprehensive studies, and it may legitimately be claimed that the time for grand syntheses has not yet come. But the surprising thing is that those ten years [1929-39] have given rise to so few specific studies. The silence surrounding history past can be explained by the indifference to history in the process of being made."[21]

Rémond is defending an element essential to any practice of history of the present time: the ability to capture a history in motion. He does so with great caution, however, since he admits that "historians trained in the proper methods of historical critique and whose aim is scientific objectivity have qualms about approaching a period that is still too close. They make it a rule to wait for the beneficent effects of time." He then turns on journalists, who according to him are equally pusillanimous on the subject.[22] Initially, then, he confines himself to calling for the study of a little-known period—"a distinct chapter in the history of the Third Republic"—a fairly common occurrence in the discipline. What attracted his attention (though he does not say so explicitly) was the period itself, its actuality, its "contemporaneity," and the possibility of drawing lessons from it for the Fourth Republic—it too in crisis—more than the conditions of possibility for a contemporary history. In fact, as he reminds us, that history already exists:

> Yet the silence of historians, the abstention of essayists—already striking when compared to the number of signs of interest they have shown in the previous years—appear even more surprising to anyone considering the period after 1939. Paradoxically, we are ten times better informed about World War II and the following years than about the end of the Third Republic. . . . The Comité d'Histoire de la Deuxième Guerre Mondiale completed a considerable amount of work, whose scientific quality has no need for our praise. Is it not inconceivable that we should be less well informed and less well equipped regarding our own political history in the years 1930-39, and that no person or institution has undertaken a study of them on the same scale? Yet that is the situation. Those

ten years, 1930-39, form a hollow between two massifs on the relief map of historical studies.[23]

Later on in the article, Rémond, explaining the reasons for the silence he denounces, even goes so far as to challenge one by one the traditional objections to any contemporary history, in particular the absence of distance:

> Perhaps, however, [these objections] are not determining. Above all, their power varies greatly with the nature of the problems under study.... There has undoubtedly been too little attention to the fact that the waiting period imposed by the administrations may entail an involuntary choice and that the advantages counted on also have a cost. One expects the last word from often questionable documents: police reports where the most interesting material has been removed beforehand, administrative correspondence that is often ill informed about the state of public opinion. Every election brings further proof of the persistent gap between the predictions of prefects based on information from their informers and the results of universal suffrage. At the same time, precious documents held by private individuals are carelessly allowed to be destroyed, and irreplaceable witnesses die.[24]

Even more combatively, he turns the need for a waiting period completely on its head, articulating one of the strongest arguments in favor of a history of the present time. It would be developed in the 1970s and 1980s, regarding, for example, witnesses to the Holocaust, who were at risk of passing away before they had told their stories to posterity:

> A nearly contemporary study does not render useless in advance a study of documents undertaken at a remove. On the contrary. The reverse is no less true: nothing can replace inquiries made among contemporaries. To expect temporal distance almost mechanically to reveal the true face of historical reality is to let slip away the possibility of finding the answer to certain riddles and to risk leaving a number of uncertainties permanently unanswered. It is an illusion to think that time necessarily works in favor of the historian and historical knowledge. Far from being too soon to undertake the study of the years 1930-39, it is high time to begin.[25]

In this text, contemporary history is not yet defined in terms of the existence of living actors, though their testimony must be collected without delay: once again we find the idea that the historian of the present time is the first witness to the witness. Without saying so explicitly, the author nevertheless reduces the witness to the "great witness": statesman, minister, diplomat, party leader or business owner, possibly member of the cabinet. This was the path that Rémond would take a dozen years later, when he organized a series of colloquia at the Fondation Nationale des Sciences Politiques on that neglected history, assembling historians and actors of the time.[26] The method attracted a large number of followers among historians of the present time and proved to be productive, though in its work with former heads of state or their designated representatives it sometimes drifted toward a historiography tempted by official accreditation—for example, at colloquia organized by the FNSP on François Mitterrand (1999) and Valéry Giscard d'Estaing (2002). At a deeper level, Rémond defines contemporary history as a history in the process of being made, which one can attempt to capture in bits and pieces but from which not all lessons can as yet be drawn. He adamantly defends the prospect of an unfinished, provisional history even while situating himself within a fairly classic view of historiography, since he acknowledges or concedes that the history of an event or of a moment finds its ultimate meaning only when the process is completed.

A contradiction in this article has never been pointed out. On the one hand, it attempts to explain why the history of recent years is possible and even necessary; but on the other, it does not explain the status it grants to the World War II period, the other "massif"—which he tells us has been widely studied—that flanks the "hollow" of the 1930s. Why develop over several pages a plea for contemporary history and not simply for that of the 1930s, if contemporary history actually exists in the scientific landscape? And why draw no consequences from the experience acquired by the Comité d'Histoire de la Deuxième Guerre Mondiale, whose praises he sings? The answer probably lies in the author's ambivalence about that period, which he always apprehended as an exception, a digression in the history of France. It may also lie in his desire not to make definitive judgments about situations he himself had lived through. It is very often with reference to the Vichy regime that he would invoke the historian's need to be "objective" and "impartial," even as he encouraged studies on the subject. In 1967, in a contribution to an issue on contemporary history published in the brand-new *Journal of Contemporary History* (to be discussed below), he returned to his assessment of the French CHGM, but this time more critically: "The committee's work offers a practical demonstration that it is not impossible for minds trained in historical method to be objective even about close events which were the theme of passionate controversy. In view of its *a priori* interest in the struggle against the invader, [however,] the committee has taken little interest in the other side, the Vichy government and the 'national revolution,' or the personality and role of Marshal Pétain. Our knowledge of the years in question suffers from this marked lack of balance. Except for a few unpartisan works, of which Robert Aron [and Georgette Elgey]'s *Histoire de Vichy* (Paris, 1954) is the chief, nearly everything that has appeared on the Vichy regime is vitiated by partisanship or concern for rehabilitation."[27]

Three years later, Rémond would hold the first major colloquium in which historians and witnesses intermingled. It focused on the Vichy "government" (and not "regime") and, prudently, confined itself to the years 1940–42, Pétain's "good Vichy" as opposed to Laval's "bad Vichy," a dichotomy defended by André Siegfried, the leading authority at Sciences Po. The colloquium completely ignored the question of collaboration and, even more seriously, that of a truly French anti-Semitism, for which it would long be reproached—I was among the critics, and I do not withdraw my criticism. A little-known text sheds retrospective light on Rémond's state of mind. In a section in the journal *Réalités* (April 1972) devoted to "France once again blessed by the gods," the author—three years after the release of the controversial film *Le chagrin et la pitié* (*The Sorrow and the Pity*)—published a brief article on the defeat and the Occupation titled "The Wound of 1940 Finally Healed," in which he concludes: "Decolonization is now completed, France is at peace with the entire world, the economy is being transformed at a pace that bears comparison to the others. The memory of our setbacks is receding and there is good reason to think that their psychological effects have subsided."[28]

Although he was one of the first to take an interest in the question of the French people's collective memory (in the 1960s he held a seminar at the Institut d'Études Politiques on the theme "History, Duration, Memory, and Politics"),[29] Rémond did not foresee the anamnesis of Vichy or even the effects of the economic crisis, persuaded as he was that France was now looking toward the future and toward prosperity. That was a trait characteristic of his generation.

In his defense (as it were), apart from the fact that in the 1990s he would contribute to a disabused history of that period, at the 1970 colloquium Rémond directly took on the most complex case in the entire history of the present time: the study of a recent conflict, in this case in combination with an internal conflict, even a form of civil war with lasting aftereffects, with the idea of comparing points of view without judgment. He was defending the notion that the lecture hall is not a criminal court. Rémond himself, however, would agree to testify in just such a court years later alongside other historians, at Paul Touvier's trial in 1994 and then at Maurice Papon's trial in 1997. In the introduction to the proceedings of the 1970 colloquium, the first of its kind in France, he wrote: "Any collective research on the near past is a risky venture, [and,] when it takes as its object a period as tragic as the years 1940–44 and also proposes to reunite men who belonged to opposing camps, it becomes a gamble or a provocation." He commended himself, however, for holding the event, which, with the most honorable intentions, invited former Vichy ministers to express themselves in complete freedom and without "petty polemics."[30] Rémond came face to face with an aporia inherent in any approach to the present time, one that is particularly acute in the case of twentieth-century history. Should one choose sides? Historians who do so will be attacked by the other "parties" and criticized by the profession, which will cast suspicion on the value of their historical work. Should one opt for neutrality? That is morally untenable and can create the sense that one is playing down the crimes committed or even establishing a sort of balance between the "parties," which do not have equal merit in our system of values. Even for the purposes of scientific research, the torturer does not have the same worth as the victim. What is possible in a judicial proceeding, which must decide the question of guilt, responsibility, and harm for each of the parties—all of whom can express themselves there in contradictory ways—is not possible at a scientific venue, whatever may be claimed. Like the Comité d'Histoire de la Deuxième Guerre Mondiale, its successor, the Institut d'Histoire du Temps Présent, maintained close and sustained relationships with a large number of Resistance fighters and survivors, who consistently attended its seminars and colloquia until the early 2000s. By contrast, though former Vichyists or collaborators were also sometimes sought out by researchers in their inquiries, none was ever invited to a public event, despite the fact that Vichy and the collaboration were subjects of choice.

In that respect, the experiment of the 1970 colloquium was never repeated. There is no correct stance on the matter, as Rémond truly sensed when he spoke of a "gamble" and of "provocation." Historians of the present time who worked on terribly sensitive questions had to invent, if not methods, then at least a way of situating themselves in the landscape. They had to create their hierarchies of witnesses, had to attempt to control their display of feelings but without denying their emotions. They had to accept the fact that "evil" would be embodied in flesh-and-blood individuals whom historians had to approach, win over, and question, without losing sight of what these individuals had done; and that heroic figures, martyrs, the vanquished of History, could not be considered untouchable or excused from critical scrutiny, even if a few precautions had to be taken in that regard. Contrary to the position Rémond defended in 1970, the solution usually lies more in the deliberate choice of subjectivity than in a forced objectivity. Rather than ignore their own inclinations or identity, historians must put them to use in a personal way, to raise problems that cannot be treated "neutrally": a loathing of Pétainist values must incite greater rigor in analyzing Vichy, without a misrepresentation of the facts or silence about what does not square with current prejudices; political engagement can—and must— lead to the same critical vigilance in the study of one's own political family. For most (though not all) researchers, the worst thing is often to lose credibility, and that fear can act as a counterweight to the blind pursuit of one's own ideological inclinations. That is especially true now that the procedures of verification available even to nonprofessionals make outrageously partisan scientific statements vulnerable.

In any event, historians who attempt to capture history in motion are themselves caught up in the march of time and must accept the fact that their viewpoint will be partial, limited, fragile, the exact opposite of the illusion of mastering the ultimate meaning of History by means of science. Yet Rémond has remained attached to the positivist credo, declaring that, in spite of everything, time will ultimately make it possible to write a "true" history of one or another event or historical process. Although he has professed a great attachment to historical contingency and has fought against dogmatic or systemic history, he retains a predilection for the idea of "deep forces," which he inherited from Renouvin and Siegfried. I submit as proof his constant refusal to take into account the impact of Fascism, Nazism, and the two world wars in his view of the French Right after 1945. According to him, it has remained heir to a tripartite scheme that originated in the nineteenth century and was itself the consequence of the French Revolution. That position is difficult to maintain.[31] On the one hand, he accepts the incompleteness of any historical writing on the present time; on the other, he continues to think that the last word will come later on, even secretly hoping to have it himself. In the 1982 preface to a new edition of his history of the Right, he wrote: "The facts themselves have come to provide the beginnings of empirical verification for the interpretation put forward in 1954. Confrontation with the real is a tremendous risk for books that deal with a history that is not over: it is also a possibility for experimentation that the human sciences too often lack."[32]

Here he is on the side of the uncompleted, the deliberately provisional. Historians who adopt that stance analyze an evolving past and formulate pending interpretations. Rémond even dares mention the experimental dimension of the discipline, its observation of the most recent present. In other circumstances, conversely, he takes refuge in the orthodoxy of the discipline: "Every period receives subsequently the answer to the questions it poses; it acquires its meaning only long after it has ended. The disaster of 1940 affixed its final seal on the last years of the Third Republic. The history of our century, since it is not over, has not yet revealed all its implications or had its last word. Is it not therefore premature to fix and freeze the view of these few decades? [And historians of the present time] expose themselves to being disproved both by contemporaries and by events to come, while helping their contemporaries to understand their own time, to decipher complexity, and preparing the way for historians of the future."[33]

Here, by contrast, Rémond venerates the historian who has the last word. But then how, why, and at what moment does a history in motion become a history past?

A HISTORY ENGAGED IN ITS ERA

In Great Britain, the situation evolved in the 1960s after the decline of the colonial empire, within a context where the predominant question was that of the Europeans' place in what was perceived as an increasingly "globalized" world. As elsewhere, it was initially raised outside or on the margins of the establishment. In 1964 the historian Geoffrey Barraclough published *An Introduction to Contemporary History*, which in the following years would become the standard reference work on the subject in the English-speaking world.[34] A fifty-six-year-old medievalist and a specialist in Germany, Barraclough had taught in Liverpool, London, and California. Deeply marked by the war, which he spent in the Royal Air Force intelligence services, he turned to contemporary history in the 1950s and 1960s. He did so not merely out of intellectual curiosity. Barraclough was also concerned about the metamorphosis under way in world history: the end of European domination and the emergence of new powers that were contesting its hegemony, the development of mass democracy, and scientific and technological innovations. That led him to take an interest in the present and to think differently about history: "We are beset by a sense of uncertainty because we feel ourselves on the threshold of a new age, to which previous experience offers no sure guide," he wrote in 1955, an idea clearly influenced by both Tocqueville and Benjamin.[35] Hannah Arendt would take up the same idea a few years later in *Between Past and Present* (1961). The historian must face up to that profound shift. Although all history since Thucydides is "contemporary" (a purely rhetorical concession on Barraclough's part), and though there was truly a revival of that notion after 1918, Barraclough denounces the persistence in the 1950s of nineteenth-century paradigms: objectivism, causality, Eurocentrism. He calls for a completely different way of apprehending the present time. Influenced by Marxism, he argues for a global history that would not be simply the sum of all national histories. That thesis structures his entire book and part of his body of writing generally. According to him, contemporary history, though an integral part of general historiography, is of a different nature: it obliges historians to direct their attention to the transition under way and to look back systematically. He cites examples from the recent history of Russia, Asia, and the United States:

> These few examples are sufficient to show that contemporary history does not signify—as historians have sometimes contemptuously implied—nothing more than scratching about on the surface of recent events and misinterpreting the recent past in the light of current ideologies. But they also show what is fundamentally more important—why we cannot say that contemporary history "begins" in 1945 or 1939, or 1917, or 1898, or at any other specific date we may choose. . . . [Granted,] the years immediately before and after 1890 were an important turning-point; but we shall do well to beware of precise dates. *Contemporary history begins when the problems which are actual in the world today first take visible shape*; it begins with the changes which enable, or rather which compel, us to say that we have moved into a new era—the sort of changes . . . which historians emphasize when they draw a dividing line between the Middle Ages and "modern" history at the turn of the fifteenth and sixteenth centuries. Just as the roots of the changes which took place at the time of the Renaissance may lead back to the Italy of Frederick II, so the roots of the present may lie as far back as the eighteenth century.[36]

In that sense, contemporary history is less the history of a period than a way of proceeding—a stance shared by a number of historians today with respect to the history of the present time, which in that view is not limited to the contemporary period. Following up on Bloch's reflections on the need to begin from the present to understand the past, Barraclough outlines a way of thinking that tackles the present time as such in its structural singularity and in its conjunctural particularity. He insists more on the second aspect, however: the contemporary ultimately belongs to a new periodization, whatever arguments he may put forward for moving away from that positivist legacy.

Barraclough was perceived as an iconoclast. Commenting on his writings, A. J. P. Taylor, one of the major figures of English historiography, notes that "it is one thing to say that our view of the past changes in the light of the present; quite another to claim that the past itself changes"—a good illustration of the persistence of the very same objectivist paradigm that Barraclough is denouncing.[37] Barraclough develops quite a personal point of view on contemporary history, which looks in retrospect—to follow his own method—like an outline of what would develop in the 1970s. In some cases, he is even remarkably prescient: more than a decade before Jean-François Lyotard, Barraclough sought to characterize his own era as "post-modern" to distinguish it from the "modern" period (which according to him ended in the 1940s), in the same way that the term "modern period" was devised to distinguish that era from the Middle Ages.[38] He sees it as a "climacteric" moment, in the sense of a critical period, and develops a sort of radical presentism—"no one has a duty to the dead except in relation to the living"—one way of reminding us that the post-1945 world is a world of survivors.[39]

It was also in 1964 that the Institute of Contemporary History opened at the Wiener Library of London, a documentation center established in 1947. Its founder, Alfred Wiener, was a German Jewish refugee who fled Nazism in 1933 and founded the Jewish Central Information Office in Amsterdam, which then moved to London in 1939. The Wiener Library did not only have the objective of assembling documentation on Nazi persecutions; after the war it also became a major site for reflection and consciousness-raising about the risks of a resurgence of anti-Semitism. Two years later, in January 1966, the new institute launched a review, the *Journal of Contemporary History*, run by two other German Jewish refugees, the historians George L. Mosse, who taught in the United States, and Walter Laqueur. That new venue for research would ultimately contribute to the development of contemporary history in the English-speaking world. Originally, however, it too was on the margins of academia, particularly because its first priority was the history of Nazism and Fascism, hence a continental history to which the English still believed they did not really belong.[40] On the editorial board of the new review were English, American, German, and French academics, all well-known or poised to become so: Karl-Dietrich Bracher, Allan Bullock, Norman Cohn, Bernard Lewis, Hugh Seton-Watson (son of Robert William Seton-Watson, the advocate of contemporary history mentioned in chapter 2), Eugen Weber, Alfred Grosser, and Pierre Renouvin. In the first issue, the editors note that the opponents of the history of the near past had become rare, either because there was a greater tolerance for that practice in the milieu or because the limits inherent in any historical writing appeared more sharply, weakening the force of the criticism formerly directed at the study of the contemporary. The end of the scientist ideal of the nineteenth century and the impact of the two world wars had thus cleared the way for a broader and more pragmatic vision of the discipline. In a few lines, the authors swept aside the traditional objections: the scarcity of archives, the lack of distance, the still-keen passions. It was rather the abundance of archives and documents that threatened the historian of the twentieth century. The rule of a fifty-year waiting period prior to any access to the public archives may have prevailed at the time in Great Britain, France, and elsewhere, but it could not prevent state secrets, at least in democracies, from being aired after a few years. As for the absence of distance, it no longer had any pertinence once the objectivist credo was abandoned. These two counterarguments would be repeated constantly in the following years everywhere that a historiography of the present time developed. What was more original was that not only did the new journal not deny the risk of a historical writing caught up in the passions of the time; it fully assumed that risk and even embraced it as an ethical postulate:

> The historical journals of the nineteenth century excluded the "discussion of unresolved problems of current politics" (*Historische Zeitschrift*), announced that they would "avoid contemporary controversies" (*Revue Historique*), or even that they would refuse "contributions arguing still burning questions with reference to present controversy" (*Historical Review*).
>
> The Journal of Contemporary History, unlike its more distinguished predecessors, while not actively looking for controversy, will certainly not eschew it; it will not shy away from the still unresolved questions of the recent past. "Academic" is not, at any rate should not be, a synonym for "neutral," "noncontroversial," or "irrelevant to today's world."[41]

That position was all the more remarkable in that not all the members of the new board were fierce opponents of the objectivity paradigm: Pierre Renouvin is a case in point. The argument replicated in its main lines Robert William Seton-Watson's ideas, expressed in his founding article of 1929. Two other dimensions were added to that deliberate engagement with the present time. First, contemporary history had to be a transnational history, and, though the journal's top priority was the history of Europe, it did not intend to isolate that continent from the rest of the world. Secondly, the journal was not addressed solely to specialists but sought to reach a broader readership. It was attempting to fight against the overspecialization of history, a postulate that took into account the growing interest of the general public.[42] Finally, with remarkable intuition, the editors of that issue, which was devoted primarily to the genesis of Fascism, warned against a potential risk that continues to threaten the world of contemporaneists nearly forty years later: that of a historiography focused exclusively on the tragic or catastrophic dimension of the century. "Although the historian cannot or should not forget the essentially tragic nature of his subject—the nearness of death and oblivion—the study of contemporary history does not justify a descent into total pessimism about human affairs. Gibbon ... described history as a record of the crimes, follies, and misfortunes of mankind. Our own age has added more than a normal share to this grim catalogue, but the age has also been marked by heroic action on an unusually wide scale and by a most remarkable development of intellectual power in many fields."[43]

Despite an across-the-board development of the historiography of the present time, the place occupied even today by the study of Nazism, Communism, the world wars, and the colonial wars—even in the *Journal of Contemporary History*—demonstrates, if there were any need, that these catastrophes have not ceased to produce their effects over the long term.

THE REINVENTION OF THE PRESENT TIME

In the following decade, the history of the present time underwent a dual development still more or less characteristic of its current situation: it now constitutes a large, sometimes even dominant branch of historical studies, and it occupies an unprecedented place in the public space and popular culture. The general public's appetite for and interest in history are nothing new, of course, especially in France, Germany, and Italy. But, beginning in the 1970s, a new form of curiosity about the past emerged. History in general became an object of mass consumption, cultural investment, and entertainment. The signs are well-known and have given rise to a vast body of literature: the emergence of memory as a new intellectual, social, and cultural category; the proliferation of commemorative events; the establishment of national heritage sites almost everywhere; the success of literature and films with a historical component; the omnipresence of history on television; and, in the last decade, the explosion of Web sites and discussion forums dedicated to history. Nevertheless, that passion for a new sort of history or memory—two terms that would gradually become confused in popular conceptions—would come to focus on the recent past and give precedence to the major catastrophes of the twentieth and twenty-first centuries, almost the sole objects of major polemics and "policies of the past" in the last two decades. After 1989 that interest considerably increased on a global scale in the countries of Central and Eastern Europe that transitioned to democracy, in the countries of Latin America liberated from dictatorships, in a South Africa delivered from apartheid, and in a number of countries still marked by colonial legacies (Algeria, South Korea). But that phenomenon had begun much earlier and is part of an evolution much more profound than simply the effects of the fall of the Berlin Wall.

The development of the history of the present time belongs to that context. It resulted from an evolution specific to historiography and to the scholarly world, but it has also been accompanied by a "social demand" for history. The creativity of historians and of social scientists in general—their capacity to identify phenomena, to give them a name, to inscribe them in time and space—have shaped an expectation, a need to understand the near past, which in turn has fueled their inquiries. The social demand for history that has emerged in the public space of contemporary societies goes a long way toward explaining the development of contemporary history in the last thirty years or so. There are many signs of it, but here I will give only a few examples taken from the situation in France, where the changes are in fact more visible, if not really different from what is happening in other countries. "The explosion of the new history was spectacular, beginning at the turning point of 1968-1969," writes François Dosse. "It took the place of psychoanalytic and anthropological publications. In 1974 the number of volumes devoted to history was six times what it had been in 1964; and the key positions indicated an absolute preponderance of the *Annales*. That craze for history in the 1970s was fairly similar to the interest sparked by anthropology in the 1960s. Here again, the object was to discover the figure of the Other, not in remote places but within Western civilization itself, in the deep recesses of the past."[44]

At the time, what was known as the "new history" current consisted almost exclusively of medievalists or modernists: Georges Duby, Jacques Le Goff, Emmanuel Le Roy Ladurie, Pierre Chaunu, and many others. In their books, which often sold well, these highly renowned historians contributed toward creating a heightened awareness within an enlightened readership, which discovered a history of mentalities or a different view of the Middle Ages very remote from the usual forms taken in mass-market historical works. These authors benefited from the general appetite for culture in all its forms characteristic of the post-1968 period. In historical works, readers sought to discover new, unfamiliar worlds, though questions of identity—and therefore a preoccupation more rooted in the present—were beginning to appear. The interest in identity was attested by Le Roy Ladurie's *Montaillou*, published by Pierre Nora (Éditions Gallimard, 1975) with the eye-catching subtitle *Village occitan* (*An Occitan Village*) in the midst of a wave of regionalism; and, a decade later, by Braudel's evolution, marked by the publication in 1986 of his last magnum opus, *L'identité de la France* (*The Identity of France*). The same year, Georges Duby, one of the main historians in that current, was named president of the Société Européenne de Programmes de Télévision (La Sept; European Society of Television Programs), the first channel devoted almost entirely to cultural programming and the precursor of the Franco-German channel Arte. It was an unmistakable sign of the importance history and historians had taken on as transmitters of a new contemporary mass culture, a history experienced in this case as a positive referent, an anchorage in a world where temporal frames of reference were shifting.

Contemporary history was almost absent from that movement. It developed in parallel fashion, however, in niche publishing and print journalism, since a demand and even a nascent economic market existed there as well. Not surprisingly, it was the so-called sensitive periods and subjects that attracted growing numbers of readers, a sign that the cultural dimension and the identity question were far from the only explanations for that renewed interest in the past. It can even be said that there was a rift between the public's expectation of a history of twentieth-century "battles" and the overt contempt by most historians in the dominant current for that form of history, a rift somewhat reminiscent of the situation in the late nineteenth century. No doubt there was also—already—a kind of fascination with the century's violence, even a form of voyeurism, which was openly expressed during the so-called retro wave in the ambiguous success of Liliana Cavani's film *The Night Porter* (1974). The phenomenon endured, however, and even intensified in the following decades, affecting both the generations marked by the major catastrophes of the twentieth century and later generations, whose members had been spared to a greater degree but who suffered from the aftereffects. It is therefore likely that the phenomenon is not merely conjunctural. The events of 1968 also played a role, creating an increasingly marked demand for a history that was less deferential, more critical of the gray zones and other taboos, real or proclaimed, of recent history. An inquiry into the lethal dimension of the twentieth century therefore took shape in the 1970s and continued to expand. In my view, this was very different from the attraction to medieval or modern history or even to the legacy of the French Revolution, which would preoccupy the French people during the bicentennial in 1989. That inquiry did not belong to the order of positivity, of traditions revived and reclaimed, of an exemplary history that ought to guide the present and the future, but rather to the order of negativity: the past took the form of a burden that had to be assessed so that it could be faced or possibly escaped. Contrary to a certain *doxa* formulated in the wake of Nora's reflections on the "era of commemoration" at the end of *Lieux de mémoire* (*Realms of Memory*), or of Hartog's discussion of the question of presentism, I do not think we can understand the regime of historicity in effect since the 1980s without taking into account the strong tension, which varies by time and place, between the positive and negative poles. The obsessive presence of the past in which we live does not stem solely from a loss of tradition, an ill-considered rupture with the past, an almost Promethean unconsciousness that would confine postmodern and even "post-postmodern" societies to a perpetual present and thus make us consume history the way we consume high technology. It stems as well, perhaps even more, from the pressing need to free oneself from the weight of the dead, the tens of millions of dead, the unprecedented destruction occasioned by human folly and not by fate. That explains the other tension, between the imperative to remember and the need to forget, that characterizes the recent debates surrounding the latest catastrophes.

It was in that context that contemporary history would experience a kind of apogee. Initially the public, for lack of a steady supply of scholarship, turned to journalists, literary writers, and "amateur" historians. These writers usually had no real contact with academia, which partly abandoned these subjects to them. In 1961 Henri Amouroux, who got his start in a pro-Pétainist journal, *La Petite Gironde*, before joining the Resistance network and participating in the creation of the newspaper *Sud-Ouest*, published a first general history of the French people during the Occupation. It appeared in a series brought out by Fayard called "Les grandes études contemporaines" (Great Contemporary Studies).[45] In 1968 the same publisher issued volume 1 of the first comprehensive account of the Algerian war, written by the famous reporter Yves Courrière—a war that had officially ended barely four years earlier.[46] Based on many testimonies, especially from the "defeated"—military officers, members of the police, militants in the Organisation de l'Armée Secrète (OAS; Secret Army Organization)—the book introduced a new historical genre that privileged life stories, the anecdotal, and the military dimension of that subject, what Benjamin Stora calls the "Courrière effect."[47] A few years earlier, in 1963, a journalist named Jean Lacouture had brought out a new series at Éditions du Seuil called "L'Histoire immédiate" (Immediate History), which would be continued by Jean-Claude Guillebaud. The term "immediate history," destined for a certain success, is said to have been invented by the publisher Paul Flamand, who wanted to produce well-documented books on recent events while at the same time making a distinction between historical study and investigatory journalism.[48] The series set out to promote contemporary history, and its very first titles referred to the latest catastrophes: Jean Plumyène and Raymond Lasierra's *Les fascismes français, 1923–1963* (1963; *French Fascisms, 1923–1963*), no doubt the first book on the subject, and Saul Friedländer's *Pie XII et le IIIe Reich* (1964; *Pius XII and the Third Reich*). In subsequent years, the series came to include works in ethnology (Germaine Tillion) and political science (Maurice Duverger) as well as recent documents, such as a series of interviews with the top leaders of the 1968 movement (Jacques Sauvageot, Alain Geismar, Daniel Cohn-Bendit): *La révolte étudiante: Les animateurs parlent* (1968; *The Student Revolt: The Organizers Speak*). It also included books on sociology, with Edgar Morin's famous *La rumeur d'Orléans* (1969: *Rumor in Orléans*).

Initially, the expression "immediate history" was the result of an editorial decision and was not an epistemological concept. Not until fifteen years later did Lacouture, riding the success of the series in a context where contemporary history was beginning to make a name for itself, attempt to formalize the term in an article appearing in a book on the "new history." He conferred on "immediate history" the beginnings of scholarly legitimacy. In that article Lacouture inquires about the appropriateness of the expression: "Immediate—really? Which is to say, instantaneous in its grasp, simultaneous in its production, pure of any mediator? To imagine it is practically to deny it—or to reserve for it a few extreme cases."[49] A brilliant argument follows on the issues of contemporary history, one that demonstrates a shrewd ability to see into the future. That history, whether written on the spot by actors or witnesses, by journalists, or by historians seeking to understand the roots of an event or a process under way, is less about "immediacy" than about the observation of a change occurring before the observer's eyes. This idea is simple but central, since it shows that contemporaneity does not define a moment frozen in time but rather a movement under way: "In the quest for a definition, the 'immediatist' would be tempted to suggest that the discipline he is striving to practice does not exactly have to do with these changes and even less with the 'changed,' but rather with the 'changing.' Just as Malraux paved the way for tragic and literary existentialism by having the hero of *La voie royale* [*The Royal Way*] say that what counts is not death but 'dying,' so the 'immediatist' gives priority to that existential passing."[50]

In the years following, the concept of immediate history was elaborated in the scholarly world parallel to and sometimes in competition with the notion of the history of the present time. In the next chapter, I shall explain why in my view the term "immediate history" has epistemological disadvantages. But it does have the merit of underscoring the fundamental aporia of any contemporary history: analysts are obliged to create their own distance, which explains the close relation to the other social sciences, a position defended by the Belgian sociologist and economist Benoît Verhaegen:

> Two traits characterize that discipline at the confluence between history, anthropology, and sociology. First, it sets out to overturn the traditional univocal relation between the scholar and the object of knowledge, a relation based on the passivity of the object and on a maximum distance between it and the scholar. It substitutes a relation of exchange that entails real participation on the part of the object—as historical actor—in knowledge of itself and, at the limit, the disappearance of the scholar as an individual. Secondly and correlatively, the method of immediate history aspires to be resolutely oriented toward a social and political practice and engaged in a revolutionary transformation of the world.[51]

If journalists were the first to occupy the field of a popular contemporary history, academics followed, allowing that history to definitively leave the margins where it had been confined. We saw earlier the pioneering role of René Rémond, committed to defending the scientific possibility of a recent history. In the early 1970s Pierre Nora, who was a generation younger than Rémond (he was born in 1931), followed suit, briefly sketching out a few of the possible features of a new historiography of the contemporary. In 1972 he published an article destined for a certain future, "The Monster Event," in which he develops the idea that "the mass media now have a monopoly on history," which is to say, in substance, on the creation and diffusion of events.[52] "Television is to modern life what the steeple was to the village, it is the Angelus of industrial civilization." But like all cool media used passively at home, at a remove, television bears something unexpected within itself and turns history into "aggression," through constant outbursts of the new and sensational—hence its "monstrous" character. That postulate, which remains as fresh as ever, has several consequences. First, it changes the position of historians and the very nature of their work, since events are no longer intelligible only long after the fact, when the passage of time and the judgment of posterity have had their say. They take on a "historical" dimension in the moment itself, and contemporaries themselves can thus characterize them as events, can even participate in their emergence and in the name given to them:

> But it is for historians that the modern monstrous event grows ever more monstrous. Indeed, of all initiates, they are the most ill equipped. In a traditional system, the event remained the privilege of the historical profession. Historians gave it its place and value, and no one delved into history without their stamp of approval. The event is henceforth presented to historians from the outside, with all the weight of a given, before their elaboration, before the work of time. And all the more forcefully in that the media immediately impose lived experience as history, and the present imposes more lived experience on us. An enormous promotion is occurring, from the immediate to the historical and from the lived to the legendary, just as historians find their habits disrupted, their powers threatened, find themselves face to face with what they elsewhere take care to bracket. But is this the same event?[53]

Not only is the event becoming, or becoming again, an essential element of historicity, against the grain of the dominant historiographical current; it is also changing in nature. It now concerns the masses, hence everyone. Events can no longer be perceived as the froth of slower movements. By virtue of their number and their repetition, they bear multiple meanings. As a result, a new space for analysis opens up:

> Therein lies the good fortune of the historian of the present: the displacement of the narrative message to its imaginary, spectacular, parasitic virtualities has the effect of underscoring the share of non-event in the event. Or rather, of making the event only the temporal and neutral site of the abrupt, isolable emergence of a set of social phenomena that have surged up from the depths and that, without the event, would have remained buried in the recesses of the collective mind. The event bears witness less by what it conveys than by what it reveals, less by what it is than by what it activates. Its meaning is absorbed by its impact; it is only an echo, a mirror of society, a hole.[54]

The originality of Nora's position with respect to a new reflection on contemporary history is that, unlike a number of his predecessors, he does not make a plea. He is not advocating a practice that ought to have its place in what is in fact an immutable system. It is simply because, as it is being made, history changes in nature, and because historians, interpreters of time, must not leave to others the task of producing the sole account, that the historian must also evolve and must appropriate the event, here envisioned more as a symptom (this is my term) than as a historiographical end in itself.

Nora would elaborate that initial idea in several other writings. In 1974 he served with Jacques Le Goff as coeditor of three volumes on the new ways of doing history (*Faire de l'histoire*). Contemporary history occupies a place there, still modest but real, particularly in Nora's own article on the event—reprinted, revised, and further elaborated—and in articles on new objects, such as Marc Ferro's analysis of the relation between film and history.[55] In 1975 Nora left the Institut d'Études Politiques, where contemporary history had had its beginnings, for the École des Hautes Études en Sciences Sociales. There he held a chair that its president, Le Goff, identified as being on "the history of the present time." Nora's proposal was titled (a slight nuance) "The History of the Present." This was unquestionably an evolution in the tradition of one of the meccas of historical research at the time. In the proposal he presented, as in an article written on the same subject three years later, Nora explained what he intended to do in practicing a "history of the present," which had overcome the discredit it had had in the late nineteenth century, and he remarked on the development of the social sciences: "Now that this revolution has largely called into question the practice of history as the science of the past, it is logical that the historian's inquiry should naturally broaden its horizon to the present time, a present whose own density and transparent opacity raise quite particular problems of method. It is the original characteristics of that new historical consciousness that, for lack of resources, one would aspire to illuminate. . . . I would like to study the weight of the past on the present through a comparative inventory of the different historical legacies, based on types of contemporary society."[56]

The historian of the present, after the media and the event, must take an interest in what is not yet identified as "memory" but as "the weight of the past on the present." In this preliminary version of Nora's *Lieux de mémoire*, the first volume of which would appear ten years later and would not concern contemporary history alone, one can detect Rémond's influence. In reality, almost everywhere in France and throughout Europe, the outline of a particular historiographical configuration was taking shape. The revival of contemporary history was the expression of a cultural evolution and no doubt of a change of historicity that would rely on elements heretofore abandoned, even held in contempt by historians: the event, conceived differently and occupying a place of choice in the contemporary imaginary; the media, taken as sources of information and objects of history and, soon after, as modes of transmission of a new practice of the discipline inscribed in a public space; and finally, memory, an object whose social weight would gradually appear but that initially had the strategic interest of linking the study of the past to that of the present, hence of allowing a "history of the present" to be inserted into a scholarly system where medievalists and modernists were still hegemonic.

Nora, however, like most other French authors involved in that field at the time, did not take into account the founding texts of the German and English historians who had put their stamp on the discipline outside France. Although pioneering in his call for a history of the present, he does not mention the German institute by that name created in Munich twenty-five years earlier; and while defending the principle of a contemporary history, he does not mention the journal of the same name created in London a few years prior. Similarly, the catastrophic dimension of the twentieth century appears only in the margins of his reflection; except for a few allusions, he even seems consistently to avoid it. Yet it is precisely this dimension that dominated in places where a contemporary history was being written at the time. Wars, conflicts, and revolutions are certainly part of the general context of Nora's article, but his "monster event" is not the Holocaust, which he had personally escaped. Nor is it the Algerian war, to which he devoted a critical and politically engaged book called *Les Français d'Algérie* (1961; *The French of Algeria*), which grew out of his experience in Oran as a young teacher. The monster event is an abstraction, an epistemological figure, more than an object of study. This deserves to be pointed out because Nora's career path would lead him in a different direction, away from the implementation of a new history of the present time, which would come to thrive elsewhere.

By the late 1970s, thinking had evolved considerably. Most of the institutions created after 1945 for the historical study of World War II underwent a similar evolution at about that time, a little earlier or later depending on the case. They were encouraged to institute reforms, to introduce innovations in their problematics, to deal with a field larger than the history of the war alone: first by moving forward chronologically to tackle the history of the postwar period, then by going back to the early part of the century to include World War I. For contingent reasons but also because of a favorable historiographical context, the French now appeared to be precursors. In 1976-77 the General Secretariat of the Government decided that the Comité d'Histoire de la Deuxième Guerre Mondiale, which it had overseen since 1951, would henceforth fall under the sole auspices of the CNRS, which financed its staff and activities. The unusual measure of government oversight had been taken to facilitate access to particularly sensitive archives controlled by various ministries (Foreign Affairs, Interior, Finances, and others). The strategy bore fruit, despite the impossibility of gaining access to the collections of the Vichy regime and to wartime documents dating to July 10, 1940, and after. The government put an end to that system for two reasons. First, the state anticipated the effects of a pending law on the archives that stipulated a waiting period of thirty rather than fifty years, automatically offering the possibility of opening the archives of the Occupation. That law of January 3, 1979, allowed for a real historiographical breakthrough, though it would take some time for the majority of the documents from that period to become available for use by researchers. Secondly, the government believed that France now had to look to the future and clear away the last aftereffects of the world war, as indicated by President Valéry Giscard d'Estaing's decision in 1975 to eliminate the May 8 national holiday commemorating the end of World War II. The state, based on the belief that France had to move on, thus set out to normalize an institution created in urgency just after the end of the war and treated as a special case for several decades. The CHGM (and this was quite unusual) had had only one secretary-general, Henri Michel, a permanent fixture from 1951 to 1978. He therefore escaped the usual modalities of appointment and evaluation in force in the scholarly world, a trait he shared with other European historians, who were perceived at the time as expert officials holding a monopoly: for example, his colleague Louis de Jong, longtime director of the RIOD (the Dutch Institute on the History of the War) and author of a monumental twenty-nine-volume history of the Netherlands.[57] True, the results of the French committee speak for themselves: many studies on the Resistance were completed and the first surveys were conducted on French public opinion during the Occupation, on the political and economic situation, and even on the purge and liberation of the country. These achievements could all be exploited by the following generation (to which I belong), despite a tenacious cliché that the history of the period began only "belatedly." It was rather the history of Vichy that was an innovation in the 1970s—not that of the war, since that history had been undertaken in 1945.

The Secretariat General of the Government therefore negotiated with the CNRS to hand over the committee in the first half of 1977, a transfer made necessary by Michel's retirement. The idea arose at the time that this contingent situation ought to be exploited to promote the creation of a "research center on the history of the contemporary world," the first of its kind in the French scholarly landscape. As the preliminary statement of intent that would fuel discussion explained, "The fact is, there exists a vast field of knowledge that has heretofore been inadequately covered and which, with determination, method, and persistence, could be developed."[58] The richness of the period, which extended "from World War II to our own time," the fact that it lent itself to a multidisciplinary approach better than any other period, and the end of the discredit attached to that form of history would incite the CNRS to support and set up a new research center, one of its raisons d'être at the time. The role of that center was all the more necessary in that practical obstacles persisted: the difficulty of gaining access to the public archives especially, as well as, conversely, the presence of a "huge mass of sources already available," which required specific resources and methods and, in particular, the pursuit of large collective inquiries. More surprisingly, the statement of intent invokes a kind of scholarly patriotism: "Let us add that, because of the deficiencies long obvious in that area, the field, neglected by the French, has been so to speak 'colonized' by foreign researchers, foremost among them American researchers. Is it not paradoxical that a large proportion of the most pertinent studies on twentieth-century France are the work of English-speaking historians? Although it is a delight to see the increase in the number of foreign historians who are devoting themselves to French history, one may nevertheless wish that, in the future, French research will better manage to cover a field so essential for knowledge and understanding of our own future."[59]

The unnamed American researchers were undoubtedly Eugen Weber, author of the first history of Action Française, which was published in the United States in 1962 but not translated into French until 1985; Stanley Hoffmann, the great Franco-American political scientist, a professor at Harvard and the author of many influential essays on France; and Hoffmann's student Robert O. Paxton at Columbia University, whose book *Vichy France* was translated into French in 1973. The tone of the note is all the more remarkable in that it was written in 1977, a decade before the constant refrain arose that the study of the sensitive periods of recent French history had all been written by foreigners.

The solution ultimately adopted stipulated the gradual absorption of the CHGM by the new institute: the committee would cease to exist after a few years. Beyond the personnel problems, which would greatly complicate matters, the central question was the fate reserved for studies of the war and, more generally, the very definition of the new institute's activities. Three main avenues were defined at the time. First, the way had to be cleared for a history of France since 1945. That little-known history would incidentally shed "light helpful for understanding the nation's future." Secondly, studies had to be undertaken that would "open windows to the outside" and to comparatism, to remedy the tendency of French historiography to remain too "Hexagonal," that is, too confined to the borders of metropolitan France. And thirdly, the new institute, lacking the capacity to cover the entire history of the twentieth century, would therefore privilege certain "geocultural" areas (the *Europe des Neuf*, the nine member states of the European Community at the time; the United States, the United Kingdom and the Commonwealth; and Southeast Asia) or certain essential subjects: "Inasmuch as the period under consideration was dominated (at least in its first phase) by the phenomenon of decolonization, it would appear desirable to pay particular attention to the former colonial territories that have now become independent countries." Emphasis would therefore be placed on Francophone Africa. This was still two decades before the controversies about the "colonial unthought" of French historiography and society, proof that this "unthought" may deserve to be put in perspective rather than brandished as a slogan. Finally, research on World War II, a field in which French historiography held a preeminent place—thanks especially to the International Committee for the History of the Second World War—would have to be continued and even expanded. In addition, the statement of intent situated the new organization precisely: it would have the status of an "autonomous unit" and would hence be under the sole oversight of the CNRS and not of any institution of higher learning, in keeping with the classic division peculiar to France. "Far from beginning from scratch, the new institute will in the first instance make use of everything that has already been achieved. As a result, it will maintain close and amicable relations with all the universities and major institutions (Fondation Nationale des Sciences Politiques, École des Hautes Études en Sciences Sociales, and so on) where research centers that are pursuing studies on recent history exist." That diplomatic wording was designed to avoid the impression that the center was making hegemonic claims and to show that its mission would be to provide a place to meet and to coordinate activities. Indeed, many academics, jealous of their prerogatives (especially that of directing theses), observed the negotiations under way with a certain mistrust.[60]

Last but not least was the problem of what to name the new research center. The question was obviously essential, since it had both epistemological and historiographical implications, though the decision was ultimately the result of a kind of institutional pragmatism. Several names were suggested: "Institute for the History of the Contemporary World," "Institute for the History of the Present," "Institute for the History of the Present Time." The author of the note, who at one point even mentions the notion of "ultra-contemporary," expresses a preference for the first option, "contemporary world," but without explaining why. At the time, the CNRS was also considering the creation of another autonomous unit—the "Institut d'Histoire Moderne et Contemporaine" (Institute for Modern and Contemporary History)—to conduct research on the seventeenth, eighteenth, and nineteenth centuries (here the word "contemporary" had its traditional meaning in French academia, that is, "since 1789").

The name finally chosen was the "Institut d'Histoire du Temps Présent." After years of discussion with François Bédarida, I have still been unable to clarify the precise reason for that decision. No doubt it was made in the first place by default. Despite the desire for reform that presided over the creation of the institute, tampering with the major canonical divisions of historical time is simply not permitted, and the term "contemporary history" would continue to define a period that was now almost two hundred years old. The existence of two institutions working on different periods with two etymologically related names ("contemporary" and "present time") was to exacerbate the indetermination of that form of historiography, but it was also to have a major advantage: it gave rise to an enduring epistemological reflection on the relation between formal definitions, theoretical foundations, and actual practices with respect to the question of contemporaneity. That reflection has been the mark of the IHTP and of researchers working within its constellation, to which this book directly attests. In addition, the notion of "present time" had made its appearance in the lexicon of historians a few years earlier. François Dosse even explains that it was the choice of Jacques Le Goff, head of the history section at the CNRS, who would participate in the creation of the new unit. The name may have thus been an echo, as it were, of the program of studies at the EHESS to which Nora had been appointed some time before.[61] It is true that the great medievalist Le Goff played an essential role in the creation of the IHTP, proof that the development of contemporary history was now an object of interest to the entire discipline. But Le Goff was far from alone. Rémond, having been one of the first to practice a new kind of contemporary history, also brought all his influence to bear. For example, from 1979 to 1990 he was head of the IHTP's scientific board, which, along with the laboratory council, is one of two review agencies common to all CNRS units.[62] A body specific to the new institute was added: the coordination board, which Bédarida promoted as a way to integrate eminent members of the political world, administrative elites, and former Resistance fighters. Furthermore, the term "history of the present" had had a prominent presence in German historiography for a very long time and since 1949 had been incarnated in a seminal institution, the Institut für Zeitgeschichte in Munich. Although not all the French participants in the creation of the IHTP had read Hans Rothfels and his successors, they knew of the existence and mission of that institution. It had close ties to the French committee being restructured and would partly serve as a model for the new IHTP. Indeed, since 1967 the IfZ had represented West Germany on the International Committee for the History of the Second World War, chaired by Henri Michel.

Finally, the choice of a name, and especially the fact that it was subsequently able to achieve prominence, owed a great deal to the new director's personality, though that designation was no doubt not his first choice. Bédarida, born in 1926, was a specialist in the contemporary history of Great Britain, where he spent part of his career, and a *maître de conférences* (lecturer) at the Institut d'Études Politiques in Paris. He was familiar with the historiography written in English, which made him atypical in French academia. Bédarida had been given the task of establishing a critical edition of the minutes of the Conseil Suprême Inter-Allié (Anglo-French Supreme War Council), the military coordination organization in 1939–40, based on selections Renouvin had made in 1972 from Édouard Daladier's archives, held at the Fondation Nationale des Sciences Politiques.[63] A good friend to the somewhat older Rémond, Bédarida shared his Catholic faith. In 1944 his religious convictions had led him to participate (along with his wife, Renée) in the venture of *Témoignage chrétien*, the underground newspaper of the spiritual resistance. He therefore had a suitable background. And in that resistance milieu in close proximity to personalism, the notion of the present time had a more profound sense than the mere designation of a historical sequence. It connoted a temporal engagement in the here and now, which not only assured respect for faith in all its dimensions, but also gave that faith its full significance: that of working for a better world here below and not simply waiting passively for the hereafter. Bédarida has sometimes mentioned the kinship of the institute's name to that of two weeklies from the 1930s that had emerged from the personalist current: *Sept: L'hebdomadaire du temps présent* and its successor, *Temps présent*. *Sept* was founded by the Dominicans at Éditions du Cerf in 1934, and it sided with the Spanish Republicans and the Spanish Popular Front, provoking the ire of Rome and leading to the review's dissolution. *Temps présent* was created, notably, by Jacques

Maritain and François Mauriac in 1937.[64] That indirect legacy would play a determining role in how Bédarida conceived of the new institute's missions, particularly through a continuous reflection on the social role of historians, their responsibility in public debate, and the connection between "science and society," as it was called at the time.[65] He would do so by choosing paths different from those taken by the "organic intellectuals" close to the Communist Party and their heirs, who ceaselessly denounced the role of social demand in the emergence of the history of the present time, even while defending the idea that historians had to place themselves in the service of the people's cause.[66]

This discussion about the name of the new institute may appear to be a secondary matter. It was so at the time, in fact, since other options might have prevailed. The creation of the IHTP, and consequently, of a "history of the present time" track in French historiography, was not a result of a preliminary theoretical labor, which might have culminated in the institutionalization of a more or less well-defined concept already put to the test. It was the reverse. In accordance with a still-diffuse need, an ad hoc institution was created; and because that institution elaborated a unique practice of history under the banner of "history of the present time," this notion ultimately took on meaning and became rooted in the historiographical lexicon. There is, then, a pragmatic dimension to the concept, which I fully accept, though since the beginning of this book I have tried to show that a more or less comparable reflection on the place of the present in historical time can be identified over the *longue durée*, whatever the terms used in different times and places. What this means is that discussions of the history of the present time are not unique to one conjuncture—the need to explain the twentieth century—but raise much more universal questions about the place of the historian, the writing of history, and what is at stake in the relation between observers and actors. Nothing of that was expressed clearly in 1978, but almost all these questions would be raised in the following years.

In the decision that created the IHTP, the CNRS specified that the institute "has the aim of covering a field of historical research inadequately explored by French historians before now: the recent history of France and of other countries since 1945. [And] even as it includes within it the Comité d'Histoire de la Deuxième Guerre Mondiale, the Institut d'Histoire du Temps Présent will also study the period 1939–45."[67] The handover did not go smoothly: Michel made a fuss and took the *Revue d'histoire de la Deuxième Guerre mondiale* with him to the Ministry of the Defense. That proved to be a stroke of luck for the IHTP, which in 1983–84 participated in the creation of a new journal, *Vingtième siècle*, the first French scholarly journal of contemporary history. Nevertheless, the staff, the library (minus its photo library), the collected archives (which would later be stored at the National Archives), the inquiries under way, and the general office of the International Committee for the History of the Second World War all went over to the IHTP. I have explained in a different book how that institution (which I joined in 1981), created primarily to elaborate a history of the post-1945 period, encountered head-on the anamnesis of World War II in Europe in the 1980s and 1990s. That explains its considerable investment both in the history of the poorly covered aspects of the war and the Occupation (collaboration, anti-Semitism, the Vichy regime) and in the history of its memory. For example, IHTP's first project was to study the period spanning the May 8 commemoration.[68] From the start, and for reasons different from those of Nora and the EHESS, the IHTP (with Jean-Pierre Rioux, Danièle Voldman, Denis Peschanski, and a few others) would become involved in, among other things, the historical field of collective memory and oral history. Likewise, from the outset it encouraged research on decolonization and the Algerian war, thanks to Charles-Robert Ageron. He found an auspicious place and suitable resources at the new institute, which the university where he had been working had not offered him at the time and which would allow him to publish several major works on these subjects before the historiographical revival of the 1990s. Finally, the IHTP welcomed not only historians but also sociologists and economists.

By the 1980s, then, the historiographical landscape for that area of research had changed considerably. There were now several sites in France working on recent history around a network of personalities: the Université de Nanterre, where Rémond served as president between 1971 and 1976; the Institut d'Études Politiques in Paris; and various departments of social history, the history of international relations, economic history, and even Germanics. The diversity of the areas of specialization, historiographical and ideological sensibilities, and academic locations shows that this history was truly on the rise at the time. During the 1980s "contemporaneists" (including, it is true, specialists in the nineteenth and twentieth centuries) constituted nearly 30 percent of the 1,155 professional historians employed in France in higher education and at the CNRS, compared to 22 percent of historians of antiquity, 18 percent of medievalists, 18 percent of modernists, and 12 percent of art historians (all periods combined).[69] They had had the highest growth rate in the preceding years. Among contemporaneists in the 1990s, specialists in the twentieth century came to be in the majority, a trend that stabilized in the following years.[70] Although no one realized it immediately, that represented a real change in the profession, its way of conceiving of research and teaching, its relation to society, and the nature of its visibility. Finally, though I have here concentrated on France, the same evolution could be observed elsewhere. Most historical centers on the war in Europe broadened their focus of interest, with World War II serving as a foundation for studies on World War I, decolonization, and the Cold War, and for reflections on the epistemology of contemporary history, especially notable in Germany.

The methodologists of the nineteenth century had imagined they could exclude the contemporary from scientific history and relegate it to a form of civic and patriotic education. In that respect, they were following a tendency that, in the wake of the French Revolution, arose in Germany, the country that "invented" history in the modern sense of the term. The proponents of the new history, practitioners of the *longue durée*, had thought—in the name of an equally scientistic ideology—that they could hold at bay a history of the present time, judged too political and event based. But the event took its revenge, though perhaps only temporarily. All of historiography must now reckon with the weight of the present time and with the difficulty of classifying the catastrophes of the twentieth century as a bygone past.

CHAPTER FOUR

Our Time

The major catastrophes of the twentieth century produced new historio-graphical figures, serving to root a history of the present time in the field of historical scholarship and in the public space. World War I contributed to the decline, even collapse, of the paradigm of objectivity that had developed in the nineteenth century, following the wholehearted engagement in the ideological war by historians and academics in general from every camp. It also saw the rise of the figure of the historian as expert, charged with as-sisting in the redefinition of borders. As a result, historians became actors, though still minor ones, in a process under way—or even witnesses, survi-vors of an experience of extreme violence who spoke in the name of their deceased comrades. They claimed a place for themselves in the public space, in osmosis or conflict with scholarly discourses, which were themselves per-vaded by the direct experience of the war. In general, a new relation to the past emerged, one marked by a political and moral obligation to construct a collective memory—a "debt," Paul Ricoeur would say. That memory was fueled by the proliferation of accounts by war veterans, the erection every-where in Europe of monuments to the dead of a new kind, commemorations of mass mourning, and the first large-scale public policies of memory. These were all unprecedented elements of historicity that kept the near past alive and rooted it in the social imaginary, without seeking to abolish the distance from the original emotion. After 1945 another model of historicity made its appearance: that of the great tribunal of history, with the collection of an unprecedented volume of testimonies and documents and the first juridical and judicial interpretations of a history that had only just ended. Likewise, the first accounts of the war were elaborated within official organizations created for the circumstances. The writing of the history of the conflict was an integral part of wartime culture before becoming a central element of the postwar era in the context of the Cold War and of European construction. Exchanges among university students and courses of study on recent history were a driving force in that process.

The revelation of the major mass crimes, foremost among them the extermination of the Jews, no doubt played a central role in the importance granted to recent history. We saw in the previous chapter how the need to understand, to retain the traces and testimonies of the destruction of European Jewry, began during the extermination process itself. The shaping of that history and the levels of awareness evolved remarkably after 1945 and displayed some original aspects—for example, the longevity of the problem, its transmission from one generation to the next. In fact, the problem became more acute the further one moved *away* from the event. Although the supposed silence about the Holocaust was most likely a myth forged after the fact, it was truly in the 1960s in Germany and Israel, in the 1970s in France, and in the 1980s in the United States—hence with varying time lags—that the memory of the Holocaust became a major public problem at the national and international level. It was a good twenty to thirty years after the war that the major official commemorations were set in place, that officials apologized or expressed remorse (Willy Brandt in 1970, Jacques Chirac in 1995), that this history became the object of a considerable investment in primary and secondary education, and, above all, that what I have called a "second-wave purge" was launched (not without serious difficulties and resistance). In particular, French prosecutions of crimes against humanity turned traditional judicial time on its head and as a consequence profoundly changed our relation to history. Imprescriptibility, effectively applied to crimes of a political nature, is not simply a category that has always existed in certain legal systems (in the United States, for example, there is no statute of limitations for murder). It also belongs to a singular regime of historicity in that it obliterates the distance between the past and the present. For the duration of the trial, it artificially makes us contemporaries with the suffering endured not by a few but by an entire collectivity. It obliges us as well to apprehend the past once again from the angle of norms and moral categories, as in the immediate aftermath of the event. Imprescriptibility, though it involves applying terminology forged after the catastrophe, belongs to a temporality in which it is not so much the present that dominates, but rather the persistence of the past—or, more exactly, of an insuperable, unprecedented, and therefore germinal event.

The anamensis of the Holocaust, more or less belated, underwent another development that is even more significant for my argument here. That anamnesis, perceived as an effect of the very singularity of the genocide, its unprecedented character, itself became a precedent, almost a model to be imitated and sometimes envied in a different conjuncture, that of the fall of the Berlin Wall and the end of the Cold War. These events led not only to the end of the Communist dictatorships in Central and Eastern Europe but also indirectly to the end of other authoritarian systems—in South Africa and Latin America, for example. Although there are still no studies that would allow us to establish with certainty the existence of a direct connection between the two phenomena, it is possible to observe a remarkable historical concomitance: it was at the very moment that Europe undertook on a large scale a new wave of legal, moral, and financial reparations for the crimes perpetrated by the Nazis against the Jews that similar questions arose almost everywhere in the world, even in Europe, where the war in the former Yugoslavia raised dilemmas similar to those still unresolved from 1945. Must one purge, in the name of morality and security, the civil servants, police officers, and magistrates of defunct regimes, at least those who committed identifiable offenses, or must they be kept on to assure the continuity of the state? Must those guilty of acknowledged crimes be given amnesty, or must they be put on trial? How are they to be judged, and how is formal law to be respected in the face of these often inordinate crimes? By what laws and in what courts? Must the archives of the crimes committed be made public in the name of democratic transparency, or must a waiting period be observed to keep the peace? Such are a few of the questions raised in the 1990s when the fight for acknowledgment of Holocaust victims and of the crimes committed against them—exclusion, dispossession, deportation, extermination—finally saw some results, thanks to the actions of a few victims' associations and relentless militants (Simon Wiesenthal, Beate and Serge Klarsfeld). And yet, even if we concede only a concomitance and not a linkage between the two processes, a debate has arisen between the proponents of memory and those of forgetting, between those who demand justice in the name of an ethic of human rights and those who advocate amnesty in the name of traditional *raison d'état*, between those who recommend speaking out and bearing witness against silence and those who want to move on. Granted, these questions had already been raised in 1945, after Nazism and the war had come to an end. But after 1990 they arose with greater clarity about the stakes involved and especially with a new place granted to the voices laying claim to a right to memory, which became a true human right. These voices existed in the immediate postwar era, but they were in the minority and found little support, as attested by the passage of amnesty laws relatively early on in many European countries. If the situation turned out differently in the 1990s from Cape Town to Santiago, it was because many political actors, members of the legal profession, and interest groups feared reproducing the example of the memory of the Holocaust, which had taken two generations to be fully acknowledged. That very general hypothesis leads, ipso facto, to the following observation: everywhere in these countries the need to write a history of the present time, whether by historians, witnesses, tribunals of a justice system now characterized as "transitional," truth and reconciliation commissions (a novelty in postwar narratives), museums, or memorials, was self-evident. It was in fact an actual social practice that would have been impossible to curb in the name of the opposite necessity: that of waiting for history to be written exclusively by future generations of scholars. Not only has the catastrophe changed how contemporary history is written, but its long aftereffects have contributed to changing in a lasting manner the relation to the past and to the present.

A radical change has thus occurred almost everywhere in the historiography of the last thirty years: contemporary history has become a major preoccupation in the scholarly world and in the cultural and political sphere. But must we reduce that change to the direct or indirect consequences of wars and conflicts? Of course not. Pleas for contemporary history have multiplied since the end of World War I, and they ultimately found a hearing and a base of operation in the academic world, even as the objections raised to that branch of history gradually lost their pertinence. Other elements came into play, such as progress in the methods used: oral history, for example, with the spread of devices for recording and preserving testimonies; the appearance of new themes, such as the history of memory; and interdisciplinary studies, which have become a factor for all historians but have no doubt given a bit more credibility to those working on the political, social, or economic history of recent periods, since they can now draw on data and studies in political science, sociology, or economics. The general public's appetite for recent history also played a role, as we have seen. One would have to add the role played by film, television, radio, and online venues. True, investments in history by these media target all periods. It is fairly easy to see, however, that the history of the twentieth century greatly predominates in audiovisual productions of every kind. In addition to the general context analyzed here, there are particular reasons for that state of affairs that deserve at least a mention. For the history of the last 150 years, we have at our disposal moving images, now recorded and used in legally and technically accessible databases. In France, for example, the Institut National de l'Audiovisuel (INA; National Audiovisual Institute) benefited from a groundbreaking law on copyright registration for audiovisual productions, introduced in 1992 by the historian Jean-Noël Jeanneney. Such databases also exist at the major international press agencies, which cater to the historical documentary industry. The explosion in audiovisual supply and demand has encouraged the systematic exploitation of these archival collections (by definition nonexistent for earlier periods). Naturally, filmmakers and authors privilege the periods and events for which a large store of images and sounds exists, notably historical catastrophes from World War II (omnipresent on television screens around the world) to September 11. I was on the advisory board of the French cable channel "Histoire" for a few years and can therefore attest to the debates regarding the relative difficulty, for lack of moving pictures, of dealing on TV with subjects prior to the late nineteenth century. The idea that only the image really "speaks" to the television viewer gives added weight to that argument.

Be that as it may, the success of contemporary history can be explained by factors that undoubtedly run deeper. These lie in the very evolution of regimes of historicity, though it is not easy to distinguish between cause and effect: has our current regime of historicity changed because the contemporary and the present occupy a greater place in it, or is the interest in the contemporary a consequence of an evolution in the relation to history? Often cited among these factors is the argument that the decline of ideologically oriented "grand narratives" has changed how history is perceived and written. The end of modernity and the postmodern condition that emerged in the 1970s may in some way have made us more sensitive to contemporaneity, sharpening our sense that we are living in a present devoid of meaning, deprived of a structuring idea of progress or a finality of History.

> In the course of the past fifty years, each grand narrative of emancipation—regardless of the genre it privileges—has, as it were, had its principle invalidated. *All that is real is rational, all that is rational is real*: "Auschwitz" refutes the speculative doctrine. At least this crime, which is real, is not rational. *All that is proletarian is communist, all that is communist is proletarian*: "Berlin 1953," "Budapest 1956," "Czechoslovakia 1968," "Poland 1980" (to name but a few) refute the doctrine of historical materialism: the workers rise up against the Party. *All that*

is democratic is by the people and for the people, and vice versa: "May 1968" refutes the doctrine of parliamentary liberalism. Everyday society brings the representative institution to a halt. *Everything that promotes the free flow of supply and demand is good for general prosperity, and vice versa:* the "crises of 1911 and 1929" refute the doctrine of economic liberalism, and the "crisis of 1974-79" refutes the post-Keynesian modification of that doctrine.

The investigator records the names of these events as so many signs of the failing of modernity. The grand narratives have become scarcely credible.[1]

In reality, it is less the "end of ideologies" that has come into play as a factor in the emergence of a contemporary history (on the contrary, ideological commitments, including the most partisan, have led some to become historians of the present time) than the decline of holistic interpretations of History. Once each of the events that had been analyzed in terms of a single and mechanical explanatory principle—"class struggle," "the market"—turned out to be suspended in time, as it were, deprived of the place previously assigned it in the system, a historical substantiality would have to be returned to it. These events had to be reintroduced as sui generis elements of a narration that, once it had been deconstructed, had to be reconstructed. Furthermore, it was not enough to say that Auschwitz was after all a real crime and not an abstract category. It was also necessary to understand its underlying causes and intrinsic complexity, hence to return to a singular history, especially since the last avatars of these grand narratives were now assuming degenerate forms such as negationism. According to Lyotard, it was truly a certain reading of recent history (1956, 1968, 1974) that collapsed with the "grand narratives." The collapse therefore opened the way for a reassessment of that history on different foundations, without the guiding thread(s) that had prevailed since the beginning of the Cold War. I might add that uncertainty about the interpretation of the past, the present, and the future returns cyclically in the history of thought and historiography. The "grand narratives" that arose in the 1950s only filled a void left by the catastrophe of World War I (temporarily compensated for by the "promise of dawn" in 1917), then by that of 1939-45, which no "positive" element came to attenuate. From that standpoint, the situation of the 1970s was not a novelty, nor is it an explanation in and of itself.

Likewise, it is possible to posit the existence of a connection between the major epistemological shift represented by the "linguistic turn," an aspect of postmodernity born in the United States, and the emergence at the same moment of a new history of the present time. A real weapon of war directed against a social history that was hegemonic at the time and against materialist interpretations of History, that movement aspired to revolutionize the social sciences by proposing a different paradigm. In the definition formulated by Gérard Noiriel —following in the footsteps of Paul Ricoeur, Hayden White, and many others—"All reality is mediated by language and texts, therefore all historical research is dependent on a reflection on discourse." Noiriel took issue with the supremacy of various forms of social determinism in that movement, setting out to substitute for it the supremacy of narrative.[2] In any event, the debate had an impact on the entire discipline and somewhat incidentally came into play in the nascent epistemology of a history of the present time. On the one hand, the "linguistic turn" was among the changes that, in the social sciences generally and in history in particular in the 1980s, created a favorable context for calling into question the dominant paradigms—including determinist social history and the *longue durée*— and thus favored the emergence of new ways of doing history, including a revived contemporary history. On the other hand, the reassessment of narrative in the historian's craft unquestionably encouraged the development of a history of the event, of memory, of representations, of opinion, all approaches and objects that would contribute toward giving the history of the present time a more problematic configuration than a mere "return"— caricatured for a time—to traditional political history. These new or revitalized objects, which gave credibility to the new history of the present time, owed as much to the political and cultural context as to a specifically scholarly context, which also evolved at its own pace.

Still another argument is recurrently cited to explain the new importance of the present time in historical studies: the "end of the national paradigm." By definition, a history that is essentially national privileges vertical time, which runs from the origins to our own era—in France, from Hugues Capet to François Hollande. Or it gives precedence to singularity, even exceptionalism, as in the notion of the *exception française* or the German *Sonderweg*. The more ancient the nation's roots, the greater its tendency to valorize them, and the less relative weight given to the most recent period. Conversely, if the national aspect diminishes, horizontal time will more readily be privileged. That "global time" is less dependent on the obsession with origins, more marked by transversality, and therefore more oriented toward recent periods. The first pleas for contemporary history by historians such as

Robert William Seton-Watson in the 1930s or Barraclough in the 1960s already expressed the idea that the historical discipline had to evolve in two directions, to take into account both the present time and globalization, phenomena they described as intimately linked. There is a share of truth in that observation, but it also has its limits. First, it is disputable whether that "globalization" began with the second Industrial Revolution and the scientific and technical upheavals of the last third of the nineteenth century. It can be identified much earlier, for example, in the Age of Discovery. Globalization—in actuality, if not in historical accounts—would then have predated the national paradigm, which for its part emerged with the formation of modern nation-states. Secondly, experience has shown that the writing of a national history, especially if it has a civic purpose, has almost always included the contemporary period, even when that period was left out of historical scholarship. Furthermore, it took time for the history of the present time that emerged after 1945 to depart from the national framework, and the importance given to that framework has not followed a linear evolution. In the 1960s the history of World War II was an internationalized history; in the 1980s it tended once more to become nationalized, focusing on the phenomena of domestic collaboration; and in the 1990s it became Europeanized and open to comparisons with World War I. In reality, the thorniest question is why, even on subjects unfolding in a transnational space, the national prism has remained so important and so attractive. Finally, it would be risky to transpose the situation of American, German, or French history to that of other countries without an analysis of some sort. National history has many good years ahead of it in states that, since the end of the Cold War, have sought to forge or repair an identity of their own, such as the countries that emerged from the former Soviet Union (the Baltic states, Ukraine, Belarus). National and identity-based practices, then, have by no means disappeared from recent historical writing, though they are being deployed in a context where the need to face the "dark pages" of the past dominates.

Last but not least, the history of the present time developed within the context of a crisis about the future in a "presentist" regime of historicity. It may even have contributed toward reinforcing that disproportionate attention to the present, as François Hartog wrote:

> As a historian trying hard to be attentive to my time, I, like many others, have observed the rapid rise of the category of the present, to the point where the

self-evidence of an omnipresent present has taken root. That is what I am call-ing "presentism" here. Is it possible to define that phenomenon better? What is its import? What meaning ought to be attributed to it? For example, within the context of professional French history, the appearance in the 1980s of a history claiming to be a "History of the present time" has gone hand in hand with that movement. . . . The profession has been called upon, sometimes commanded, to respond to the multiple demands of contemporary or very contemporary his-tory. That history, present on different fronts, has in particular found itself in the spotlight of current judicial proceedings, during trials for crimes against hu-manity, whose foremost characteristic is that they deal with the new temporality of the imprescriptible.[3]

"Crisis about the future"? Without a doubt. Part of this book is written more or less from that perspective, since I am trying to show that the ap-pearance, in stages and without linear logic, of a new history of the present time in the Western world, and therefore of a new form of contemporane-ity, has corresponded to moments of great uncertainty—in the aftermath of 1918 or 1945, for example—regarding the possibility of maintaining a con-nection with the bygone past and of envisioning a somewhat open future. Hartog notes, among the signs of that presentism, the social rejection of aging, the need to keep both death and the dead away from our immediate environment, and the establishment of national heritage sites, viewed as an all-out frenzy for preservation and hence as a fear of the alterity of passing time. He includes the investment in memory as opposed to history, that is, the desire to relive the past in the present rather than observe it from afar, with detachment. I would add a few others, such as the desire to define the crimes of the past in legal terms and to atone for them in accordance with the standards and values of the present. It has been forgotten that these very standards and values owe their current configuration partly to the difficulties after 1945 of coming to terms with the unprecedented nature of these crimes. That attitude has led to a form of constant, retrospective judgment of past generations, who are accused of not having "understood" the real nature of the events they were living through, since they did not draw all the conse-quences from them that we draw thirty, forty, or fifty years later.

The historiographical category of the present did not originate in the 1980s, however, and it had its birth not in France but in Germany. Likewise, the idea of a breach opened between the past and the present did not rise up at the end of the last century but after the French Revolution: "Since the past has ceased to shed its light upon the future, the mind of man wanders in obscurity," Tocqueville wrote in 1840, a line Hannah Arendt discusses in

Between Past and Future.[4] That sense of uncertainty already seems to have been perceptible in the postrevolutionary regime of historicity, which gradually put an end to the imperious reign of a history marked by divine providence or reason. It can even be suggested that that perception of time, that uncertainty, was characteristic of modern contemporaneity, which was only reinforced by the catastrophes, as yet unforeseeable, of the century following Tocqueville's. There is, then, truly a connection between the attention given to the present time and a change in the perception of the future; but that connection may be more structural than conjunctural or specific to our own time.

Hartog is no doubt right as well to point to the thorny question—of a different order, however—of the role the historian has played in the area of expertise, legal or otherwise. But it is not so much the historian's intervention (which can obviously be criticized) that I consider the explanatory element. Rather, what seems to me to move in the direction of presentism is the very existence in the first place of an area of experience where the historian's services would be needed. Whether or not historians accept the role they are called upon to play in "historical" trials does not change the existence of a demand. The prevailing idea is that actors in the present, in this case a tribunal convened fifty years after the events, purport to intervene retroactively, to atone for the past, by enlisting every sort of technique and field of knowledge, including that of historians.[5] It therefore seems to me that, from the standpoint of its intentions if not its actual achievements, the history of the present time as it has unfolded over the last thirty years is rather a form of resistance to presentism, an aspiration to restore, as all historians do, a depth to the near past and to current events, a way of inserting it in time. Whether or not it has succeeded is another matter, and it may share some of the responsibility for the domination of certain themes in recent historiography and public debates. But if, as Hartog writes in a passage quoted in the introduction to this book, the present, detached from both the future and the past, privileges the immediate, then the history of the present time is an antidote and not a symptom.

APPELLATIONS CONTRÔLÉES?

Given the various ways of approaching the history of the near past, it is not surprising that the same practice has been given a multiplicity of labels— *appellations contrôlées*, as it were—both in a single language and in different languages. Furthermore, the translation of a term into another language can change its meaning. Especially in English (now the dominant language in the human and social sciences), the term most frequently used is "contemporary history," taken in its etymological and pragmatic sense, since over the last forty years the legitimacy of that approach has not really been in question. The English-speaking world, especially in North America, tends more readily to argue about concrete objects and approaches to recent history than to inquire into its epistemology, legitimacy, and political or moral significance. Nevertheless, an increase in interest in such subjects can be observed among a younger generation of American and Canadian researchers, thanks to the emergence of a popular history, written by the people and for the people, as the saying goes—an expression of the current development of "public history." That movement, which arose in response to the social demand for history in the early 1980s, has sought to train professionals to participate in the creation of local museums and national parks and to aid businesses in organizing their archives and holdings. In some American universities, it thus established "applied history" programs, which have attracted great interest in the nascent field of the history of the present time in Europe, caught up in the social-demand paradigm.[6] For a few years, that movement has worked with and encouraged ordinary citizens, or rather communities, to produce a "historical" knowledge about their families, schools, cities, and regions outside the frameworks of traditional academic history. Vast surveys of these popular, more or less spontaneous practices of history in the United States, Australia, and Canada have in turn led to innovative and original epistemological reflections.[7] Likewise, there is a new interest in the concept of "historical consciousness," partly because of the infelicity of the notion of "collective memory," which historians and sociologists have overused in recent years, and partly because the phrase belongs to the basic history curriculum and to cultural history, which seek as well to understand the evolution of "historicity," a term still not very widespread in the English-speaking world.[8]

As for the notion of *Zeitgeschichte*, or "history of the present time," it has spread widely both in the German-speaking world where it originated, then in the French-speaking world beginning in the 1980s and 1990s. It has also had a fairly marked development in Latin America, especially in Brazil, where centers and reviews of the *tempo presente* multiplied in the 1990s and 2000s.[9] That interest can be explained by the attention French and German historiography has shown in the crises of the twentieth century, in wartime violence and political violence, in the aftermath and the aftereffects— all themes that by definition are of interest to countries emerging from dictatorships and civil war, hence the persistence of such very similar notions, invented in the Spanish-speaking world, as *historia actual* (which is closer to "immediate history"), *historia vivida*, and *pasado vivo*. The adjective "living" refers both to the persistence of the past and to the presence of living actors.[10] The last thirty years, then, have seen a circulation of concepts and notions expressing the need to tackle head-on the legacy of recent catastrophes, to analyze them or grasp their impact over the medium term.

Since the "history of the present time" is sometimes associated with a certain way of practicing contemporary history on which there is not complete agreement and which is obviously not free from flaws, some French researchers prefer to use the apparently more neutral expression "very contemporary history." That usage is primarily a reflex action, an effort to mark one's distance or opposition to a school of thought.[11] As of this moment, no text has given that expression a conceptual content. Lacking any real pertinence, it introduces further imprecision when it is clarity that is needed. Above all, it once again reduces the notion of contemporaneity to mere temporal proximity, which distorts its meaning, since the task is not simply to measure historical time but to understand the relation between the past studied and the historian's present.

The expression "immediate history" is also still in use. As we have seen, it appeared in France before "history of the present time." "Immediate history" has been the occasion for theoretical reflection, particularly by Jean-François Soulet, a specialist in Communism who founded the Groupe de Recherche en Histoire Immédiate (GRHI; Research Group in Immediate History) at the Université de Toulouse–Le Mirail in 1989.[12] Despite long-proclaimed differences between history of the present time and immediate history, the evolution of real practices indicates a close proximity between the two currents. Neither treats subjects more "recent" than the other, and both met with the same academic suspicion before becoming the object of the same sort of craze. Both encounter the same obstacles and are conversant with the same epistemological questions, though the answers vary by sensibility and focus of interest. Guy Pervillé, Soulet's successor, has in fact written that the two expressions are synonymous because they designate the same historiographical sequence, "the one for which witnesses still exist."[13] But is the debate over? About content, yes, given the absence of concrete differences between the two approaches. But about the meaning of the term "immediate," no.

If words have meaning, neither contemporary history nor the history of the present time nor any sort of history can claim to be situated in the "immediate," for the good reason that, since the Renaissance and the emergence of a mediate knowledge, to do history is precisely to create a mediation, to establish a bridge between a past—often unintelligible to later generations—and a present that needs to be embedded in time, in a depth of field, regardless of how long it lasts. It is imperative to pay attention to words, since immediacy is one of the great illusions of our time. Seeing the Twin Towers collapse in real time is a form of apparent instantaneousness that originated with modern means of communication. We must not forget, however, that this so-called instantaneousness required the presence, fortuitous or not, of movie cameras capturing the event from particular angles and shots framed by lenses. We must not neglect the fact that these images, which traveled around the world in a few seconds, were therefore transmitted by an eye that not only "sees" but also shields, a reminder as banal as it is essential. William Safire, the famous American journalist and essayist and former adviser to Richard Nixon, once compared immediate or "instant" history to instant coffee.[14] He denounced the risks of assessments that come too early, those we have become accustomed to see spreading everywhere a few minutes after the first projections of the electoral results (and now even weeks before) or a few hours after the outbreak of a conflict in the world. Our era consumes these rhetorical exercises ad nauseam. They are only the more long-winded when information is lacking: for hours, "political commentators" with impeccably coiffed hair hold forth as soothsayers; retired army officers come in to explain the outcome of a war that may last several years; "specialists" in international relations, based on their morning reading of a few articles in the foreign press, explain the evolution of the future world to us, beginning with the event of the day. In our societies there is certainly a strong demand for immediacy, for "analyses" that are forgotten almost as soon as they are uttered: they are designed to be consumed on the spot, without preparation and without effort, like instant coffee. Our age abhors both a vacuum and uncertainty; it cannot stand to wait or to proceed slowly. As a result, historians of the present time must by definition position themselves outside that temporality, which follows a logic other than that of knowledge. The objection that it is too soon, formulated by nineteenth-century historians in opposition to contemporary history, does after all contain a certain amount of common sense, as all historians know. But the "necessary distance" should not be understood as a waiting period: it is a construction, a state of mind, a way of analyzing the present differently in a world that seems to have banished all temporal, spatial, and physical distance. The effort to write on the spot the history of an event with potentially weighty consequences, and a fortiori that of a catastrophe unfolding before our eyes, does not simply reduce them to their present forms or freeze them in an immediacy—which is impossible to capture and in fact has no meaning for the historian. On the contrary, doing the history of the present time means postulating that the present has a substantiality, a depth, and that it cannot be reduced to an accumulation of snapshots taken on the fly. As with any good history, the matter at hand is to restore a genealogy, insert the event in a time span, propose an order of intelligibility in an attempt to escape the emotion of the instant, or—to use a Lacanian vocabulary—to introduce a little symbolic where the imaginary has invaded everything. That is one of the essential tasks of history and one of the most important missions of the history of the present time.

WHAT DOES IT MEAN TO BE CONTEMPORARY?

The task of defining the contemporary appears to be more essential than simply choosing the right label, though that question belongs to a register more philosophical than historiographical. "To belong to the same time," as we have seen since the beginning of this book, can mean several different things. "To be contemporary" is to belong biologically to the same era, a basic fact that has to be taken into account, though it is far from sufficient. As in all the other social sciences, particularly sociology and anthropology, direct contact, exchange, dialogue, confrontation, the mere presence of witnesses or actors, of their memory, of their possible reactions, and hence of the transference that can occur between protagonists from the same era constitute a singular aspect of contemporary history, despite the intellectual contortions that deny such particularity in the name of a unique and indivisible historical science. If all history is contemporary, the history of the present time is a little more so than the others.

For actors with divergent positions, "to be contemporary" is also to maintain a relation to an actuality, a present perceived as "common" in a space that has varied considerably over the last half century. It is to participate together in the affairs of the world, despite differences in age, place, situation, and perception of lived time.

> The contemporary is not a property, a quality, or a set of qualities that one might hope to fix as an ideal type. All attempts to define an archetype of our contemporary share the error that there is a historical essence common to all the actors present on the stage. The error lies in believing not that there are many points in common among historical actors, but that these points in common could constitute their modernity. For there is a bit of everything on the stage: traditional, modern, very ancient, even archaic, very new—and, above all, a great deal that is mixed. The contemporary is rather a relation between all the ingredients of actuality.[15]

Contemporaneity must therefore be conceived as a relationship to both time and space. The crucial question for the historian is to situate the place of the dead or the place of the bygone within that totality. A society that grants great importance to memory, even at a superficial level, ipso facto attributes a more pronounced presence to the dead and the bygone past. It assigns them a different place from that which has traditionally been theirs, since it gives them a ceaselessly reactivated actuality: that is the principle at work in a "commemorative" age, especially our own, which claims moreover to atone for all the sufferings of the past, having reintroduced them into the present in the mode of an impossible forgetting. In a world where the line between the past and the present has been reduced, historians of the present time find themselves facing a dilemma precisely because of that desire to bring back and preserve in actuality the sufferings or crimes of the near or remote past. Historians must either be "of their time" and hence go along with the illusion that history can be atoned for, participate in the collective emotion, and, for example, place their art in the service of "memorial" causes; or they must fall out of step, at the risk of being misunderstood, in order to create distance. In the latter case, they will be at odds with the very principle of an emotion seeking to revive the suffering of the dead as a form of empathy. Are historians of the present time "presentist"? Would they not be closer to the "miscontemporary" Alain Finkielkraut speaks of with reference to Charles Péguy, or of the Nietzschean "untimely"? "Those who are truly contemporary, who truly belong to their time, are those who neither perfectly coincide with it nor adjust themselves to its demands. They are thus in this sense untimely. But precisely because of this condition, precisely through this disconnection and this anachronism, they are more capable than others of perceiving and grasping their own time."[16]

There is no doubt a certain amount of aestheticism in that posture. But that approach to contemporaneity exactly coincides with the posture that historians of the present time have sought to adopt in recent years. They create distance from proximity to avoid sinking into the illusion of an understanding of the same by the same, on the pretext that we are breathing the same air as the actors being studied. Paradoxically, to work on recent history is to permanently take the measure of the constantly shifting distance from the object or subject studied. There is proximity, because one is studying a process under way, unfinished by definition, or because there is a living, accessible actor, an actor who is likely to react to the historian's words. There is relative distance, because the process is dated in spite of everything, or because the subject is older than the observer: here again is the central idea that "present time" defines a significant interval of time and not a fleeting instant. Finally, there is a greater or lesser degree of alterity, because the experience described is often alien to the historian, especially in the case of an experience of extreme violence. Historians of the present time, like all historians, thus experience a structural tension between proximity, distance, and alterity, but they do so with a different polarity: *it is more difficult for them to be far away.* Their practice consists not of moving closer to what is a priori remote, like an anthropologist considering a Caduveo Indian or a historian a medieval peasant woman. On the contrary, it consists of moving away from what appears close by, such as a resistance fighter or a survivor who is the same age as the historian's father or grandfather, who speaks the same language, who may live in the same neighborhood, and, often, who regularly attends or attended the seminars at which the historian speaks.

I insist on this point because it explains the confusion that often surrounds the very project of the history of the present time. It truly belongs to the discipline of history and has no intention of fleeing its family or origin. Although it lays claim to a few specificities and even singularities, it does not seek to impose itself as an autonomous discipline or to merge with sociology or with an "anthropology of the present," a discipline that appears very close to it in appearance, if only because it too takes an interest in the contemporary world—which is also that of the observer—and also raises the question of intentional distance-taking. The anthropology of the present, which appeared in the early 1990s, is actually a further sign of the growing preoccupation with the present or the contemporary in the late twentieth century. Having taken note of the recent emergence of a history of the present time, that form of anthropology did not aspire to take its place or to reignite the old debate about history and structure. As Marc Augé wrote in 1994: "The history of history, which is in part the history of the relationship between history and anthropology, led at the end of this century to a definition of the conditions for a 'history of the present.' Anthropology, however, must not interpret that development as the imperialist sign of unfair competition, but rather as a symptom that is only the more significant in that its source lies in the reflections of historians, specialists in time by definition."[17] In that sense, the evolution of both history and anthropology toward inquiries about the present constitutes the beginning of a response to the evolution of contemporary societies, where "immediacy," lived experience, and "direct" testimony have taken on increasing importance in a public space dominated by the emotion of the moment. As a result, mediate, distant, indirect analysis increasingly has difficulty getting a foothold—hence the risk that lies in maintaining that illusion within the disciplines most concerned.

In a dazzling text in which he imagines a dialogue between an anthropologist and a historian crossing swords on the comparative merits of direct and indirect observation, the anthropologist Gérard Lenclud reminds us that, by definition, his discipline cannot abolish all distance: "[The anthropologist] would like to remind the historian that though the ethnographer 'is there,' that is, shares the existence of the people he studies, he is not 'one of them.' He looks on them from afar, participates from a distance. His vantage point is thus not a cave, since it is already open to the point of view of the other, already confronted with another point of view, already called into question, disoriented. The historian is grateful to the anthropologist for that reminder but affirms immediately that the 'I was there' thereby loses part of its force. The ethnographer cannot be everywhere at once."[18]

It is not so much the presence of the observer on the ground as one event or another is unfolding that will create the conditions for a better knowledge. Rather, it is the ability to establish one's distance from the events or people observed, the quality of articulating and shaping a narrative, the possibility of relating a preliminary knowledge, a first act of questioning, to the observations in the field. Just as historians cannot lay claim to someday having the last word, since they can in no way predict how what they have personally observed of the past here and now will be perceived by their colleagues two or three generations in the future, anthropologists cannot claim the privileged position of "contemporaneity," since that expression, understood in its primary sense ("of the same time"), in no way abolishes alterity and thus the necessity of laying the foundation for a regard from some way off.

By contrast, for both the anthropologist and the historian of the present time, the contemporary scene is a place where their writings can have almost immediate effects, because, like those of a journalist, they become part of a process under way. That is quite a striking singularity. It is not a new idea. "Every 'immediatist' . . . is both a collector of facts and a producer of effects, of immediate effects."[19] And it is not so much a question of the consequences that one historical interpretation or another may produce in the here and now: a discussion on archaeological sites in the Holy Land or of the religious manuscripts of the Middle Ages can be just as heated as a controversy about September 11. It has to do rather with the consequences that the historical analysis occupying—deliberately or not—the space of expertise can have on a process under way. In general, that is where the history of the present time proves to be most difficult, and most risky.

For example, the report compiled by the Nederlands Instituut voor Oorlogsdocumentatie (NIOD) on the massacres in Srebrenica in 1995 brought down the Netherlands government in 2002 by pointing to the responsibility of a United Nations team of Dutch peacekeeping forces. Although it conducted a thorough investigation, the report sometimes missed its target, applying paradigms used for the history of Nazism to the wartime situation in the former Yugoslavia. It did so not only by reflex—that was its field of expertise and even the reason it had been sought out, based on the principle of a possible analogy between the two historical situations—but also to escape the dominance of legal categories by trying to "displace" the problem as it had been raised before the International Criminal Tribunal for the Former Yugoslavia in The Hague. But that analogy with the Nazi period, despite its inappropriateness, increased tenfold the political effects of the report, which could only have a devastating impact once Nazism was at issue.[20]

Similarly, and still within the register of expertise, the report compiled by Christian Bachelier in 1998 within the framework of the IHTP on the role during World War II of the Société Nationale des Chemins de Fer Français (SNCF), the French railroad company, was not merely a scholarly or expert interpretation of a question debated in the public space. It profoundly changed the nature of the problem being considered.[21] Initially, that report sought to establish its distance not only from the historical period itself (that went without saying) but also from the way the problem had been posed in the early 1990s. Called upon by the SNCF to do an expert assessment of a single matter—the deportation trains (about a hundred of them)—the IHTP proposed to broaden the field of inquiry. It would conduct an investigation of the overall strategy of the railroad company and of the control exerted by the French government and the German occupation authorities in order to assess the SNCF's potential for autonomy. In 1992, at the start of the inquiry, it appeared that charges might be brought against the company for crimes against humanity; hence the historians' need to depart from an exclusively juridical or judiciary logic, itself inscribed in the temporality of debates over memory. The IHTP therefore proposed something other than a mere factual history seeking to determine the guilt or responsibility of one individual or department or another, focusing instead on a political and economic analysis of the company's strategy and thus placing the questions of the deportation convoys within a broader context. Once the report was submitted, in 1998, the organizations that were making a case against the public enterprise, unable to pursue criminal prosecution, decided to appeal to the administrative justice system. That system does not judge individuals; it had to determine the responsibility of the public enterprise itself in order to decide whether payment of damages was justified. Almost the only supporting evidence for these new complaints, some of which were judged valid, was the Bachelier report. That did not prevent certain protagonists from accusing the historians of wanting to "conceal the truth," an outright lie that was both tactical and political. In other words, the Bachelier report, solicited to lend support to an eventual criminal defense, was used as evidence for the prosecution in an administrative procedure in France—and also in all the judicial proceedings in the United States seeking damages against the French company. And the historians, though aware of the risks and having distanced themselves from the possible use that might be made of their work, could not really anticipate these effects. Granted, similar examples may be found in medieval or modern historical studies, but experience has shown that consideration of the possible effects of that type of expertise on the process being studied, insofar as it is not "over," has been a structural fact in the history of the present time. Historians may well establish distance in order to escape their own contemporaneity, but it will catch up with them, though exactly when or where they will not know.

A DEFINITION ON THE BASIS OF INVARIABLES

Apart from the question of labels and the multiplicity of definitions of contemporaneity, in the actual practices of historians there are two ways of identifying contemporary history, and they are not mutually exclusive. First, one may seek out the invariables that allow one to distinguish that segment of historical time from other periods. These factors do not depend on a particular historiographical context or a given conjuncture. This method has the advantage of allowing comparisons in time and space among the various practices that have claimed to be concerned with recent history; therein lies the interest of taking the long view. Secondly, one may define the "present time" or the "contemporary" in terms of periodization. That is the historiographical operation par excellence: periodization seeks to identify a starting date and to isolate a historical segment with characteristics peculiar to it. Unlike the first approach, this definition entails interpreting the segment being considered and thus depends on variables: authors, schools of thought, scholarly or cultural contexts.

It is difficult at first glance to distinguish major historical sequences except by establishing noteworthy boundaries. That tradition, as we have seen, dates back to the Renaissance and even to the very first historical narratives. These boundary markers are generally memorable events that were significant for contemporaries or for their descendants: wars, revolutions, crises, or dynastic or constitutional changes. The habit is solidly rooted in the perception of time across the ages, at least in the Western world. Similarly, the choice of a historical periodization always stems from a reading or rereading of the past from the vantage point of a given era, whether by historians, the government authorities, or the public at large. Only contemporary history partly escapes that characterization, since it is possible to define it by invariables, which are not dependent on a reading situated in a certain time and place.

A Mobile Period

In the 1980s several historians of the present time, myself included, advanced the idea that, because the boundary closest to us is constantly moving, this mobility ought to have consequences for the research to be conducted. In particular, it called for a sort of permanent vigilance about the current situation. Although historians of the present time remain attentive to their own time, especially for the reasons mentioned earlier, that idea of a constant mobility of time did not survive for long and had only a very limited impact on actual historical work. Historians of the present time are not historians of the instant, and their role is not to chase after current events. Furthermore, it is a truism that historical studies must face a permanent prolongation into the future of human societies, though the question is not without its effects on the organization of programs of study. In many European countries, especially if the hours for history instruction have been reduced, these programs face a dilemma: either deal with the history of the present and reduce every year the time devoted to other episodes from the past, or refuse to make a selection and avoid controversy about the idea that one period or another is no longer taught, at the risk of making the curriculum incoherent. These difficulties reached an acute stage in the 1980s, especially in France, when school policies on history instruction decided that students in the last two years of *lycée* ought to be exposed both to recent history and to what was termed "current events," a development linked to the very emergence of a new awareness of the contemporary. This is a special problem, however, and has not had any impact on the development of a history of the present time. Conversely, the very instability of any periodization of contemporary history, which usually ends "in our own time," cannot simply be swept aside. That is a first invariable for any contemporary history.

A Significant Time Frame

Doing the history of the present time always entails choosing a significant time frame, a "period" in the most classic sense of the term: for instance, "from 1945 to our own time," "from 1989 to our own time." Experience has shown, however, that this time frame will often be shorter in duration than in medieval or modern history. The nearer one gets to the present, the closer together the demarcations will be. This phenomenon is easily observable in the rubrics for exams, thesis topics, and historical research. For example, in the new general history of France published between 2009 and 2012, the thirteen volumes are divided in a rather traditional manner: four volumes cover the Middle Ages, from the advent of Clovis (481) to the end of the Hundred Years' War (1453); four cover the modern period, from the Renaissance to the dawn of the French Revolution; and five cover the contemporary period, in the institutional sense of the term, from 1789 to 2005.[22] Simple arithmetic shows that each volume of medieval history covers on average 250 years, each volume of modern history 80 years, and each volume of contemporary history about 45 years—sometimes even less, such as the one on 1914-45. It therefore took a larger number of volumes to cover the more than two centuries that separate us from the French Revolution than to cover a millennium of medieval history or three centuries of modern history. That history of France can be compared to a recent history of Germany in twenty-four volumes, a series published between 2004 and 2010. Aside from an introductory volume, eight volumes are devoted to the Middle Ages (from the fourth century to the end of the fifteenth); four to the modern period (1495-1806); five to the nineteenth century (until 1914); and seven to the "short twentieth century" (1914-90) in and of itself, including three volumes devoted specifically to the Third Reich, the Holocaust, and World War II and half a volume on the history of the German Democratic Republic.[23] Although there are clear differences between the German series and the French, given the greater place of medieval history in Germany and the still-considerable impact there of the years 1933-45, analogous disparities exist. It takes eight volumes to cover ten centuries of medieval history and almost as many to cover less than a century of the history of the present time. These two examples illustrate a phenomenon well-known to researchers, teachers, and publishers of textbooks: the closer one gets to the present, the shorter the sequence of time, and the greater the density of the material studied.

The reasons for this situation, here observed empirically, could be discussed at great length. The sum of our knowledge obviously decreases as we move further back in time. That rule may not apply to historians of the future who look back on our era, so anxious to preserve traces of every kind—though the unreliability of the media used to preserve them may raise the same kind of problems that historians have always encountered. By necessity, the most recent events have more weight in historical memory, hence in historiographical choices. Furthermore, these histories of France and Germany were conceived within the cultural context of the late twentieth and early twenty-first centuries, a period that grants great attention to the history of the present time. Finally, the density and compactness of contemporary history lie in the "acceleration" of history itself, a consequence of the increase in the speed of communication, the gradual disappearance of the spatial limits that even a few decades ago could limit perceptions of the present time, and the multiple forms of globalization—all processes that make us witnesses to and contemporaries of what is happening at every instant all over the world. That is currently a major challenge for historians of the present time and will continue to be so in the future. Some will object that I am presenting contextual elements to explain a criterion that is supposed to be invariable. But a quick glance at a few precedents will show that this is not a trait specific to the late twentieth century. Ernest Lavisse and his collaborators devoted seventeen volumes (plus an index volume) to the original edition of *Histoire de France, depuis les origines jusqu'à la Révolution* (1903–11), which covered fifteen centuries, and nine volumes (including an index volume) to *Histoire de France contemporaine depuis la Révolution jusqu'à la paix de 1919*, a "present" time that covers barely 130 years.

A Political Waiting Period

Whether contemporary history goes back "fifty years, a month, or a minute," to borrow Croce's phrase—that is, whatever the periodization or the demarcation adopted—the question will arise of a waiting period, which by definition does not exist for other historical sequences. Granted, I have just shown that this obstacle has been partly removed from historiography over the course of recent decades. It has not entirely disappeared, however, as attested by the recurrent discussions about the waiting period imposed on public archives, during which access to information is controlled, even prohibited.[24] In France, that latency period was bitterly debated by deputies and senators whenever legislative bills on the archives were brought up for a vote. It has gradually been shortened over the last three decades from fifty years (the situation prevailing in the 1960s) to thirty years (law of 1979) and finally to twenty-five years (law of 2008) for documents of public interest.

Nevertheless, the waiting period varies greatly for certain types of documents considered "sensitive" by legislators or the executive branch.[25] The same is true in most European countries, which have generally agreed on a waiting period of about twenty-five to thirty years, with exceptions made for certain documents. In the United States a "declassification" system for different types of public archives prevails, which has the advantage of allowing gradual access to many public documents rather than making them subject to an across-the-board waiting period. But in all cases, and though the obstacle of temporarily inaccessible archives is often circumvented, this means there is at least a political and normative definition of contemporary history. That singularity when compared to other periods of history, though quite obvious, is not without ramifications, especially with respect to the relationship historians maintain with the state. It should be added, however, that this remark is fully valid only for public archives, that is, written traces, images, or sounds produced by states and established authorities of all sorts. It is partly valid for private archives, communication of which can also be restricted by laws. But it does not apply to all the sources accessible to contemporary history, whose diversity and abundance constitute both a pitfall and a major asset for the discipline.

Division by Century

Since the nineteenth century, in the historian's practice and in other disciplines as well, historical time has frequently been cut up into "centuries," which allows one to define more easily the territories to be distributed, the exams to be given, and the lessons to be delivered. Quite naturally, then, there are specialists in the twentieth century just as there are in the sixteenth. These divisions are apparent in the titles of textbooks, research centers, and scholarly journals. For example, the first issue of the review *Vingtième siècle* (*Twentieth Century*) appeared in 1984. It was created by historians from, among other places, the Institut d'Études Politiques in Paris (René Rémond, Michel Winock, Jean-Pierre Azéma, and Jean-Noël Jeanneney), the Université de Paris X Nanterre (Jean-Jacques Becker and Jean-François Sirinelli), and the new Institut d'Histoire du Temps Présent (François Bédarida, Jean-Pierre Rioux, Danièle Voldman, and Henry Rousso), where the editorial office was initially located. In the months preceding the journal's launch, the youngest of the editors raised the question of whether we ought not to anticipate the possibility of its success and consider the pertinence of its title. At the time, the end of the century was barely seventeen years away, and in the event that *Vingtième siècle* caught on in the world of scholarship, its name could rather quickly become obsolete. The argument was swept aside by the more distinguished editors. It was impossible to use a name already taken by another review, namely, the older *Revue d'histoire moderne et contemporaine*. There was also no question of calling the fledgling journal "Review of History of the Present Time," since that would have created the sense that it had only one father when in fact it had several (that problem would later give rise to a few pointless quarrels about legitimate paternity, for which academia has such a gift). The name was therefore kept as it was. Seventeen years later, success having in fact been achieved, the review faced a dilemma: change its name and thereby cloud an image well established in the field, or keep it and lose something of the substance of its original message. The aim, in fact, was to study not only the twentieth century but also the present time, which was about to spill over into the twenty-first century. The original name was retained.

> Our review felt duty bound to mark the transition from the twentieth to the twenty-first century. It does so here in its own way, without misplaced vanity and without regrets. In the first place, it avoids any notion of an overly slick assessment that would affix the seal of truth, hastily cobbled together, such as those that have appeared in so many publications in the last few months. The only truth that this special issue wishes to suggest is the following: time, our time, is not over, the heaviest chains of causality and the most "striking" events (in the first place, according to some, 1989) have not been sufficient to unbind us from the twentieth century, with its hazy chronology, whose sources go back long before 1914 and which, before our opened eyes, runs down "to our own time" without tragic fatalism or a euphoric "sense" of History. In short, the crepuscular problematic (in black and white, in rose or blood red) does not convince us, and the various events that in the past year have marked our entry into the third millennium have not made us change our minds. History in the present, history of the present time, history of the presence of time, history of a past that is not past—contemporary history, therefore, in the most precise sense of the adjective—has nothing to do with calendar obligations and artificial remembrances, since by definition it rejects boundaries and closure.[26]

If we set aside the last assertion—which is rather strange in the context, since the name of the review refers precisely to the boundaries of a century—the interest of this argument lies in the statement that historians of the present time are first and foremost historians and therefore work on significant intervals of time. They do not wish to be subject to the tyranny or the fashions of the immediate and the actual. Inasmuch as the review did not choose a more conceptual or general name, it would have been a risky choice to call itself *Vingt-et-unième Siècle* (*Twenty-first Century*) with the first issue of 2001.

Nevertheless, a more "structural" and more ambitious choice from the outset would have avoided that drawback.

In terms of the division into "centuries," historians of the contemporary are thus those who work on the most recent century: that is an invariable. But behind that somewhat mechanical partition of time an implicit vision is concealed—namely, that a century constitutes the commonsensical temporal horizon and may be a pertinent category for scientific analysis. A hundred years is now barely longer than a human lifespan. It is a symbolic interval, at least for civilizations that have adopted the Gregorian calendar and for which the passing of centuries and millennia constitutes a time perceptible to the social imaginary. A century is a segment within reach of memories, individual or collective, direct or transmitted, of the first or second generation. Nevertheless, in hypothesizing that common sense perceives the century as a natural historical horizon, are we not called upon as historians, if not to reject it, then at least to introduce a shift in perspective? It may be noted, in fact, that specialists in a given century rarely raise the question of whether the century in itself constitutes a pertinent choice and, if so, for what reasons. That is true especially of twentieth-century specialists, not to mention those who are already positioning themselves as specialists in the twenty-first century barely under way.[27] Most are aware of the lack of pertinence of these demarcations and have imaginative ways of making the flow of the centuries coincide with a subjective interpretation of History. They situate themselves in an interpretive register, the other way of defining the present time. Sometimes they cheat a little with the numbers: European historians have the habit of beginning the nineteenth century with the fall of the Napoleonic Empire in 1815 and ending it with the outbreak of World War I in 1914. Geoffrey Barraclough, one of the pioneers in contemporary history mentioned in the previous chapter, locates the start of the twentieth century and modernity in about 1890, with the technological revolutions. And the great historian Eric Hobsbawm has defined a "short" twentieth century that supposedly began in 1914 and ended in 1991, with the fall of the Soviet system.[28] As for the September 11 terrorists, they had the good taste to launch their attacks at the very beginning of the new century, thus offering historians a ready-made starting date.

The Actor and the Witness

Finally, the presence of living actors who can bear witness to their lived experience constitutes the invariable most readily applied. Historians of the present time often delimit their territory by referring to the "duration of a human life," that is, about seventy to eighty years, a calculation that retro-actively takes into account recent biological advances.[29] Unlike a century, which is a fixed limit, the idea here is again that of a moving boundary line, in any case a slippery and relative temporality that is in reality very difficult to master. In 1978-80, when the IHTP was created, it initially adopted that sort of criterion: contemporary time thus extended back to about 1900. As luck would have it, the institute's historians could thus enter into direct dia-logue with their colleagues who specialized in the twentieth century. Nei-ther side really understood as yet the differences between them, since the present time was indistinguishable from the century under way. That being the case, what could someone born in France or in the rest of Europe in about 1900 "bear witness" to in 1980? To her childhood before the outbreak of World War I? To his activity as an adult, beginning in the 1920s? To the noteworthy moments of her life, for example, living through World War II, beginning in 1939? To the start of an era of relative peace and prosperity after 1945—if, that is, he was born on the right side of the Iron Curtain and did not live in a colonial territory? That is a naïve view of things, since the process of speaking out about the past conforms to infinitely more complex criteria than simply the restitution of historical memory, in the sense in which Maurice Halbwachs understood it: that is, of a collective past more or less internalized by the individual's experience and by the first social frame-works in which it was inserted (the family, living environment, and so on). What comes into play is the very capacity of subjects to remember and for-get, their wish to express themselves or not to express themselves about the past, their responsiveness to the eventual questions of the historians who think to question them, the various experiences they had depending on their location, their gender, the chance events of existence, their temperament, their social position. An essential element must also be added: the differ-ence in generation between the historian and the potential witness. The act of questioning someone who is older and who has had an experience inac-cessible to the historian (a former deportee, for example) will certainly raise difficulties inherent to any interview in the social sciences, but it will at least have the advantage of being an obvious situation of alterity. By contrast, questioning someone closer to one's own age will require an increased vigi-lance, by virtue of the principle articulated several times in this book: the task of a historian of the present time is to create distance out of proximity.

Consequently, the presence of living witnesses is not to be confused (as has too often been done) with the possibility that a historian has to question them and thus to produce oral historical sources. There is no homothety between oral history and the history of the present time, though there are obvious historiographical links. On the one hand, many historical sources of the most remote past are oral sources that were collected, then inscribed on a support able to withstand the passage of time and to persist in the form of a trace. There is, for example, the famous case of judicial and police archives used to understand the popular imaginary. These entail the well-known risk of reproducing the viewpoint not of the interrogated but of the interrogator.[30] On the other hand, the historian may work on a recent event, but without being able to gather enough testimonies to make a significant difference. All those who work on the history of genocides and large-scale massacres of the recent period are familiar with that difficulty. Nearly all the actors may have disappeared, or those who survive may have no desire to bear witness, out of fear or for reasons linked to their own psychic economy. This has sometimes happened in international criminal tribunals that were judging recent crimes committed by neighbors, peers, sometimes even family members (as in Rwanda), and not by strangers.[31]

How, then, are we to justify putting forth such a criterion to define the history of the present time, and what does it mean to do the history of a period for which living witnesses exist? In the first place, though there is no perfect equivalence between the writing of the history of the present time and the possibility of using oral testimony, such a possibility is an important, if not decisive, reality in actual practice. The earliest accounts of a tragic event (war, revolution, and so forth), even if there are only a few of them, are almost always direct testimonies that historians will use later on, while sometimes viewing them critically. The information available on authoritarian or totalitarian systems, of which there has been no shortage in the recent period, very often comes first from clandestine witnesses, who are more reliable than any official document. Second, whatever the proclaimed unity of the historical method, a situation where the historian is dealing with the words of a dead person cannot possibly compare to a situation in which the witness and the historian are face to face in a direct interpersonal relationship, in a friendly or tense confrontation between two consciousnesses, two unconsciouses, two imaginaries, where the words of one are shaped for the ear of the other, its capacity to listen or, on the contrary, its "resistance" to alterity. That is true even when the historian's mission is to bring the dead person back to life for an instant by means of the traces left behind, including words recorded in an archival document. *Pace* the critics of the history of the present time, there are essential differences between the two situations, beginning with the nature of the phenomenon of transference. Working on a remote past obviously does not keep the historian from making a transference onto a person who died centuries ago, or the deceased person from passing on his legacy. But such a transference can work in only one direction, whereas in direct confrontations between a historian and a witness in person, questions of transference play a determining role, especially if the historian wants to get the witness to talk about his or her past. The misunderstandings and even serious conflicts that can arise in such circumstances can often be attributed to an ignorance of these elementary psychic mechanisms, especially on the part of historians. Conversely, when an informed observer takes into account the witness's unconscious expectations, very strong bonds can be created between the two, and great intelligibility may result. Filmmakers and documentarians, those other producers of historical knowledge, have understood perfectly that specific, direct, intersubjective relationship with interlocutors in the flesh. These witnesses are often incapable of speaking without being prodded, sometimes mercilessly so, by the likes of Marcel Ophuls or Claude Lanzmann. The talent and success of these filmmakers rest in great part on their capacity to "make" the most reticent speak, even by shamelessly manipulating them and using an aggressiveness completely incommensurate with what historians are sometimes reproached for doing. It is striking in this respect that academics are often accused of "appropriating" the words of their witnesses, while the methods of Lanzmann, who almost physically and morally substituted himself for those whose testimony he was supposed to be presenting, are held to be sacrosanct.[32] By contrast, there would be a great deal to say about the orthodox and pusillanimous ethics of the social sciences interview, which almost always privileges the open-ended question over the leading one, which in appearance offers the witness solicited more freedom. In reality, that method often leads to an erasure of the researcher's subjectivity and to unremarkable results and information gathering. Social scientists ought rather to be taught to master their subjectivity while at the same time allowing it to manifest itself, one of the only ways to create desire in the witnesses being questioned, to lower their guard, and to produce a little transference. And transference alone can produce surprises and provide access to a truth that might extend beyond the agreed-upon frameworks. The practice of documentary filmmakers cannot be adopted by scholars, who are duty bound to respect protocols set out beforehand. In addition, images will always have more force for the general public than the written word. Nevertheless, there are a few lessons to be learned from the impact of these filmed testimonies, when compared to those collected by researchers, historians, or sociologists armed with a theoretical arsenal that is sometimes both wordy and pointless. That apparatus hampers their ability to consider themselves subjects listening to other subjects and therefore to allow themselves to be affected by the words of others.

In the end, the history of the present time is distinguished less by the question of living witnesses than by the very presence of the actors, whether or not they are questioned or sought out. It is their physical presence, their existence in the flesh, that creates an obligation for the historian completely different from that of a researcher who works with traces. No lengthy demonstration is needed to make that point. Historians of the present time, more than other historians, are subjected to the gaze of their objects of study, to their friendly "surveillance," sometimes even to their condemnation, if by chance the historians are taken to court for defamation. You have every right to say anything you like about the dead (though the trend seems to be moving toward restrictions), but not about the living, hence the greater risk of self-censorship. These are extreme cases, however, and the singularity in this instance is situated elsewhere. Actors who turn into historians of the events in which they participated frequently compete with researchers born later, raising objections based not only on the knowledge they have acquired, comparable to that of the researchers, but also on experience that the others by definition do not have. Although participant historians may have more difficulty taking their distance, they may also have more accurate arguments, greater factual precision, and keener psychological penetration. In their lucidity and critical thinking, the writings of Jean-Louis Crémieux-Brilhac, a former member of Free France who became a historian of the movement, or of Daniel Cordier, former secretary to Jean Moulin who became his biographer, have more merit than many academic writings on the Resistance, where narrow-mindedness is coupled with a facile hagiography. In addition, for the historiography of Fascism, Nazism, and the Holocaust, many of the great books written before the 1990s and the rise of a new generation were by historians who had themselves lived through the period (Saul Friedländer, Walter Laqueur, George Mosse, Léon Poliakov, Zeev Sternhell, Martin Broszat). Their experiences, all very different, played an essential role in their choice of a vocation and in their manner of writing history.

The actors themselves can sometimes turn into observers—of the historians. Take the case of an astonishing book of recollections, published in 2008 by Renée David, a former resister and Raymond Aubrac's cousin.[33] She was interned at the Montluc Prison in Lyon in 1943, at the age of twenty-two, and later in Drancy. A senior research assistant at the Sorbonne, she participated in almost all the seminars and colloquia that the IHTP devoted to the history of the Occupation, from the institute's creation to the early 2000s. For nearly a third of the book she speaks about that experience, sizing up the positions of each of the parties, seeking to understand the dialectic at work between memory and truth, continuing in her writing a dialogue she had had in person for more than twenty years with historians of several generations, myself included. She indicates the achievements of a historiography that took shape before her eyes, celebrating the warm bonds that actors and historians, considered as individuals and not simply in terms of their status, maintained with one another for years. She also shows the deadlocks and conflicts that historiography faced—after the "Aubrac affair" in 1997, for example. At the time, a meeting organized and publicized by the daily newspaper *Libération* to discuss slander being spread about Raymond and Lucie Aubrac turned into a confrontation between one actor and another, between one researcher and another, between actors and researchers, and between generations.[34] The crisis was painful but no doubt necessary to mark the rift that ultimately exists on such subjects, between those who think the historian must serve a cause (political, moral, or something else) and who demand that servitude despite the risk of a justificatory writing, and those who think the historian's task consists of looking critically, autonomously, and subjectively at any object or subject that seems worthy of interest. That stance requires that the historian be responsible, the high price of freedom. Despite these conflicts, David thinks the dialogue was fruitful because the historians "encouraged, 'drove' the witnesses themselves to take a difficult look backward."[35] Here she puts her finger on an essential element, if not an original one from the epistemological standpoint: not only can historians of the present time create their own sources by, for example, putting together collections of testimonies, but they can also act on these sources. They can even do so with living actors whose view of history, including their own history, may change as a result.

An Unfinished History

"Acts that have already been completed [*faits accomplis*] appear to us with a great deal more clarity than acts in the process of being completed," wrote Fustel de Coulanges.[36] That view was repeated by Raymond Aron in an even more incisive formulation: "The object of history is a reality that has ceased to be."[37] In that deliberately teleological view, human actions assume their meaning only after the fact. We have just seen that that stance may have

some legitimacy—in terms of periodization, for example. That said, the practice of historians of the present time entails the opposite stance: they dare
to form a blurry picture of events in the process of being completed and of
a reality that continues to live in their own present. They interpret an unfinished history and accept responsibility for the provisional nature of their
analyses.

> What is specific to a history of the present time—and to a history of the present
> time that is inextricably social and cultural more than to a political or economic
> history or a history of cultural productions (theater, film, magazines, and so
> on)—is to be a wobbly, shaky, incomplete, unfinished history. The proper way
> to do that history is not to attempt to remedy or mask that incompleteness, by
> reestablishing by some artifice overly appealing continuities that would make
> the present emerge logically from the past. It is to accept that very incomple-
> tion, to work through it in order to highlight, by virtue of the inadequacy of the
> representations vis-à-vis the social realities they claim to express, the very nov-
> elty of these realities.[38]

I endorse word for word the conclusion of this text by Antoine Prost, published in 1993 in a book that pays tribute to François Bédarida. Not only does
Prost here clearly accept the idea of a singularity of that form of history—
which he would later deny—he also points out the most obvious singularity. In this respect, the history of the present time is truly part of a general
movement of contemporary historiography, all periods combined. Having
turned away from the objectivist paradigm, historiography now acknowledges almost naturally that a historical era can have many lives, by virtue of
the different historians and different observers who will examine it in the
future. That does not entail, however, defending a relativist position in which
every postulate about a past that "actually existed" has disappeared and in
which any knowledge acquired at a given moment would be subject to complete revision twenty or thirty years later. To accept the incompleteness of a
historical statement is not to deny the dimension of a cumulative acquisition
of knowledge within the discipline. That said, though every history can now
be considered unfinished, the history of the present time is a little more so
than the others. Its difficulty lies precisely in that greater uncertainty about
the statements it utters. That aspect links it to the other social sciences, at
least those disciplines that do not claim to explain reality by laws but rather
strive to understand individuals or social facts in motion, with all the risks
that entails.

Finally, I would add that the historian of the present time has become caught up in a contradiction within objectivism that has rarely been pointed out. "To historians who wish to relive an era, Fustel de Coulanges recommends that they blot out everything they know about the later course of history. There is no better way of characterizing the method with which historical materialism has broken," wrote Walter Benjamin, a denigrator if ever there was one of positivist conceptions.[39] That posture of a historian who does not know the last word remains largely a mainstay of the profession, including among historians who are neither positivists nor materialists. It even constitutes the usual antidote for the sin of anachronism, which consists of explaining the actions of one age with categories that belong to the historian's own time. Yet there is a blatant contradiction between the principle of a history that can be written only when it is "over" and the principle of empathy—both of which are methodological postulates of positivism. On the one hand, historians are enjoined to write nothing until the events are over, until the story has come to an end, because they will be unable to understand the ultimate meaning of an era if it is studied too soon. But on the other, they are asked to observe that same past—which is therefore over—while bracketing the knowledge they have of how things turn out, so as to better empathize with people from the past and to understand their actions "as if they were there." Historians must therefore establish their distance but, in the same gesture, forget what that distance allows them to see. Historians of the present time do not have that problem. They easily overcome the contradiction because they do not in fact know the end of the story and are therefore in an ideal situation to empathize with their contemporaries without straining their imagination. True, it is more difficult—but all the more necessary—for them to "brush history against the grain," as Benjamin invites them to do.

A DEFINITION ON THE BASIS OF VARIABLES

As a general rule, the time-honored historical periodizations are based on founding moments: the fall of the Western Roman Empire (476), the taking of Constantinople (1453), the French Revolution (1789). Despite the critique of political and "event-based" history, and despite scientific advances and the close relation history maintains with the other social sciences, it is not profound economic, social, or cultural changes that structure "official" historical time—that of courses of study at schools and universities—so much as events, in the most traditional sense of the term. It is not the first Industrial Revolution that launches the contemporary era in the French tradition, but rather the French Revolution, though historiography is now less rigid about chronology than it once was. The borderline between modern history (late fifteenth to late eighteenth century) and contemporary history has thus occasioned many disagreements. To be more precise, it is the beginning of contemporary history rather than the end of the modern that is problematic: there is little controversy about the break represented by the fall of the ancien régime in France. Although differences have always existed when establishing the line between antiquity, the Middle Ages, and modern times, depending on which event is given precedence, the disagreements between the various schools about when contemporary history begins may involve a span as long as 150 years and may therefore profoundly change the meaning of the word "contemporary." Below I give a few of the most significant examples, following the order in which the starting points still in use for defining the contemporary period appeared over about a century and a half.

1789

Logically, the earliest date in time is also that of the oldest tradition still persisting into the twenty-first century. The year 1789 and the revolutionary event in the broad sense have constituted a starting point for the contemporary period since the late nineteenth century. At the time, that way of dividing up time corresponded to an intellectual and political reality in many European countries. At present, however, the survival of that tradition tends to be peculiar to France. It persists in spite of later historical developments, the profound changes in historiography during the twentieth century, and even the reinterpretation of the revolutionary event itself. Although French historians played a prominent role in all these transformations, the obsolete demarcation was not really called into question until the emergence in the 1980s of the notion of a history of the present time. Although the founding fathers of the French Republic had every reason to place their actions within the tradition of the Revolution (albeit with the contradictions indicated in chapter 2), and although present-day France, like a good part of Europe, remains beholden to the long-term effects of that major fracture in the course of history, what could such an expansive definition of contemporaneity now mean? At an anthropological level, it is self-evident that an event remote in time may continue to live on or may be revived in the imaginary of the present, in national or global memory, in traditions, or in political or cultural heritages. But that is not sufficient for continuing to assert that an event more than two hundred years old remains the decisive turning point of "our time" and even less so for artificially holding onto it as a contemporary event, especially in the demarcations in force in higher education. In fact, the historical demarcations in secondary education are proving to be more rational, restricting the contemporary period to the twentieth century and thus making use of a more acceptable criterion.

Moreover, the distinction in use among historians between the adjectives "modern" and "contemporary" no longer makes much sense. The two terms belong to different registers and, logically speaking, should not designate successive historical sequences: "modern" refers to the advent of a new order with respect to an old one, whereas the primary sense of "contemporary" is "that which belongs to the same era." Modernity belongs to our own time, inasmuch as, since the Renaissance, it has been a way of marking a change. Contemporaneity carries within it something of the modern and something of the ancient. A further complication: some contemporary epistemological reflections make the eighteenth century and the revolutionary moment the *beginning*—not the end—of a modernity that confers a determining place on historicity, that is, on the awareness that the human condition is evolving. And that modernity may have weakened in the last third of the twentieth century with the crisis about the future. In addition, not only is it absurd to believe that the French Revolution belongs to the "same time" as the beginning of the twenty-first century, but that demarcation also neglects the fact that later events that were just as important have had notable and lasting effects both on "modernity" and on the way of conceiving "contemporaneity."

1917

One revolution drives out another. Among the other dates that have constituted a starting point for the contemporary world and that continue to be used at times is the year 1917, or rather, the sequence 1917-18. This demarcation arose in German historiography especially, after World War II and the fall of the Third Reich, with the writings of Hans Rothfels and the creation of the Institut für Zeitgeschichte. That periodization associates in a single movement the Russian Revolution, the entry of the United States—a nascent great power—into World War I, and the end of the war (not its starting point), a major defeat with weighty consequences for the history of Germany and Europe. Not without valid arguments, it valorized the emergence of a first form of globalization. But it was also a way of reducing the importance of national criteria at a time when German historiography, like the rest of German society, had to confront the terrible toll of Nazism. The demarcation was abandoned by later generations in favor of a more fluid periodization that focused on the history and prehistory of Nazism. That had a different disadvantage, the object of fierce debates in the 1980s: it isolated the sequence 1933-45, singling it out in the extreme, to the point of granting it the status of a kind of historical extraterritoriality.

1945

Whereas 1789 and 1917 refer to specific historiographical traditions, both marked by a strong sense of national exceptionalism (whether the *exception française* or the German *Sonderweg*), other starting points for the contemporary world took root more simply and more "naturally," at least in appearance. Such is the case for the year 1945, which can be found in a large portion of English historiography of the 1980s, especially with the creation of the Centre for Contemporary British History (CCBH) in 1986, whose field of investigation begins just after World War II. Unsurprisingly, similar demarcations are found in American historiography. Furthermore, the distinction between "modern history" and "contemporary history" is almost absent from the English-speaking world, for almost self-evident reasons in the case of the United States, whose national history is barely more than two centuries old, and for pragmatic reasons in the British case: "Both the 1945 and the living memory definitions are best seen, not as attempts to delimit an era but to provide a convenient description of the contemporary."[40] The same demarcation appears in France, for example, in courses of study for the last two years of secondary school, enacted in 1957 and modified in 1959. Strongly influenced by Fernand Braudel's ideas, these programs specify that the period 1914-45 be treated in the junior year, while during their senior year students will be invited to study the history of "civilizations": Western, Soviet, Muslim, Far Eastern, Southeast Asian, and Sub-Saharan African.[41] On the one hand, secondary (and primary) education has tended to be somewhat ahead of historical research as to the place granted to recent history; but on the other, it created a strange separation between most of history, approached in a traditional manner by means of facts, events, and chronology, and a "contemporary world" that appears suddenly in 1945 and for which space, culture, and the long view are privileged. Implicitly, then, the idea is still that there is not enough distance for studying, for example, the Chinese Revolution the way World War I is studied.[42] That program gave rise to many controversies, less about the 1945 division than about the question of civilizations. It was not until the reforms of 1981-82, however, that the concept would be definitively abandoned in favor of a demarcation that revived chronology and placed World War II in its proper place. Beginning with that date, the course of studies for the senior year covers the period from "1939 to our time," a result both of the emergence of a public debate about the memory of that war and of the first achievements of a reinvigorated history of the present time.

At first sight, the year 1945, like the other divisions, obviously marks the birth of a new world, indicated especially at the international level by the end of European domination, the gradual disappearance of the last colonial empires, the emergence of new great powers, and the birth of nuclear technology, with its considerable military and civilian implications. It therefore constitutes a "natural" boundary marker for historians, as it was for many contemporaries. And yet, the decision to make the contemporary world start after World War II is both a choice about and a point of view on the meaning of that event. It requires that, at least in the order of representations, we turn the page on the most lethal war in the history of humanity. It necessitates relegating to a past considered to be over the "early" twentieth century, that of Fascism, Nazism, and the mass crimes of the Soviet Union. To place the emphasis on that demarcation is to underscore the triumph—at least partial—of the democratic idea, with the advent in the postwar period of European construction, economic growth (also Western for the most part), and a welfare state that for a time stood as a universal model. All in all, it is an optimistic view of twentieth-century history, one that assumes that the generations after 1945 truly overcame physically and mentally the deleterious effects of the previous decades, marked by wartime violence and extremist politics.

After 1989, in fact, an entire historiography developed in opposition to that sometimes placating vision. It proposed a more "pessimistic" view— closer, no doubt, to the lived experience of history on the part of Europeans after 1945. In 2005, the year of the sixtieth anniversary of the end of World War II, the British historian Tony Judt published a history of Europe since 1945, characterizing those years not as a gradual triumph of the Western model but rather as an interminable exodus from the war, which did not end until after the fall of the Berlin Wall.[43] Like other historians intent on adopting a vantage point whose center of gravity is no longer Western Europe, he points out that, for millions of Eastern Europeans, the year 1945 was first and foremost the year of a new collective and individual catastrophe, the starting point for a subjection that no one could predict would end after two generations. In 2010, a short time before his death, Judt argued the case for a new European history. He made an astonishing statement:

Just what this new history will look like is unclear. We cannot say with any certainty even of what its chronology will consist. The questions which occupy us just now will not always be at the center of our attention. European history, even in our era, does not consist only of collaboration, resistance, mass murder, retribution, political justice and the memory of all of these. But until we have successfully incorporated these and related questions into our understanding of the recent European past we shall not be able to move on. The history of Europe from 1945 to the present begins with this rethinking of the war and its consequences, and we are still at the beginning.[44]

1940

That view of things prevailed until the 1970s or 1980s, when, within European societies, a major retrospective inquiry began into the scope and significance of the mass crimes perpetrated by Fascism and Nazism (but not yet Stalinism), an inquiry that Tony Judt, with a certain pessimism I do not share, considered unfinished in 2010. An entire generation realized at the time that that page of twentieth-century history may have been turned too quickly, that it may not even have been written, at least not satisfactorily, by the measure of the new questions emerging, particularly around the history of the genocide of the Jews. It was in that context that some advanced the idea that "our time" began neither in 1789 nor in 1945 and the end of the last world war but in 1940, with the defeat of France.[45] Just as German historians before them had made the roots of Nazism a starting point for the history of the present time, French historians made the outbreak of World War II a boundary marker. The main idea is to reintroduce into the present time certain aspects of the event that were insufficiently studied, when they were not purely and simply expelled from historiography: for example, the internal history of the Vichy regime. To assert in 1980 that the year 1940 constituted the "matrix of our time" was both to put into perspective the enduring consequences of the 1940 collapse and to call into question the participation, somewhat overestimated, of France in the Allied victory of 1945. Only in appearance did that choice retain a focus narrowly confined to the French Hexagon, concentrating on the French defeat of May–June 1940 and not on the outbreak of the war after the Germans invaded Poland in 1939—a date that is sometimes pushed back to July 1937 and the beginning of the Sino-Japanese War. In fact, the act of moving the cursor back to the beginnings of the war was part of a more general development in Western historiography. In those years, there began to be a reevaluation upward of the magnitude of the collaboration in France, Belgium, the Netherlands, and the

Scandinavian countries, of the impact of Fascism within the few democracies remaining on the European continent in the 1930s, and of the depths of endogenous anti-Semitism, which partly explains the ease with which Nazis were able to set the Final Solution in motion. That shift back a few years in the interest taken in the near past went far beyond the framework of historical research, as we have seen, since it was part of a broad cultural and political revision of the very meaning of the contemporary world. The mythologies constructed in the immediate postwar period, first in Western Europe and then, after 1989-91, in Central and Eastern Europe, crumbled one after another. As a result, World War II, Nazism, and the Holocaust, far from being seen as an aberration or a digression in the inexorable evolution toward a world of progress and well-being, now appeared to be milestones in a conception of humanity that must henceforth face the possibility of its own destruction, partial or total. That was also the case just after 1939. The matrix of the present time is no longer 1945, a year that was certainly terrible but that, in spite of everything, bore within it all the hope for a better world, but the years 1939-40, which sounded the death knell, as it were, of a certain optimistic conception of History. The nascent historiography of the present time came to adopt a fundamental pessimism, which remains one of its distinctive traits.

This outlook, one might add, was no doubt closer to the feelings of contemporaries than the retroactive optimism produced by the valorization of the year 1945. By way of example, consider an astonishing text written in 1938 by the conservative Swiss historian Gonzague de Reynolds, who engaged in a reflection on the end of the nineteenth century, which he situates, as it happens, just before the outbreak of World War II:

> World war, Russian Revolution, Fascism, National Socialism, economic crisis, Spanish Civil War: such are the events that dominate the contemporary, that give it a meaning. What meaning? ... The first obvious fact is that we are no longer in the nineteenth century. Everyone knows the nineteenth century is over chronologically, but very few have finally understood that it is over historically. ... Second obvious fact: the nineteenth century now belongs to the past, it now represents an outdated civilization: "bourgeois civilization." In a word, for us it is the Old Regime. What is more, the nineteenth century is itself linked to an old world, a world that is dying. The twentieth, by contrast, inaugurates a new world, the world being born. Third obvious fact. A fourth obvious fact follows from it: we are not witnessing the development of a conflict that is coming to an end, after which things will gradually return to their prior state, the prosperity of the nineteenth century! We are also not passing through one of

those crises that generally mark the transition from one century to the next, after which halted progress begins again. No: we are changing eras. Europe has known only two such changes since the Christian era: the end of the Roman Empire and the classical world, and the end of the Middle Ages. We are now experiencing the end of the modern age, the age inaugurated by the Reformation and the Renaissance. We are entering another age. . . . In effect, fifth obvious fact: Is a series of events like the world war, the Russian Revolution, Fascism, National Socialism, and the economic crises enough to destroy a society, put an end to an age? The war was already sufficient, and the economic crisis would have been sufficient in and of itself. Granted, the past underwent upheavals whose traces are still visible or from whose consequences we are now suffering. None, however, had this universal character or coincided with an intellectual and moral anarchy as profound as our own. No, not even the fall of the Roman Empire and the barbarian invasions. That is why, sixth obvious fact, between the nineteenth and the twentieth centuries, between the end of the modern age and the beginning of the new age, we are witnessing, we, the witnesses and the victims, an abrupt, violent break in continuity. So abrupt, so violent, that we find nothing like it in the past. Furthermore, seventh obvious fact, we are at war, in the midst of war. We have never ceased to be so since 1914. A twenty-two-years' war, which will soon be a thirty-years' war, which may perhaps be a hundred-years' war.[46]

1914

The idea of an apocalyptic Year Forty was appealing as a matrix. It intuited the advent of a new order of representation of the near past, in particular the weight of memory and the specific memory of that event. But historians of the present time, more than others, have learned that the paradigms in their field are short-lived. Barely a decade later, that conception was implicitly called into question, not because of its pessimistic view of history but rather because of its choice of starting date. The century of darkness began neither in 1939-40 nor in 1933, when Hitler came to power, nor in 1917-18, but at the dawn—not the end—of the Great War. It may even have begun slightly earlier, with the Balkan Wars of 1912-13, a prelude, so to speak, to the catastrophe of 1914. The same reasoning prevailed here as for the other world war. Never before had so many people (nearly 10 million) died in a conflict in so short a time. Never, or almost never, had a war crossed such a threshold of violence on the battlefield; and never had the belligerent societies been so involved in the totalization of war. The fact was massive, almost blinding, once it was put forward. But though World War I had in the past given rise to important works, had even constituted an early field of study for contemporary history in Europe, the memory of it was often relegated to the background by the impact of World War II, as attested, for example, by the mutual ignorance that long prevailed between specialists of the respective wars, as if the two events were not inextricably linked.[47] In the 1990s a crucial change occurred in historiography. World War I not only occasioned a new wave of studies devoted to societies at war, to the material and psychological conditions of soldiers, to the study of specific and differentiated forms of violence; the place of that event in the history of the century also changed in nature.[48] Having belonged since the outbreak of World War II to a somewhat distant past, World War I was suddenly reinstated as the most recent past, both historiographically and in terms of commemorations. One has only to observe the spectacular investment by the public policies of memory since 1998 (the eightieth anniversary of the armistice), especially in France, Germany, Great Britain, and Australia, in conserving the memory of World War I, or the renewed interest that many European and American literary writers and filmmakers have devoted to it in the last two decades—though that interest does not equal in intensity that directed toward World War II, which is still in a class of its own. Here is another illustration of the fact that the persistence of a historical event does not depend on its temporal proximity.

There are many reasons for that development. First, the fall of the Berlin Wall brought flooding back national, ethnic, and border problems that had not been entirely wiped out in 1918, after the dissolution of the Central Empires. These problems became entrenched after 1945 with the Cold War and Communist domination, as illustrated by the extreme case of the violent breakup of the former Yugoslavia. The collapse of the Soviet Union, somewhat unexpected at least in its modalities, called for a reinterpretation of twentieth-century history, which until then had been caught up in the idea that European Communism was destined to endure and that the world would be divided into two blocs for a long time to come. The abrupt end of the USSR obliged historians to rethink the very nature of the Soviet system and thus to go back to the source of a revolution that had erupted in the midst of World War I. In a different register, the sometimes excessive focus on Nazism by historians of the contemporary world gave rise to legitimate criticisms of the purported origins of the extreme violence that had unfolded in Europe in the 1930s and 1940s. The new historiography of World War I indirectly called into question the dogma of the uniqueness of the Holocaust, but without disputing its unprecedented character. It did so by insisting that a first threshold of violence, a violence of a different nature, was crossed in

1914–18. It also implicitly showed that the unheard-of violence in which all Europe was plunged for the four years of a very long war may have directly influenced the nature of the violence of the next war thirty years later, including the implementation of the Final Solution. World War II historians had already paved the way for a pessimistic reading of recent history, and World War I historians went even further in that direction, showing the degree to which the war had formed the horizon of the European continent for a large part of the twentieth century. The belated and posthumous success of the historian George Mosse, inventor of the controversial but thought-provoking concept of brutalization, is one indication. Thanks to that notion, historians have come to better understand that the impact of a war is not limited to the death toll, the material destruction, and the difficulties of reconstruction: one does not "disengage oneself" (*se déprendre*) from a war (an idea I borrow from Stéphane Audoin-Rouzeau) just because an armistice or a peace treaty has been signed. On the contrary, the violence of war, whether suffered, inflicted, observed, or avoided, can have a lasting effect on psyches.[49] Yet the aftereffects of the violence of World War I seemed to have been effaced by the fact that in 1939 humanity crossed another apocalyptic threshold. And that violence was rediscovered in the years 1990–2000.

In addition to the fall of the Berlin Wall and the progress of historiography, the gradual rebirth of pacifism in Europe and North America may also have given rise to a renewed interest in that conflict, even as the 1933–45 historical sequence was still monopolizing the attention of the Western societies at the time. Policies of memory were also being enlisted, especially in the struggle against "forgetting" Nazi crimes. Almost universally, the total war conducted against the Axis powers has for obvious reasons been perceived consistently since 1945 as a necessary war, a war vital for the survival of humanity, a "good war."[50] It was the epitome of the "just war," a precedent often invoked later on to justify military intervention by the Western powers, whether in Suez in 1956 or Serbia in 1999. One thing Nasser and Milošević have in common is that they were both compared, somewhat hastily, to Hitler. That precedent was implicitly accepted by all the movements linked to the anti-Fascist tradition, including the Far Left European movements of the 1970s. They opposed the war in Vietnam and portrayed themselves as heirs to the European resistance to Nazism, since, after all, "Fascism" could not have been brought down except by the use of the most brutal and most extreme war power. In 1990–2000, the reappearance of the specter of war on the Western horizon in a context completely different from that of the Cold War—with the first Gulf War, the war in the former Yugoslavia, the attacks of September 11, and the resulting interventions in Afghanistan and Iraq—gave rise to opposition and the rebirth of pacifist movements and sentiments. When war, its horrors, and its civilian victims had to be denounced once again, the reference to World War II and its memory became less effective, even counterproductive. That explains the renewed attention to World War I by a number of social actors (politicians, militants, writers) since about 2001. At the same time, thanks to historiography, people are rediscovering what a "bad war" it was. It is therefore a "good" historical reference usable for the pacifist battles of the present moment. Given that logic, it is not surprising that on an ideological level, the theses advanced by part of that new European historiography have sparked indignant reactions. These historians point to the mass consent of the combatants engaged on the front as a major argument for explaining their endurance or adaptation to unprecedented thresholds of violence. I shall not go into detail about this Franco-French dispute about "consent," but the historians' viewpoint has been perceived as a challenge to the figure of the victimized soldier. Incidentally, it undercuts a convenient historical argument, all the more convenient given the consensus throughout Europe, on the Right and on the Left, denouncing the futility of World War I.

1989, 2001?

In November 2003 Thomas L. Friedman, of the *New York Times*, wrote: "Carl Bildt, the former Swedish prime minister, noted to me in Brussels the other day that for a generation Americans and Europeans shared the same date: 1945. A whole trans-Atlantic alliance flowed from that postwar shared commitment to democratic government, free markets and the necessity of deterring the Soviet Union. America saw the strength of Europe as part of its own front line and vice versa—and this bond 'made the resolution of all other issues both necessary and possible,' said Mr. Bildt. Today, however, we are motivated by different dates. 'Our defining date is now 1989 and yours is 2001.'"[51] Can the fall of the Berlin Wall or the attacks of September 11 constitute boundary markers as well for a new contemporary period? It is still too early to say—and that remark in no way contradicts my argument. Although the attacks on American soil launched a new historical sequence of wartime violence and produced major international consequences, it is not certain that they constitute an inaugural catastrophe on the global scale. By contrast, the sequence 1989–91 has all the appearances of an event in the strong sense of the term, one that marks the disappearance of an old world, born with the

Leninist revolution in 1917 and crystallized in 1945 with the domination of Stalinism over half of Europe. But though nothing prevents us from doing a history of the present time of the last twenty years that takes into account the impact of that break, nothing obliges the historian to toss out the chronologies established at each demarcation of importance in the history of humanity. For example, the Zentrum für Zeithistorische Forschung (ZZF) in Potsdam, created in 1996 to deal with a history of the present time whose center of gravity was no longer Nazism, has conducted studies primarily on the comparative history of the two Germanies within the context of the Communist dictatorships of Central and Eastern Europe. It has produced major research on the Cold War, hence on the period between 1945 and 1989.[52] But it does not postulate the need to formalize a new period, which would in fact be difficult to define, given the lack of sufficient distance. The possibility of writing on the near past does not entail having the last word on the question, but at best the second or third word, after journalists and witnesses. Furthermore, at the risk of repeating myself, it must be kept in mind that, like any other form of history, the history of the present time, whatever its singularities, studies historical time frames that are significant enough to merit particular attention. Neither the period "from 1989 to our time" nor, a fortiori, "2001 to our time" can for the moment be characterized with the slightest relevancy, beyond the convenient concept of "post-Communism" or "post–Cold War." Furthermore, even if contemporary history can be seen to begin in 1914, 1940, 1945, or 1989, it is difficult to imagine pushing the periods prior to those respective dates back into so-called modern history. If the term "modern history" is therefore retained for the period that ends with the French Revolution, including the Napoleonic Wars, and if the term "present time" or "contemporary" is set aside for a historical sequence beginning in 1945 or 1989, what will the period extending from 1815 to one of those years be called?

In the Face of the Tragic

Qui peut dire où la mémoire commence
Qui peut dire où le temps présent finit
Où le passé rejoindra la romance
Où le malheur n'est qu'un papier jauni.

Who can say where memory begins
Who can say where the present time ends
Where the past will merge with the romance
Where misfortune is only a yellowed page.

LOUIS ARAGON,
"Les larmes se ressemblent," *Les yeux d'Elsa*

In this book I have sought to strike a balance between permanence and a conjuncture, between an ahistorical definition of contemporaneity and its inclusion within a context. Several subjects of reflection have thereby emerged, which I shall address by way of conclusion.

Not surprisingly, the historical overview over the *longue durée* revealed that the idea of contemporaneity has undergone a profound evolution. Therefore we cannot be content with the cliché that "all history is contemporary." Until the Renaissance and the emergence of a mediate knowledge, and probably even until the eighteenth century, the very idea of a recent history distinct from the rest was weak, since there was no clear separation between past and present. That does not mean, however, that there has been a continuous and immutable conception over several millennia of how to write about one's own time: the modalities, methods, and purposes for writing history changed considerably from one civilization to another. The conception of time as cyclical or as linear, the present viewed as the end of all things or as an eternal modality, the placement of the commonwealth, the lord, the sovereign, or providence at the center of the narrative: these are all profoundly different regimes of historicity. By means of a detour through a lengthy history, I have been able to identify—albeit fleetingly and breezily—a few permanent traits in the definition of one's own time, rather than simply indicate in a rote phrase that the practice of contemporary history dates back to the most remote times.

Witnesses who see, witnesses who speak, witnesses who write, even if they are themselves historians, certainly play an essential role, since they are the first if not the only mediators. Stemming from—or, rather, associated with—that observation is the idea that memory also plays a primary role, since the "I-remember" exists prior to historical narrative, the "once-upon-a-time." Here I follow in the tradition of Paul Ricoeur, who wrote: "As regards the reference to the past, we have no other resource but memory itself . . . we do not have something better than memory to signify that something took place, happened, occurred *before* we declare that we remember it." In that view of the relationship between the past and the present, "testimony constitutes the fundamental structure for moving from memory to history."[1] But in the present time, these witnesses are not out of reach, they do not exist only through the imprint they have made, they are not only the past resuscitated. Unlike witnesses from the past, who will be brought back to life only through the traces that the historian or posterity exploits, these witnesses exist apart from and prior to any historiographical operation.

Another almost constant trait is that historians of the present time maintain conflictual relations with power, whether religious or political. By virtue of their art and later their profession, they were destined to anticipate the judgment of posterity, even to orient it, in the presence of those most concerned, who sought immortality in writing because they could not have biological immortality. As a result, these historians remained ineluctably caught up in a tension between freedom of written expression, to which they aspired almost naturally, and the need to bow to the prince. Until the eighteenth century, in fact, history was above all the history of the powerful or of divine will.

After the French Revolution, new categories of historical time arose. "History as such" was now perceived as an autonomous force detached from both divine providence and the sovereign's actions. The "bygone past" was distinguished from the past in general and indicated a fracture, a "before" and an "after," marked by the upheaval of 1789. A new historical sequence therefore made its appearance in modes of thought. Depending on the place, it would become widespread under the name *Zeitgeschichte* or "contemporary history." A need was now felt to identify a new period after "modern times." Before the Revolution, the use of the word "contemporary" was relatively uncommon, and it had many meanings, including the one Pascal gave to it: a presence of the immemorial past, which has withstood time without alteration. Seventeenth-century readers of the Old Testament were contemporaries of the Jews who received the Tablets of Law. After the Revolution, the word came into general use, but with a different meaning. History ceased to be entirely contemporary, since there was no longer any continuity between the past and the present. The contemporary period now designated a more limited, more visible sequence marked by singularities. At the same moment, still among the heirs to the Revolution, history gradually constituted itself as a profession. It even aspired to be a science: it promulgated detachment and objectivity and, in almost the same movement, came to look with suspicion on the possibility of writing about the recent past in the heat of passion, since that was precisely what one had to distance oneself from. What had previously been an uncontroversial element of historical reflection—consideration of the present, a present not detached from the past—was now problematic. That explains the exclusion, from the early nineteenth century on, of the history of the present time. But though not considered a field that could aspire to scientificity, it remained a category of reflection, education, and literature.

How to think about one's own time changed. A tension appeared between the need to write a history on the spot, to give meaning to the event that had just turned the old order of things on its head, to understand its underpinnings, and the impossibility of undertaking such a narration for lack of sources, detachment, and serenity. That dilemma (necessity versus impossibility), that opposition between those who aspired to get down to business immediately and those who denied them all credibility because time had not yet done its work, was concomitant with the advent of contemporary history. Hence the paradox of the methodological school, which rejected the scientific dimension of a potential history of the present time but practiced it de facto in education and through the publication of textbooks and mainstream works. The same attitude reappeared in the wake of—sometimes even in the midst of—all the catastrophes of the twentieth century. That was the case after 1918 and after 1945, both decisive moments in the constitution and subsequent institutionalization of a long-lasting, acknowledged, and yet still disputed (if not contested) history of the present time. That tension entailed two ways of confronting historical traumas, understood here as the delayed effects of an event that has caused a break, turned values upside down, and modified everyday life. Historical traumas leave lasting traces, sometimes psychic or physical wounds, both in individuals and within collectivities. There were those who advocated a waiting or cooling-off period, in order to best fulfill the criteria of impartiality. They rejected the very idea of a history of the present time, which seemed to them presumptuous, risky, polluted by contingency and the noise of the incidental. In a sense, they placed themselves on the side of a beneficial repression, an encouragement to forget, as it were, a fiction of science, sometimes a denial reflex. According to them, the material of history had to be cold, or at the very least cooled, like ashes. Then there were those who wished to dig through the smoking vestiges of the event, to interpret the first words of witnesses seeking to tell of the catastrophe when extreme experiences were at stake, who wished therefore to fulfill the expectations of those who demanded meaning in the chaos left by a war, a genocide, mass destruction. For them, the history of the present time was an intellectual, moral, and psychological need, which more or less assumed the risk of keeping the wound open and allowed for no waiting period prior to understanding and putting into words events perceived and experienced as unheard-of.

Since the Revolution, then, there seems to have existed a structural relation between the writing of a history of the present time and the existence of a historical trauma requiring an adaptation—more or less long, more or less thorough—by the societies concerned to the crisis that has occurred. The need to reestablish a temporal continuity after the break, the need to forge narratives, even antagonistic ones, that can give meaning to the fracture suffered or provoked, the recomposition of individual or collective identities by major historical catastrophes are processes inherent in the generations that follow "monster events." In general, questions about contemporary history belong to that context. Such history, then, is not simply that of an "after"—an anachronistic position, which is that of all historians—but also of an aftermath. It is closer in time to the catastrophe and in any case much more present in the consciousness or unconscious of the actors, who have to deal with a past that is slow in passing away, and sometimes might not pass away at all. The aim of that history is not only to establish its distance from the traumatic event so as to be able to interpret it but, even more, to grasp its short- and medium-term effects, to forge the tools for interpreting its "afterlife," that is, the prolongation of the initial shock and the way to adapt to it. From that standpoint, historians of the present time do not define themselves, or at least not exclusively, by the "objective" temporal proximity separating them from the event studied, but rather by their own capacity to create for themselves the proper visual and ethical distance needed to observe a time that is only partly their own.

If, then, there has been a contemporary history identified as such since the French Revolution, the actual practice of that history in recent years has been profoundly marked by a certain configuration. The components are not new, but their combination is somewhat original. That configuration establishes a relationship between a series of elements in a reality that is all at once social, cultural, political, tangible, and concrete to concepts and notions developed by the social sciences, since history is not the only discipline at issue. These concepts include the event, testimony, memory, social demand, and "judiciarization" (the consideration of historical events in terms of judicial categories). The order of these elements is not immaterial here. Some, such as the event, are characteristic of all historical writing; others, such as direct testimony, are constitutive of a specifically contemporary writing of history; still others, such as the increasing intervention of the law and the justice system in historical interpretations, belong to the most recent conjuncture.

The link between event and the history of the present time is neither new nor original. Initially, however, one had to fight against the excommunication of the event before once could confront the aftereffects of the major traumas of the twentieth century. Obviously, historians could not leave the century of wars, genocide, and totalitarianism outside the field of scholarly historiography. In addition, the event as it has been studied by historians of the present time in the last thirty years has little in common with the event of the "event-based history" formerly denounced by the Annales School and, moreover, largely constructed as an imaginary figure of the enemy to be defeated. On the one hand, it has usually taken the form of unprecedented catastrophes coming one right after another. Each time, there is the same need to understand how humanity was able to cross a new threshold of violence or destruction—after 1918, after 1945, even after 2001. On the other hand, in studying that event, historians have given precedence not only to how it unfolded and the way it was experienced by contemporaries, but equally to its consequences, its lasting effects, its memory. The attention paid, notably, to the aftermath of these catastrophes reveals events that possess an almost autonomous life in the social imaginary long after their apparent conclusion, sometimes with an increasingly tenuous relationship to the original events. From that point of view, the interminable and impossible completion of the French Revolution throughout the nineteenth century, the anamnesis of World War II in the last third of the twentieth century, and that of World War I at the dawn of the twenty-first serve as textbook cases.

The question of testimony is no more specific to contemporary history than is that of the event, since history is by definition a permanent dialogue between the living and the dead, one way among others of preserving their memory. Furthermore, a historical actor, before being a "witness," remains fundamentally a subject, which the circumstances, or the appeals of historians, sociologists, and anthropologists, or those simply of a publisher, will transform into an expressive witness. Dialogues with the dead are not on the same order as those with the living and do not entail the same methods or the same ethics. In addition, twentieth-century history has seen the rise in power of a new figure of the witness and a new kind of testimony linked to the very catastrophes discussed throughout this book. Thinking has thus evolved toward a reflection on the victim and victimization, a central figure in the contemporary relation to the past. This is not only because the twentieth century was enduringly marked by suffering—it was the traumatic century par excellence—but also because our societies have responded to that suffering with policies of acknowledgment and reparations (especially of the material kind), which have granted actual political, legal, and social status to various categories of victims: displaced persons, political deportees, "racial deportees," victims of the anti-Semitic laws, the dispossessed, the interned, officially recognized resisters, the "Righteous," victims of forced labor, and so on. The infinitely complex elaboration of these categories, both on general principles and in their application *intuitu personae*, has in most cases required historical expertise in order to define the right to claim that status. Likewise, the enormous increase in the civil and criminal procedures intended to make amends for historical events sometimes several decades old has led to the enlistment of expertise of all sorts about past events, including historical expertise. As a result, the relation between historical actors and historians has changed in nature. It has become strained, and the old opposition between experience and knowledge has again reared its head. Actors erected into witnesses have claimed, sometimes in complete innocence, to speak in the name of an entire era, forgetting that even their most terrible and ineradicable experience was limited in time and space: those deported to Buchenwald cannot give an account of the experience of being at Auschwitz. And historians have sometimes forgotten that historical discourse consists of general statements that are often very difficult to apply to particular cases—hence the difficulty of inserting a flesh-and-blood accused (during the Eichmann or Papon trials, for example) into philosophical or historical categories. In fact, that opposition between witnesses and historians is not so simple, since some witnesses—in France, Daniel Cordier, Jean Moulin's former secretary, who became his biographer—have unambiguously sided with the historians most suspicious of testimony. Academia has split in two: one part has developed a veritable ideology of testimony that glorifies the witness and the victim, considers their word sacred, and displays toward them a false humility. In my view, that attitude masks a scientific populism whose objective is not, like that of any populism, to defend the cause of the "forgotten of History." Rather, there is a desire, more or less unconscious, to speak—loudly—in their place. Consider the virulence of the remarks made during recent historiographical disputes, especially in France, regarding the attitude of World War I combatants, or the heroization of the Resistance, or the scope of the colonial unthought and its connection to the immigration question. Not only do I reject that ideology of testimony, which appears in part to be the avatar of an ideological radicality that has lost its traditional historical frames of reference and is seeking new "wretched of the earth"; I also think that the real respect the historian owes witnesses—or rather, once again, historical actors—is to engage with them in a face-to-face encounter, a dialogue, whether friendly or polemical. That in no way prevents one from having respect for what they were in the past, yet at the same time it allows one full freedom to criticize their interpretations of history, including their own history.

We move almost naturally from the witness and the victim to "memory," one of the late twentieth century's buzzwords. Here again, all contemporary history is confronted with the actors' recollections, with a living memory that may or may not find public expression and enter into competition with scholarly discourse. But the memory in question here, as we have seen, has been of a different nature, so much so that some have spoken in reference to the last third of the twentieth century of an "age of memory," an inevitable consequence of the century of major traumas. Historians of the present time, somewhat more than others, have been confronted with the uncontrolled deployment of that notion, which ultimately subsumed all the other usual forms of relation to the past—history, tradition, heritage, myth, legend. They have therefore become particularly invested in a history of the uses and presence of the recent past, quite an illuminating example of how to establish one's distance from an issue in the present. Let me insist, however, that historians' studies on memory, while more or less dependent on the atmosphere of the time, on a preoccupation on the part of their contemporaries, have taken several directions, with different ramifications. I leave aside the oldest of these preoccupations, which rediscovers the notion of memory under cover of oral history, hence solicited testimony: it underwent a development after 1945 with the large-scale campaigns to interview U.S. veterans of World War II, then in the 1970s with collections devoted to English working-class memory (Paul Thompson), women's memory (Luisa Passerini), and French Protestant memory (Philippe Joutard). Apart from that trend, it is primarily the *lieux de mémoire* vein on the one hand, and that of "traumatic memories" on the other, that have had the most success in the last three decades. The first vein, inspired by the publishing venture that Pierre Nora devoted to France, which spurred German, Italian, Russian, Dutch, and Luxembourgeois versions, is above all a rewriting of national history at one remove. It has looked analytically at the material and immaterial patrimony of each country. That patrimony was considerably expanded to include everything that, at one moment or another, may have constituted support both for a specific imaginary and for national character. For the most part, that way of envisioning the history of memory belongs to the register of positivity; that is, it tends to consider the past in terms of permanent behaviors, traditions, and habits of mind that establish a national identity. Citizens of the country under consideration can recognize themselves in that identity and draw resources from it. It does not concern recent history alone—far from it. Like Nora's original model, it situates itself within a *longue durée* that more or less corresponds to the first appearance of national feeling. The second vein has to do primarily with studying the traumatic episodes of the recent past, often absent from the *lieux de mémoire* problematic, except in Germany. It has often been pointed out, in fact, that the two principal French debates about memory—that regarding Vichy and that regarding Algeria—were absent from the seven volumes Nora edited and published between 1984 and 1992, just when these debates were emerging in the public space.[2] Whatever the reasons, that absence casts into relief the difference between that current and the one that put its energies, sometimes to an excessive degree, into the history of the century's "human infamy": the two world wars, genocides, colonialism, and totalitarian systems, whose aftereffects, aftermath, and delayed effects became the obligatory subjects of major studies, even as a new history of the present time was taking root. That second vein accompanied and even structured the new historiographical field, which developed nearly everywhere in the world and, from the start, belonged to the register of negativity. It is a history confronted primarily with mourning, loss, resentment, and impossible atonement, imperatives to which historians, sociologists, or others engaged in that field could not really respond. Finding itself trapped, that history in response gave rise to conflicts, even a form of violence, which shows the extent to which distant observers probably (even certainly) faced the delayed effects of the original violence of the events they were studying. The project of Nora and his emulators leaned toward behavior therapies, which urge patients to look on the "sunny side" of their history; the other posture, by contrast, placed itself within the purview of analytic therapy (though I cannot really say whether it occupies the place of the analyst or that of the analysand), which attempts to historicize trauma by retracing its development after the shock, by putting words to the wounds, by making historical discourse not a resource for one's identity, but a symbolic agency able to counterbalance the invasive imaginary of an identity founded on victimization.

Social demand followed from that development, since historians were faced with expectations of a new kind from a society grappling with profound questions about the recent past. The term "social demand" itself designates a problem encountered by all the social sciences, namely, more or less explicit expectations likely to translate into research, the impetus for which arises outside academia. Social demand is not simply expertise, another innovation that has affected historians in general and those of the present time in particular. The term "expertise" designates an aspect of social demand that enlists knowledge in the service of an action, public or private, and whose purpose is not only to understand the real, but to change it. It exists, therefore, only if there is in the first place a well-defined field of action in which actors clearly and explicitly express an expectation, as in the case of a judicial proceeding. Social demand in general may simply lie in the imagination of the researcher interpreting the ambient context. These notions have long been part of the epistemology of the social sciences, even of the sciences in general. The intense debate surrounding the question of historical expertise points to a redefinition under way of the relation between power, knowledge, and society. It is part of a shift in which influence has been transferred from traditional "intellectuals"—"legislators," as Zygmunt Bauman calls them, those who seek to guide the world—to "interpreters," "specific intellectuals," to use Foucauldian terminology, hence to experts who seek rather to understand, sometimes at the risk of losing their autonomy.[3] If the historian too has become an "expert," it is because history itself, and specifically recent history, has become a field of expertise, a field of action within which certain social actors aspire to intervene retroactively on the past.

The last element in that configuration belongs to the same conjuncture. This is the tendency, recent and relatively novel, to make the past a matter of law, a field of intervention on the part of legislators and judges. Granted, that "juridification" (from "juridical") or "judiciarization" (from "judicial") of history is part of a general trend in contemporary societies, which increasingly ask the law and the justice system to intervene in fields where actions on their part were unusual in the past. In the case of history, it has assumed a particular importance: in the enormous increase in legal decisions concerning historians' research, especially the defamation of living actors of the past; in the role that scholarly studies and researchers have played in defining and implementing new criminal charges, such as "crimes against humanity"; in the active part they have taken in establishing criminal, administrative, or civil responsibility for the great mass crimes, even to the point of intervening as experts or witnesses in the major trials of war criminals in Germany, Israel, and France; and finally, in the emergence of an original way of interpreting the past, which uses the law as a normative tool to define past events retroactively, such as the provisions against negationism or, in France, the passage of what have been called "memorial laws," official positions taken by lawmakers on more or less recent episodes (the Algerian war, colonialism, the genocide of the Armenians, the Western slave trade and slavery). That trend is one of the most striking political and social expressions of what I have described throughout this book: the weight of the tragic past in our societies; the will to make amends for that past in the name of a virtuous conception of memory, the witness, and the victim; the change in the social status of the historian; and the specificity of the history of the present time, which has been particularly affected by that intrusion of the law and the justice system in interpretations of the past.

An incidental question and a reproach sometimes heard: Has the history of the present time contributed to increasing the current divide between past and present? Has it encouraged the pervading presentism by focusing excessively on the present, misconstruing the dialectical connections existing between it and the past *at every moment* in history? Throughout this study I have attempted to show that, on the contrary, in both its epistemological premises and its actual achievements, the history of the present time has contributed to attenuating that divide as it took shape in the public space and in the public mind. On the one hand, that historiography forged its theoretical tools in the 1920s and 1930s, at the precise moment when that divide, which occurred with the Revolution and was formalized by the German and later the French positivists, was being attacked head-on by the Annales School and the defenders of a new contemporary history. The very definitions of that historiographical form, though they may have led to singular methods or positions, rest on the idea that the contemporary, just like any other period, belongs to history. It therefore enters the historian's field of observation on an equal footing, as in the other social sciences. The absence of a break is therefore a precondition. On the other hand, for conjunctural reasons, in recent decades the history of the present time has been somewhat more sensitive than others to questions of memory, that is, to one of the forms that the presence of the past takes in our own time. And to study memory—its relation to other forms of representing or narrating the past, including scholarly history—is by definition to consider the strong bond that exists between the present and the past, and not only the recent past.

Both because of the particular conjuncture of the late twentieth century and the invariable traits of all contemporaneity, historians of the present time have had the task of accounting for two opposing movements at work before their eyes: first, the mutation of the present into the past; and second, the mutation of the past into the present. This is not a rhetorical game but an essential question that arises for all historians of the contemporary, though they do not have a monopoly on it.[4]

The mutation of the present into the past is simply the moment when a present event, process, or actor moves to a different temporal register. The transition can in itself be an abrupt and remarkable event, as in the performance of a memorable and remarkable deed or the death of a prominent figure. It will then be said that the deed or the figure will "go down in history," an expression signifying here a form of immortality, an eternal presence in the collective narratives of the present and future. In that popular sense, "to go down in history" means to escape oblivion, to unite with an eternal present, to become inscribed in memory. This is a rather unusual phenomenon, however, and applies to only a few events or a few figures that have taken on an exemplary value. In most cases, the transition from the present to the past comes about more fluidly, often by almost imperceptible shifts. Except in the case of violent transitions—a war or a revolution—we move from one era to another without immediately taking stock of it, without having realized that one generation has gradually passed away and another has replaced it. That passing, in fact, is in good part a representation of time more than an objective element. To go down in history can thus signify a form of relative or definitive forgetting, a way of leaving the world behind, as in the American expression "I'm history." For historians, that passing from the present to the past, far from being banal, takes on crucial importance. Not only do they experience it like anyone else; it is also part of their mission to identify it, analyze it, indicate the stakes involved. That, in fact, is what is specific to a history that purports to be of its own time and must also take into account the time passing before one's eyes. And if by chance some historians are tempted to turn away their eyes, there are people nearby to call them back to order.

"We, the last survivors of the Holocaust, are passing away one after another. Soon History will begin to speak, at best, in the impersonal voice of researchers and novelists. At worst, in that of negationists, falsifiers, and demagogues. The International Day of Commemoration in Memory of the Victims is a vital link in the transmission of our tragic legacy. If we fail to give it, collectively and judiciously, its rightful place in memory and education, as the core of the fundamental values of every belief system, spiritual or secular, the forces of darkness could again come back to haunt us."[5] These words were recently spoken by Samuel Pisar, a survior of Auschwitz who, notably, testified at the Klaus Barbie trial in 1987. The remarkable thing about this position is that it places in opposition the experience of the witness and commemoration on the one hand (understood here as an emotional communion around remembrance of the event), and any form of representation of the past, historical or fictional, on the other. It almost suggests that these are scarcely different from negationism. In that view of things, the handover from the actor to the researcher is experienced as a loss, almost an injustice. Although a radical view, it expresses a feeling very widespread among former deportees, former resisters, and all those who have survived extreme experiences. Yet the idea that the passing away of the last survivors changes the perception of an event and gives historians complete latitude to exercise a monopoly to which they so ardently aspire did not arise at the moment when survivors were becoming increasingly rare because of their age. It dates back a long time. I was personally called out on that point in the late 1970s, practically from my first writings on the period—an experience that all historians working on sensitive events have undoubtedly had. The idea is therefore not an expression of a conjunctural phenomenon linked to a biological condition. Rather, it is a perception of time linked both to the extreme experience—deportation, torture— and hence to the lived past, and to the way our societies view the relation between the past and the present. In the aftermath of the Holocaust, the shift from the present to the past has taken on a particularly problematic dimension, forcing historians to face dilemmas of unprecedented intensity. Once again, writing that history was both a pressing necessity and an absolute impossibility. The necessity was assumed right after the war, by both survivors and professionals (they are not mutually exclusive), and even allowed a new history of the present time to thrive. By contrast, the impossibility was not this time the methodological objection of a lack of distance and hence a relative impossibility, but rather a radical impossibility: to write the history of the Holocaust was in some sense to kill off the memory of it. That is Pisar's position, but also, for reasons that are likely less pure of narcissistic considerations, that of Claude Lanzmann.

These positions in no way prevented a thriving historiography of the Holocaust: it is no doubt one of the most diversified and sophisticated historiographies in the field of contemporary history. But these questions and fears played an essential role in how that history was written and therefore in how any history of the present time coping with the tragic has been conceived. They are emblematic of the difficulty of imposing historical distance while the actors are still living and a fortiori surviving. Such a difficulty shows the extent to which the passing from the present to the past, from memory to history, from the truth of a lived experience to that of an elaborated knowledge, can be deeply felt as a loss to be mourned, almost an anticipation of death. Yet the very idea of such a clear-cut transition between present and past is an illusion. Many former deportees have lived long enough to see a number of Holocaust historians meet an early death; the succession of generations, being valid only in general, unfortunately does not always apply to individual situations. Likewise, many historians are far more affected by historical events for personal reasons than are some former survivors or actors, who have decided for reasons of their own to move on. It is therefore sometimes a rather pointless exercise to establish an opposition between "historians" and "witnesses." By contrast, the public and repeated expression of that opposition illustrates the difficulty of conceiving of that shift, as if it were necessary to stop time, to prevent the alterity of forgetting, to try to keep alive for as long as possible a present that is itself only the memory of a past now seventy years old.

In certain cases, that transition from the present to the past can also confirm the failure to turn a necessary truth into action, the tendency to leave it for the near future, hoping that the historian will be able to fulfill a mission that the contemporary has been unable to perform. Recently, the leftist Italian senator Luciano Violante, former president of the Anti-Mafia Commission and of the Chamber of Deputies, commented bitterly on the definitive dismissal of charges, on April 14, 2012, against all those indicted in the bombing in Brescia on May 28, 1974. That bombing, attributed to the Far Right, had killed eight and wounded about a hundred. Violante averred that it was now the historians' turn to speak out. Free of the necessity to present clear and case-specific evidence, they would be able in a more or less imminent future to read the documents differently and to say what the Italian justice system could not. Historians thus find themselves summoned in advance to take up the cause and speak a truth that the justice system was unable to formulate (despite several decades of proceedings) in the most perfect tradition of the "upstanding and terrible tribunal" of which d'Alembert speaks.[6]

Behind its apparent banality, the shift from the present to the past in reality constitutes one of the thorniest problems in the history of the present time in recent decades. It has given rise to many controversies, such as the one in the 1980s between the German historian Martin Broszat and the Israeli historian Saul Friedländer. Broszat, director of the Institut für Zeitgeschichte in Munich, belonged to the Hitler Youth generation and was a leading proponent of the so-called functionalist interpretation of Nazism. Friedländer, a Holocaust survivor, had become one of the world's leading experts on the subject. Let me simply recall, without reopening a case over which much ink has been spilled, that the controversy started when Broszat published an article entitled "A Plea for the Historicization of National Socialism," asking that Nazism be treated like one historical object among others. He argued for a nonmoralistic and especially less rigid detachment, and proposed paradigms other than the ideological approach.[7] Neutral in appearance, the term "historicization" concealed a number of ambiguities, as his opponent pointed out. Underscoring the risks of such an approach, Friedländer wondered about the notion of distance in the treatment of such a subject and consequently about the very limits of a history of the present time:

> In my view, to put it briefly, this past is still much too present for present-day historians, be they German or Jewish in particular, be they contemporaries of the Nazi era or members of the second and perhaps third generation, to enable an easy awareness of presuppositions and of a priori positions.
>
> One may assume that, more often than not, the historian approaching the Nazi era has not made it entirely clear to himself on what specific basis, from what specific motives, within which specific ideological context, he wishes to deal with it. What, therefore, is necessary for any kind of historical analysis is a fundamental self-reflective process, one whereby the historian remains aware that—whatever his feeling of objectivity may be—he is still the one who selects the approach, determines the method, and organizes the material according to some kind of agenda. What is true for any historical writing is decisive for the study of such an era. Writing about Nazism is not like writing about sixteenth-century France. The possibly mistaken assumption in the idea of historicization as analyzed here may well be that forty years after the end of the Third Reich, Nazism can be dealt with more or less in the same way as sixteenth-century France.[8]

What was remarkable about this controversy is that it was almost impossible to decide entirely in favor of one or the other protagonist. Broszat's position and his school of thought proved to be of great value, since it not only "unblocked" the history of Nazism but gave food for thought on how to treat the history of all criminal systems of still recent memory. In France, for example, it has been used for a history of the Occupation within a perspective less determined by political and ideological explanations.[9] Friedländer's position has made it possible to perceive the risks that, in spite of everything, lay in "passing" too quickly from the present to the past, in letting objects cool off, in misconstruing the moral and ethical issues at stake in the construction of a historical problematic. Against the possibility of scientistic excesses to which historians can easily succumb, he recalled that a controlled, self-reflexive subjectivity, a consideration of oneself and one's profession, was the only guarantee that historical writing would be able to reconcile critical thinking and responsibility. Both historians in their way showed the decisive role of scholarly discourses and writings in the transition from the present to the past. In this process, historians are not passive witnesses but rather prominent actors—hence the fears they rouse and the attacks of which they can sometimes be the object. It could be added that historians are far from alone in this: survivors, artists, writers, all readers passionate about history, and all spectators at a commemoration also participate in that "historicization," whose effects are feared and denounced in advance. Historicization, sometimes identified with "memorialization," is in itself a social phenomenon of a general nature, and every collectivity has its own way of inscribing the present time into a long-lasting narrative.

Finally, there is the question of that "still much too present" past. Did it remain equally weighty from 1945 to 1987? I have explained in other works that, on the contrary, the memory of that period went through different phases of presence and absence. At the time this controversy was taking place, the memory of the Holocaust had reached a new threshold, particularly with the release of the film *Shoah* and the fortieth anniversary of the fall of the Third Reich, as well as the convening of the Barbie trial in France in 1987. That anamnesis literally constitutes a *mutation of the past into the present*, a process of remembrance that is the exact opposite of historicization. Was the Nazi era at that moment a period that still belonged to the present, or was it, on the contrary, a past that had returned to the present? The same question could be asked about other historical examples. The important thing here is the existence of a collision between two opposite tendencies, with historians caught in the middle. The task at hand is no longer to capture a linear movement, to understand a history in the process of being made, but to fight on two fronts: that of history and that of memory, that of a present we do not want to see pass away and that of a past that returns to haunt the present. The distinction between the two is sometimes elusive. The current history of the present time originated and developed within that uncertainty and instability. Observing my present time today, I see no reason why it should not persist on that path.

Notes

INTRODUCTION

1. [For the sake of consistency, I have translated the term *témoignage* as "testimony" throughout this book. As in English, *témoignage* refers both to testimony given in the courtroom and to the act of bearing witness (in a religious context, for example). It also has a broader sense, however: the French term can be used to describe a statement made by an interview subject or an eyewitness account of any kind.—*Trans.*]

2. Antoine Prost, "L'histoire du temps présent: Une histoire comme les autres," in "Bilan et perspectives de l'histoire immédiate," special double issue, *Cahiers d'histoire immédiate* 30-31 (Fall 2006-Spring 2007): 21-28. Prost's position is the exact opposite of that of Reinhart Koselleck, who wrote that *"Zeitgeschichte* is a nice word but a difficult concept." Reinhart Koselleck, *Zeitgeschichten: Studien zur Historik* (Frankfurt am Main: Suhrkamp, 2000), 246.

3. François Hartog and Gérard Lenclud, "Régimes d'historicité," in *L'état des lieux en sciences sociales,* ed. Alexandre Dutu and Norbert Dodille (Paris: L'Harmattan, 1993), 18-38, at 26.

4. François Hartog, *Régimes d'historicité: Présentisme et expérience du temps* (Paris: Éditions du Seuil, 2003), 126.

5. Hermann Heimpel, *Der Mensch in seiner Gegenwart: Acht historische Essais* (1954; Göttingen: Vandenhoeck & Ruprecht, 1957), 12. A lecture by Ulrich Raulff initially drew my attention to this text: see his *De l'origine à l'actualité: Marc Bloch, l'histoire et le problème du temps présent* (Sigmaringen: Jan Thorbecke, 1997), 19. See also Hartmut Boockmann, *Der Historiker Hermann Heimpel* (Göttingen: Vandenhoeck & Ruprecht, 1990).

6. Nicolas Berg, *Der Holocaust und die westdeutschen Historiker: Erforschung und Erinnerung* (Göttingen: Wallstein, 2003).

7. Hannah Arendt, "Understanding and Politics (The Difficulties of Understanding)," in Arendt, *Essays on Understanding, 1930-1954* (New York: Harcourt, Brace, 1994), 319.

8. Jean-Pierre Dupuy, *Pour un catastrophisme éclairé: Quand l'impossible est certain* (Paris: Éditions du Seuil, 2002), 9.

CHAPTER ONE

1. Prost, "L'histoire du temps présent," 21.

2. Antoine Prost, *Douze leçons sur l'histoire* (Paris: Éditions du Seuil, 1996).

3. Elements for reflection can be found, however, in Gérard Noiriel, *Qu'est-ce que l'histoire contemporaine?* (Paris: Hachette, 1998), which considers the subject in reference to the nineteenth and twentieth centuries; and Hartog, *Régimes d'historicité*. With Christian Delacroix, François Dosse, and Patrick Garcia, I explored that subject during a multidisciplinary seminar in 2002 at the Institut d'Histoire du Temps Présent: "L'histoire du temps présent à l'épreuve du passé," along with historians of antiquity (François Hartog), medievalists (Michel Sot, Patrick Boucheron), modernists (Jacques Guilhaumou, Nicolas Leroux, Jean-Louis Fournel, Jean-Claude Zancarini), and contemporaneists (Robert Frank, Olivier Dumoulin).

4. That criticism is explicit in Prost, "L'histoire du temps présent," and even more so in Gérard Noiriel, *Les origines républicaines de Vichy* (Paris: Hachette, 1999), especially in the introduction, titled "Pour une autre histoire du temps présent," a polemical argument that provides a critical view of the history of the present time as it was then developing, and to which I responded at the time: see my "L'histoire du temps présent, vingt ans après," in "L'histoire du temps présent, hier et aujourd'hui," special issue, *Bulletin de l'Institut d'histoire du temps présent* 75 (July 2000): 23–40. Let me note, with a touch of polemics in turn, that neither Prost nor Noiriel ever developed an analysis of the *longue durée* in their own works, which for the most part deal with the late nineteenth century and the first half of the twentieth century, proof that the objection is mere posturing.

5. Hervé Lemoine, *La Maison de l'histoire: Pour la création d'un Centre de recherche et de collections permanentes dédié à l'histoire civile et militaire de la France*, status report (Paris: Ministère de la Culture, 2008), 9.

6. Jean Leduc, *Les historiens et le temps: Conceptions, problématiques, écritures* (Paris: Éditions du Seuil, 1999), 92ff.

7. Bernard Guenée, *Histoire et culture historique dans l'Occident médiéval* (Paris: Aubier-Montaigne, 1980), 9–10.

8. Quoted in Leduc, *Les historiens et le temps*, 101.

9. Jack Goody, *The Theft of History* (New York: Cambridge University Press, 2006).

10. Michel de Certeau, *L'écriture de l'histoire* (Paris: Gallimard, 1975), 16, emphasis in the original.

11. Jacques Le Goff, Roger Chartier, and Jacques Revel, eds., *La Nouvelle Histoire* (Paris: Retz, 1978).

12. Jean Lacouture, "L'histoire immédiate," ibid., 270–93, at 274.

13. Pierre Nora, "Présent," ibid., 467–72, at 467.

14. Benedetto Croce, *Theory and History of Historiography*, trans. Douglas Ainslie (London: G. C. Harrap, 1921), 12 [translation slightly modified]. The essays composing this book were originally published in Italian in 1912–13.

15. Cicero, *De oratore*, 2.9.33, trans. E. W. Sutton (Cambridge, Mass.: Harvard University Press, 1942), 225.

16. Croce, *Theory and History of Historiography*, 19, emphasis in the original [translation modified].

17. Ibid., 20 and 21 [translation modified].

18. Robin George Collingwood, *Essays in the Philosophy of History*, ed. William Debbins (New York: McGraw-Hill, 1966), 7. The first essay is devoted to Croce's book and was published in 1921.

19. Certeau, *L'écriture de l'histoire*, 14–15, emphasis in the original.

20. Ibid.

21. François Hartog, *Évidence de l'histoire: Ce que voient les historiens* (Paris: Gallimard, 2005), 68. Cf., by the same author, *Le miroir d'Hérodote: Essai sur la représentation de l'autre* (Paris: Gallimard, 2001) and Herodotus's *Histories*.

22. Hartog, *Évidence de l'histoire*, 77.

23. Catherine Darbo-Peschanski, "La politique de l'histoire: Thucydide historien du présent," *Annales ESC* 3 (May–June 1898): 653–75.

24. Thucydides, *The War of the Peloponnesians and the Athenians*, 1.1, ed. and trans. Jeremy Mynott (Cambridge: Cambridge University Press, 2013), 3-4.

25. Hartog, *Évidence de l'histoire*, 96.

26. Ibid., 100.

27. Darbo-Peschanski, "La politique de l'histoire," 658.

28. Thucydides, *War of the Peloponnesians*, 1.22, pp. 15-16.

29. Polybius, *Histories*, 12.28.2-5, trans. W. R. Paton (London: William Heinemann, 1922-1927), 4:403. See also Hartog, *Évidence de l'histoire*, 120-21.

30. Denis Roussel, note to Polybe (Polybius), *Histoire*, ed. François Hartog, trans. Denis Roussel (Paris: Gallimard, 2003), 837 n. 122.

31. Horace, *Odes*, 2.1, trans. James Michie, with the Latin text and an introduction by Rex Warner (New York: Orion, 1963), 101.

32. Guenée, *Histoire et culture historique*, 20-21.

33. Jacques Le Goff, *Saint Louis* (Paris: Gallimard, 1996), quoted in Leduc, *Les historiens et le temps*, 139.

34. Marc Bloch, *La société féodale* (Paris: Albin Michel, 1939), quoted in Jacques Le Goff, "Pour un autre Moyen Âge," in his *Un autre Moyen Âge* (1977; Paris: Gallimard, 1999), 54.

35. Le Goff, *Saint Louis*, 289.

36. Alain Guerreau, review of Bernard Guenée, *Histoire et culture historique dans l'Occident médiéval*, *Bibliothèque de l'École des Chartes* 139, no. 2 (1981): 282-83.

37. Hanz-Werner Goetz, "Historical Consciousness and Institutional Concern in European Medieval Historiography (11th and 12th Centuries)," paper delivered at the Nineteenth International Congress of Historical Sciences, Oslo, August 6-13, 2000, theme 3: "The Uses and Abuses of History and Responsibility of the Historian, Past and Present," http://www.oslo2000.uio.no /program/papers/m3a/m3a-goetz.pdf, accessed in March 2011.

38. Ibid., 7.

39. Guenée, *Histoire et culture historique*, 84-85. The abbé Guibert de Nogent's *Dei gesta per Francos*, written in about 1114, can be cited as an example: "Although I was unable to go to Jerusalem myself or to know most of the individuals and all the places in question here, the general utility of my work will not be diminished thereby, if it is certain that I learned the things I have written and that I will yet write only from men whose testimony is in perfect conformity with the truth." Guibert de Nogent, *Histoire des Croisades*, book 4, in *Collections des mémoires relatifs à l'histoire de France depuis la fondation de la monarchie française jusqu'au 13e siècle*, ed. François Guizot (Paris: J.-L.-J. Brière Libraire, 1825), 112.

40. Remark reported by Nicolas Offenstadt in the obituary devoted to Guenée, *Le Monde*, October 2, 1010.

41. [The term *école méthodique* refers to a group of historians working in the late nineteenth and early twentieth centuries (Charles Seignobos, Charles-Victor Langlois, and others) who emphasized the importance of good scientific methods in the writing of history—*Trans*.]

42. Krzysztof Pomian, "L'histoire de la science et l'histoire de l'histoire," *Annales ESC* 5 (1975), repr. in his *Sur l'histoire* (Paris: Gallimard, 1999), 141.

43. Ibid., 148.

44. Frédérique Aït-Touati, *Contes de la Lune: Essai sur la fiction et les sciences modernes* (Paris: Gallimard, 2011), 18. See the book review by Nicolas Correard, "L'hypothèse scientifique comme fabrique de la fiction: Poétiques du discours astronomique au XVIIe siècle," in "Écritures du savoir," special issue, *Acta Fabula*, http://www.fabula.org/revue/document6947.php.

45. Aït-Touati, *Contes de la Lune*, 150.

46. Ibid., 154.

47. Jean-Marie Goulemot, *Le règne de l'histoire: Discours historiques et révolutions XVIIe-XVIIIe siècles* (Paris: Albin Michel, 1996).

48. Eberhard Jäckel, *Umgang mit der Vergangenheit: Beiträge zur Geschichte* (Stuttgart: Deutsche Verlags-Anstalt, 1989), 133-50, chapter titled "Begriff und Fonktion der Zeitgeschichte," quoted in Peter Schöttler, "La *'Zeitgeschichte'* allemande, entre révisionnisme, conformisme et autocritique," paper delivered at the international colloquium "Temps présent et contemporanéité," Paris, IHTP, March 24-26, 2011. For France, see *Le Journal ou Histoire du temps présent; contenant toutes les Declarations du Roy vérifiées en Parlement, & tous les Arrets rendus, les Chambres assemblées, pour les affaires publiques. Depuis le mois d'avril 1651, jusques en juin 1652* (Paris: Gervais Alliot & Emmanuel Langlois, 1652).

49. Blaise de Pascal, *Pensées*, trans. A. J. Krailsheimer (London: Penguin, 1966), § 437 (628), pp. 165-66. Depending on the edition, this passage occupies different places in the general organization of the paragraphs. It has received little comment by present-day historians and is almost completely overlooked by contemporaneists. The interpretation I give here is obviously very subjective.

50. Louis Marin, *Pascal et Port-Royal*, ed. Alain Cantillon et al. (Paris: Presses Universitaires de France, 1997), 174-75, emphasis in the original.

51. On this point, see Blandine Barret-Kriegel, *Les historiens et la monarchie*, 4 vols. (Paris: Presses Universitaires de France, 1988).

52. Pascal, *Pensées*, § 474 (633), p. 180.

53. Pierre Force, *L'herméneutique chez Pascal* (Paris: Vrin, 1989), 176.

54. Yosef Yerushalmi, *Zakhor, Jewish History and Jewish Memory* (Seattle: University of Washington Press, 1982).

55. Pomian, *Sur l'histoire*, 155.

56. Christian Jouhaud, *Les pouvoirs de la littérature: Histoire d'un paradoxe* (Paris: Gallimard, 2000), 151. The passage appears at the beginning of chap. 3, "Historiens du présent et pouvoir politique."

57. Ibid., 156.

58. Ibid., 170.

59. Niccolò Machiavelli, *Florentine Histories*, trans. Laura E. Banfield and Harvey C. Mansfield Jr. (Princeton: Princeton University Press, 1988), 4.

60. Michel Foucault, *The Order of Things: An Archaeology of the Human Sciences* (New York: Vintage, 1973), 219.

61. Johann Gustav Droysen, *Outline of the Principles of History (Grundriss der Historik)*, trans. E. Benjamin Andrews (Boston: Ginn, 1893), §73, p. 44.

62. Reinhart Koselleck, "Geschichte," in *Geschichtliche Grundbegriffe: Historisches Lexikon zur politish-sozialen Sprache in Deutschland*, ed. O. Brunner, W. Conze, and R. Koselleck, vol. 2 (Stuttgart: Ernst Klett, 1975), 647-717 [my translation from the French version: Reinhart Koselleck, "Le concept d'histoire," in *L'expérience de l'histoire*, edited with a preface by Michael Werner, trans. Alexandre Excudier with Diane Meur, Marie-Claire Hoock, and Jochen Hoock (Paris: École des Hautes Études en Sciences Sociales / Gallimard / Seuil, 1997), 15-99—*Trans.*].

63. Ibid., 28.

64. Ibid., 41.

65. Ibid., 38-39.

66. This passage is taken from an article that appeared in the *Mercure de France*, July 7, 1807, repr. in François-René de Chateaubriand, *Mémoires d'Outre-tombe* (Liège, 1849), 2:102.

67. Pierre Vidal-Naquet, *Mémoires*, vol. 1, *La brisure et l'attente, 1930-1955* (Paris: Seuil / La Découverte, 1995), 113-14.

68. See François Hartog, Pauline Schmitt, and Alain Schnapp, eds., *Pierre Vidal-Naquet: Un historien dans la cité* (Paris: La Découverte, 1998).

69. Stéphane Courtois, Nicolas Werth, Jean-Louis Panné, et al., *Le livre noir du communisme: Crimes, terreur, répression* (Paris: Robert Laffont, 1997). Quoted from the "Bouquins" edition (1998), 36.

70. Ibid., 9–18.

71. Voltaire, *La philosophie de l'histoire: Texte intégral d'après l'édition de 1765*, ed. Catherine Volpilhac-Auger (Geneva: Slatkine, 1996).

72. Jean le Rond d'Alembert, "Réflexions sur l'histoire, lues à l'Académie Française dans la séance publique du 19 janvier 1761," in *Oeuvres complètes de d'Alembert*, 4 vols. (Paris: A. Belin, 1821–1822), 2, pt. 1: 1–10. Text reproduced in *Réflexions sur l'histoire, et sur les différentes manières de l'écrire*, http://www.eliohs.unifi.it/testi/700/alemb/reflect.html, online edition by Guido Abbattista for *Cromohs (Cyber Review of Modern Historiography)*, January 1997, emphasis in the original.

73. See Patrick Garcia and Jean Leduc, *L'enseignement de l'histore en France de l'Ancien régime à nos jours* (Paris: Armand Colin, 2003), 38–44. See also Reinhart Koselleck, *Futures Past: On the Semantics of Historical Time*, trans. Keith Tribe (Cambridge, Mass.: MIT Press, 1985; 1st ed. Frankfurt am Main, 1979). My thanks to Sylvie Aprile and Emmanuel Fureix for their advice on this period.

74. "Instruction relative à l'enseignement de l'histoire contemporaine dans la classe de Philosophie des Lycées impériaux," September 24, 1863, quoted in Garcia and Leduc, *L'enseignement de l'histoire en France*, 79.

75. Koselleck, *L'expérience de l'histoire*, 83.

76. Quoted ibid. In a discussion with two of his colleagues, Johann Georg Rist and Friedrich Christoph Perthes, Gustav Poel wondered about the possibility of writing, in about 1820, a "history of the European states."

77. Koselleck, *L'expérience de l'histoire*, 83 and 84. The aphorism may bring to mind Guenée's position cited above.

78. Christian Delacroix, François Dosse, and Patrick Garcia, *Les courants historiques en France XIXe–XXe siècle*, rev. and augmented ed. (Paris: Gallimard, 2007), 12 [1st ed. Armand Colin, 1999].

79. Emmanuel de Toulongeon, *Histoire de France depuis la Révolution de 1789 écrite d'après les mémoires et manuscrits contemporains, recueillis dans les dépôts civils et militaires* (Paris: Didot, 1803), quoted in Sophie-Anne Leterrier, *Le XIXe siècle historien: Anthologie raisonnée* (Paris: Belin 1997), 20.

80. Numa-Denys Fustel de Coulanges, "Leçon inaugurale en Sorbonne" (1875), repr. in François Hartog, *Le XIXe siècle et l'histoire: Le cas Fustel de Coulanges* (Paris: Presses Universitaires de France, 1988), 341–42; quoted in Delacroix, Dosse, and Garcia, eds., *Les courants historiques en France*, 76.

81. Madeleine Rébérioux, preface to Charles-Victor Langlois and Charles Seignobos, *Introduction aux études historiques* (Paris: Kimé, 1992), 54. Seignobos's text was originally published in 1897.

82. Wilhelm von Humboldt, "Über die Aufgabe der Geschichtschreibers" (1821), translated as "On the Historian's Task," *History and Theory* 6, no. 1 (1967): 57. The line was borrowed by Leopold Ranke in 1824. It is the first sentence of the lecture that Humboldt, founder in 1810 of the University of Berlin (which now bears his name), delivered to the Prussian Academy.

83. Nora, "Présent," 467, emphasis in the original. Nora adopts the view developed in Charles-Olivier Carbonell, *Histoire et historiens: Une mutation idéologique des historiens français, 1865–1885* (Toulouse: Privat, 1976).

84. Cf. Noiriel, *Qu'est-ce que l'histoire contemporaine?*, 52.

85. Ibid., 13. Noiriel takes up Louis Halphen's analysis in *L'histoire en France depuis cent ans* (Paris: Armand Colin, 1914), which shows that the new generation of historians took an interest first and foremost in the study of antiquity and the Middle Ages.

86. Llewellyn Woodward, "The Study of Contemporary History," *Journal of Contemporary History* 1, no. 1 (January 1966): 1–2. I shall return in the next chapter to the creation of this journal.

87. Peter Novick, *That Noble Dream: The "Objectivity Question" and the American Historical Profession* (Cambridge: Cambridge University Press, 1988), 3.

88. Ibid., 37–38 and 34, respectively.

89. Ibid., 75–78.

90. Halphen, *L'histoire en France depuis cent ans*, quoted in Noiriel, *Qu'est-ce que l'histoire contemporaine?*, 13.

91. Charles Seignobos, *La méthode historique appliquée aux sciences sociales* (Paris: Felix Alcan, 1909), 2–3.

92. Droysen, *Outline of the Principles of History*, §5, p. 11.

93. Numa-Denys Fustel de Coulanges, *Questions d'histoire* (Paris: Hachette, 1893), 408. See also Leterrier, *Le XIXe siècle historien*, 282.

94. Fustel de Coulanges, *Questions d'histoire*, xv. See also Leterrier, *Le XIXe siècle historien*, 284.

95. Stéphane Mallarmé, "L'action restreinte" ("Quant au livre"), originally published in *Divagations* (1897), repr. in *Igitur; Divagations; Un coup de dés*, ed. Bertrand Marchal (Paris: Gallimard, 2003), 265.

96. Friedrich Nietzsche, "On the Uses and Disadvantages of History for Life," in *Untimely Meditations*, ed. Daniel Breazeale, trans. R. J. Hollingdale (New York: Cambridge University Press), 60. Cf. Werner Paravicini, "Nietzsche et les sciences historiques: Autour de la Deuxième considération intempestive," *Francia* (Institut Historique allemand de Paris) 29, no. 3 (2002): 151–91.

97. On this subject, see the aforementioned studies by Gérard Noiriel, Christian Delacroix, François Dosse, and Patrick Garcia; and Pascal Ory, *Une nation pour mémoire, 1889, 1939, 1989, trois jubilés révolutionnaires* (Paris: Presses de la Fondation Nationale des Sciences Politiques, 1992).

98. See Noiriel, *Qu'est-ce que l'histoire contemporaine?*, 14, which takes up the analyses of Carbonell in *Histoire et historiens*.

99. Victor Duruy, "Lettre au général Coffinières de Nordeck [director of the École Polytechnique]" (1862), repr. in his *Notes et souvenirs* (Paris: Hachette, 1901), 122–25, quoted in Leterrier, *Le XIXe siècle historien*, 239.

100. In 2009 Éditions des Équateurs began to reissue Lavisse's *Histoire de France depuis les origines jusqu'à la Révolution*, with a preface by Pierre Nora.

CHAPTER TWO

1. See Novick, *That Noble Dream*, 112ff.; and Olivier Dumoulin, "Histoire et historiens de Droite," in *Histoire des Droites en France*, ed. Jean-François Sirinelli, vol. 2, *Cultures* (Paris: Gallimard, 1992), 327–98.

2. Émile Durkheim, *"L'Allemagne au-dessus de tout": La mentalité allemande et la guerre* (Paris: Armand Colin, 1915), 42; Henri Bergson, "Discours prononcé devant l'Académie des sciences morales et politiques," speech delivered on August 8, 1914; Ernest Babelon, *Le Rhin dans l'histoire*, 2 vols. (Paris: Ernest Leroux, 1917–18); Pierre Vidal de La Blache, "La frontière de la Sarre d'après les traités de 1814 et 1815," *Annales de Géographie* 28, no. 154 (1919): 249–67. For a general analysis, see Nicolas Beaupré, *Les Grandes Guerres, 1914–1945* (Paris: Belin, 2012).

3. Anne Rasmussen, "La 'science française' dans la guerre des manifestes, 1914–1918," *Mots: Les langages du politique* 76 (2004): 9–23.

4. Novick, *That Noble Dream*, 117.

5. J. Franklin Jameson, quoted ibid.

6. Cf. Michaël Bourlet, "Les officiers de la section historique de l'état-major de la Grande guerre," *Revue historique des armées* 231, no. 2 (2003): 4–12. See also Agnès Chablat-Beylot and Amable Sablon du Corail, "Les archives de la Grande guerre: Mise en ligne d'un guide," *Revue historique des armées* 254 (2009): 132–34.

7. Antoine Prost and Jay Winter, *Penser la Grande guerre: Essai d'historiographie* (Paris: Éditions du Seuil, 2004), 16–17.

8. Quoted in Jules Isaac, *Jules Isaac, un historien dans la Grande guerre: Lettres et carnets, 1914–1947*, ed. with notes by Marc Michel, introd. by André Kaspi (Paris: Armand Colin, 2004), 302. The passage is taken from an unpublished proposal for a second volume of Isaacs's memoirs (*Expériences de ma vie*), the first volume of which was published in 1959.

9. Lucien Febvre, "L'histoire dans le monde en ruines," inaugural lecture published in *Revue de synthèse historique* 30, no. 4 (February-June 1920): 1-15.

10. Peter Schöttler, "After the Deluge: The Impact of the Two World Wars on the Historical Work of Henri Pirenne and Marc Bloch," in *Nationalizing the Past: Historians as Nation Builders in Modern Europe*, ed. Stefan Berger and Chris Lorenz (London: Palgrave Macmillan / European Science Foundation, 2010), 404-25.

11. Cf. David Reynolds, "The Origins of the Two 'World Wars': Historical Discourse and International Politics," *Journal of Contemporary History* 38, no. 1 (January 2003): 29-44, cited in Karoline Postel-Vinay, "Dire l'histoire à l'échelle du monde," *Esprit* (June 2007), http://www.esprit.presse.fr/archive/review/article.php?code=14083.

12. See Jean-Jacques Becker, *Dictionnaire de la Grande guerre* (Brussels: André Versaille, 2008), 108-10. On Harry Elmer Barnes, see Novick, *That Noble Dream*, 178-80. For a comprehensive view, see Keith Wilson, ed., *Government and International Historians through Two World Wars* (New York: Berghahn, 1996). See also Prost and Winter, *Penser la Grande guerre*, 16-29.

13. Robert William Seton-Watson, "The Historian as a Political Force in Central Europe," inaugural lecture upon the creation of a chair in Slavonic Studies at the University of London, November 2, 1922, School of Slavonic Studies, University of London, King's College, 1922.

14. Antoine Marès, "Louis Léger et Ernest Denis: Profile de deux bohémisants français au XIXe siècle," in *La France et l'Europe centrale, 1867-1914*, ed. Bohumila Ferenčuhová (Bratislava: Academic Electronic Press, 1995), 63-82.

15. Cf. Olivier Lowczyk, *La fabrique de la paix: Du comité d'études à la Conférence de la paix* (Paris: Économica, 2010).

16. Cf. Jonathan M. Nielson, *American Historians in War and Peace: Patriotism, Diplomacy and the Paris Peace Conference, 1918-1919* (Palo Alto, Calif.: Academia Press, 2011).

17. On Pierre Renouvin, see the articles his heirs dedicated to him: Jean-Baptiste Duroselle, entry in *Encyclopaedia Universalis*; and René Girault, "Pierre Renouvin, la BDIC et l'historiographie française des relations internationales," *Matériaux pour l'histore de notre temps* 49, no. 5 (1998): 7-9. See also Delacroix, Dosse, and Garcia, *Les courants historiques en France*, 358ff.; and Noiriel, *Qu'est-ce que l'histoire contemporaine?*, 56ff.

18. A large body of literature exists on this subject. See especially Paul Fussel, *The Great War and Modern Memory* (London: Oxford University Press, 1975); George Mosse, *Fallen Soldiers: Reshaping the Memory of the World Wars* (New York: Oxford University Press, 1990); and Jay Winter, *Sites of Memory, Sites of Mourning: The Great War in European Cultural History* (Cambridge: Cambridge University Press, 1995).

19. Maurice Halbwachs's *Les cadres sociaux de la mémoire* was first published in 1925. See the recent edition (1994) as well as the new edition of his *Mémoire collective* (1997), both edited by Gérard Namer (Paris: Albin Michel). See also Annette Becker's biography *Maurice Halbwachs: Un intellectuel en guerres mondiales 1914-1945* (Paris: Noêsis, 2003).

20. On the notion of moral witness, see Avishai Margalit, *The Ethics of Memory* (Cambridge, Mass.: Harvard University Press, 2002).

21. Jean Norton Cru, *Témoins: Essai d'analyse et de critique des souvenirs des combattants édités en français de 1915 à 1928* (Paris: Les Étincelles, 1929; new ed. Presses Universitaires de Nancy, 1993); and *Du témoignage* (Paris: Gallimard, 1931; new ed. n.p.: Jean-Jacques Pauvert, 1967), at 26, quoted in Frédéric Rousseau, *Le procès des témoins de la Grande guerre: L'affaire Norton Cru* (Paris: Éditions du Seuil, 2003), 68. Rousseau's book is well documented but adopts a position marked, paradoxically, by devotion to a figure considered one of the inventors of "hypercriticism," a manifestation of the ideology of testimony still persistent in contemporary historiography.

22. Jules Isaac, "De la véracité dans les récits de guerre qui émanent des combattants et des garanties que nous en avons: Entretien tenu au siège de l' 'Union' le 16 novembre 1930 à propos du livre de M. Jean Norton Cru 'Témoins,'" *Bulletin de l'Union pour la vérité* (February-March 1931): 68-69.

23. It is now the Bibliothèque de Documentation Internationale Contemporaine (BDIC), located on the campus of the Université Paris Ouest Nanterre La Défense, partner to the Musée d'Histoire Contemporaine located at Les Invalides. See Jean-Jacques Becker, "La Grande guerre et la naissance de la BDIC," *Matériaux pour l'histoire de notre temps* 100 (October-December 2010): 5-6.

24. Walter Benjamin, "Theses on the Philosophy of History," in Benjamin, *Illuminations*, trans. Harry Zohn (New York: Schocken, 1968), 257-58. See also Michael Löwy, *Walter Benjamin: Avertissement d'incendie; Une lecture des thèses "Sur le concept d'histoire"* (Paris: Presses Universitaires de France, 2001), 71.

25. Paul Ricoeur, *La mémoire, l'histoire, l'oubli* (Paris: Éditions du Seuil, 2000), 649-50.

26. Crane Brinton, "The 'New History' and 'Past Everything,'" *American Scholar* 8, no. 2 (1939): 153, quoted in Novick, *That Noble Dream*, 141. Brinton was an American historian known for his work on the French Revolution.

27. Robert William Seton-Watson, "Plea for the Study of Contemporary History," *History (Journal of the Historical Association)* 14, no. 53 (April 1929): 1-18.

28. Ibid., 2.

29. Ibid., 9. The passage from Joseph de Maistre is taken from correspondence sent to Baron Vignet des Étoles in December 1793.

30. Seton-Watson, "Plea for the Study of Contemporary History," 17.

31. Ibid., 13.

32. André Burguière, *L'École des Annales: Une histoire intellectuelle* (Paris: Odile Jacob, 2006), 33.

33. Henri Hauser, "Un comité international d'enquête sur l'histoire des prix," *Annales d'histoire économique et sociale* 2, no. 7 (1930): 384-85.

34. Wesseling, "The Annales School and the Writing of Contemporary History."

35. Raulff, *De l'origine à l'actualité*. See also Raulff's biography of Bloch: *Ein Historiker im 20. Jahrhundert: Marc Bloch* (Frankfurt am Main: Fischer, 1995), translated into French as *Marc Bloch: Un historien au XXe siècle* (Paris: Éditions de l'École des Hautes Études en Sciences Sociales, 2005).

36. See the converging points of view of Schöttler, "After the Deluge"; Annette Becker, preface to Marc Bloch, *L'histoire, la guerre, la Résistance*, ed. Annette Becker and Étienne Bloch (Paris: Gallimard, 2006), xiii; and Burguière, *L'École des Annales*, 41.

37. These are the respective titles of paragraphs 6 and 7 in the first chapter of Marc Bloch's *Apologie pour l'histoire ou Métier d'historien*, an unfinished manuscript written for the most part in 1942, published posthumously in *Cahier des Annales* 3 (Paris: Librairie Armand Colin, 1952), and reissued by Gallimard as *L'histoire, la guerre, la Résistance*. "Understanding the Present through the Past" and "Understanding the Past through the Present" are subheads added by Febvre that accurately sum up the author's thesis. On the advice of Peter Schöttler, one of the foremost experts on Bloch's work, I have here used the version published in 1997 by Armand Colin, annotated by Étienne Bloch with a preface by Jacques Le Goff, which, it appears, is closer to the original manuscript notes.

38. Marc Bloch, *Apologie pour l'histoire ou Métier d'historien* (Paris: Armand Colin, 1997), 58-59.

39. Ibid.

40. Ibid., 63.

41. Noiriel, *Les origines républicaines de Vichy*, 33-34.

42. Bloch, *Apologie pour l'histoire*, 60. The earliest and the most recent versions of *Apologie pour l'histoire* often include the first draft of this passage: "The remarkable thing is that the question can now be raised. Until a time very close to us, in fact, it seemed almost unanimously to be resolved in advance."

43. Hannah Arendt, *Between Past and Future: Six Exercises in Political Thought* (New York: Viking, 1961), 3.

44. Ibid, 3. The quotation from René Char is taken from *Feuillets d'Hypnos* 62 (1946).

45. See Emmanuel Ringelblum's posthumously published *Notes from the Warsaw Ghetto*, ed. and trans. Jacob Sloan (New York: Schocken, 1974; 1st ed. 1958) and also the most recent study on the

subject: Samuel D. Kassow, *Who Will Write Our History? Rediscovering a Hidden Archive from the Warsaw Ghetto* (New York: Vintage, 2009). See also Laura Jockusch, *Collect and Record! Jewish Holocaust Documentation in Early Postwar Europe* (London: Oxford University Press, 2014).

46. On the origins of the CDJC, see Renée Poznanski, "La création du Centre de documentation juive contemporaine en France (avril 1943)," *Vingtième siècle: Revue d'histoire* 63 (July–September 1999): 51–64.

47. Tom Segev, *The Seventh Million: The Israelis and the Holocaust*, trans. Haim Watzman (New York: Henry Holt, 2000), 104. See also Mooli Brog, "In Blessed Memory of a Dream: Mordechai Shenhavi and Initial Holocaust Commemoration Ideas in Palestine, 1942–1945," Shoah Resource Center, http://www.yadvashem.org/odot_pdf/Microsoft%20Word%20-%205423.pdf.

48. I am alluding here, of course, to the arguments in Yerushalmi, *Zakhor, Jewish History and Jewish Memory*.

49. On that history, see Pieter Lagrou, "Historiographie de guerre et historiographie du temps présent: Cadres institutionnels en Europe occidentale, 1945–2000," *Bulletin du Comité international d'histoire de la Deuxième Guerre mondiale* 30–31 (1999–2000): 191–215, http://www.ihtp.cnrs.fr /spip/php%3Farticle515.html. See also his comparative study of France, the Netherlands, and Belgium: *Mémoires patriotiques et Occupation nazie: Résistants, requis et déportés en Europe occidentale, 1945–1965* (Brussels: Complexe; Paris: IHTP-CNRS, 2003).

50. Quoted in Gerrold van der Stroom, "The Diaries, *Het Achterhuis* and the Translations," in *The Diary of Anne Frank: The Critical Edition*, ed. David Barnouw and Gerrold van der Stroom, trans. Arnold J. Pomerans and B. M. Mooyaart-Doubleday (New York: Doubleday, 1989), 59. This critical edition contains the three different versions of the *Diary of Anne Frank*, first published in 1947.

51. Anne Frank, *The Diary of Anne Frank*, 578. The "Secret Annexe" is the name of the attic where the Frank family hid. Here I reproduce the text from the first edition of the *Diary*.

52. For a brief summary of its history, see the Web site of the successor to the NIOD, the Netherlands Institute for War, Holocaust, and Genocide Studies: www.niod.knaw.nl. See also Paul Stoop, "Das 'Rijksinstituut voor Oorlongsdocumentatie' in Amsterdam," *Jahrebibliographie der Bibliothek für Zeitgeschichte* 58 (1986): 455–65; and especially Gerhard Hirschfeld, "Niederländische Zeitgeschichte: Fragen und Perspektiven der Forschung," *Jahrbuch des Zentrums für Niederlande-Studien* 16 (2005): 141–57. Cf. Pierre Lagrou, *Mémoires patriotiques et Occupation nazie: Résistants, requis et déportés en Europe occidentale, 1945–1965* (Brussels: Complexe; Paris: IHTP-CNRS, 2003), 77–78.

53. Marie-Thérèse Chabord, "Le Comité d'histoire de la Deuxième Guerre mondiale et ses archives," *La gazette des archives* 116, no. 1 (1982): 5–19. See also Laurent Douzou, *La Résistance française, une histoire périlleuse: Essai d'historiographie* (Paris: Éditions du Seuil, 2005). The author shows that, during the war, some French Resistance fighters also imagined writing their history. Nevertheless, the book does not mention the European context within which the CHGM was created or the decisive role it played in the internationalization of that historiography in the 1960s. The same bias toward a Francocentric history can be found in Laurent Douzou, ed., *Faire l'histoire de la Résistance* (Rennes: Presses Universitaires de Rennes, 2008).

54. Valeria Galimi, "De l'histoire de la Résistance à l'histoire du XIXe siècle: L'Istituto nazionale per la storia del movimento di Liberazione in Italia' et le réseau des Instituts associés," in "L'histoire du temps présent, hier et aujourd'hui," special issue, *Bulletin de l'Institut d'histoire du temps présent* (July 2000), http://www.ihtp.cnrs.fr/spip.php%3Frubrique89.html.

55. Lagrou, "Historiographie de guerre et historiographie du temps présent."

56. Ibid.

57. Lucien Febvre, "Avant-Propos," *Cahiers d'Histoire de la guerre* 1 (January 1949): 1–3.

58. Lucien Febvre, "Par manière de préface," *Cahiers d'Histoire de la guerre* 3 (February 1950): 1.

59. See Henri Michel, "Une enquête sur la Résistance par la Commission d'histoire de l'Occupation et de la Libération de la France," *Cahiers d'Histoire de la guerre* 2 (June 1949): 45–55.

60. René Rémond, "France: Work in Progress," in "Historians on the Twentieth Century," spe-

cial issue, *Journal of Contemporary History* 2, no. 1 (January 1967): 43. See the citation in the following chapter. Elsewhere in this article, the author praises the CHGM.

61. Léon Poliakov, "Une grande institution française: Le Comité d'histoire de la 2e Guerre mondiale," *La revue du Centre de documentation juive contemporaine* (April 1956): 19-22. Six years after the war ended, Poliakov published one of the very first surveys on an international scale of the history of the genocide, based on the archives of the Nuremberg trial: *Le bréviaire de la haine* (Paris: Calmann-Lévy, 1951).

62. See the first issues of *Bulletin du Comité international d'Histoire de la Deuxième Guerre mondiale*, first in French only, later in English and French, published under the aegis of the CHGM until 1978, then of the IHTP, each having served as its headquarters in turn. The French committee was responsible for its directorship until 2010 (Henri Michel, 1967-1980; François Bédarida, 1980-90; Henry Rousso, 1999-2000; Pieter Lagrou, 2000-2010). Since 2011, the position of director has been held by Chantal Kesteloot of the Centre d'Études et de Documentation Guerre et Sociétés Contemporaines (Ceges/Soma) in Brussels, successor to the Belgian center (CREHSGM) created in 1967.

63. I have dealt with this point in *La hantise du passé: Entretien avec Philippe Petit* (Paris: Textuel, 1997), translated by Ralph Schoolcraft as *The Haunting Past: History, Memory, and Justice in Contemporary France*, preface by Philippe Petit, foreword to the English-language edition by Ora Avni (Philadelphia: University of Pennsylvania Press, 2002).

64. Norbert Frei, "The Federal Republic of Germany," in *Contemporary History, Practice and Method*, ed. Anthony Seldon (Oxford: Basil Blackwell, 1988), 122.

65. Karl Jaspers, *The Question of German Guilt*, trans. E. B. Ashton (New York: Fordham University Press, 2000; 1st ed. Zurich, 1946); and Friedrich Meinecke, *Die deutsche Katastrophe: Betrachtungen und Erinnerungen* (Wiesbaden: Brockhaus, 1946).

66. Sebastian Conrad, *The Quest for the Lost Nation: Writing History in Germany and Japan in the American Century* (Berkeley and Los Angeles: University of California Press, 2010; 1st ed. Göttingen, 1999), 125. The quotation from Martin Broszat, who was director of the Institut für Zeitgeschichte in the 1980s and one of the founders of what is known as the "functionalist" school, is taken from "Aufgaben und Probleme zeitgeschichtlichen Unterrichts: Am Beispiel der nationalsozialistischen Zeit," *Geschichte in Wissenschaft und Unterricht* 8 (1957): 529-50.

67. Jäckel, *Umgang mit der Vergangenheit*.

68. Passage taken from the history of the IfZ on its Web site, http://www.ifz-muenchen.de /geschichte/html?&L=2, accessed in December 2011. On the history of that prestigious institution, see Horst Möller and Ugo Wengst, eds., *50 Jahre Institut für Zeitgeschichte: Eine Bilanz* (Munich: Oldenbourg Verlag, 1999).

69. Information provided in *Bulletin du Comité international d'histoire de la Deuxième Guerre mondiale* 1 (February 1968): 3.

70. Figure cited by Nicolas Le Moigne, "L'histoire du temps présent à l'allemande: L'*Institut für Zeitgeschichte* de Munich," *Bulletin de la mission historique française en Allemagne* 40 (2004): 186-92.

71. Conrad, *The Quest for the Lost Nation*, 124-25.

72. Hans Rothfels, "Zeitgeschichte als Aufgabe," *Vierteljahrshefte für Zeitgeschichte* 1 (1953): 1-8, at 6-7. Also on the IfZ Web site, http://www.ifz-muenchen.de/heftarchiv/1953/_1_1_rothfels.pdf

73. Johannes Hürter and Hans Woller, *Hans Rothfels und die deutsche Zeitgeschichte* (Munich: Oldenbourg Wissenschaftsverlag, 2005). See also Andreas Wirsching, "'Epoche der Mitlebenden'— Kritik der Epoche," *Zeithistorische Forschungen / Studies in Contemporary History* 8 (May 2011), http://www.zeithistorische-forschungen.de/16126041-Wirsching-1-2011.

74. See especially Berg, *Der Holocaust und die westdeutschen Historiker*, whose accusations occasioned a heated controversy. See also Peter Schöttler, ed., *Geschichtsschreibung als Legitimationswissenschaft 1918-1945* (Frankfurt: Suhrkamp, 1997), one of the first to have exposed a nerve; Jean Solchany, *Comprendre le nazisme dans l'Allemagne des années zéro (1945-1949)* (Paris: Presses

Universitaires de France, 1997); Édouard Husson, *Comprendre Hitler et la Shoah: Les historiens dans la République fédérale d'Allemagne et l'identité allemande depuis 1949* (Paris: Presses Universitaires de France, 2000).

75. Conrad, *The Quest for the Lost Nation*, 127.

76. See the key work by the historian Norbert Frei, who began his career at the IfZ in the 1980s under Martin Broszat and early on moved toward a history of memory: *Vergangenheitspolitik: Die Anfange der Bundesrepublik und die NS-Vergangenheit* (Munich: C. H. Beck, 1997). See also Pierre-Yves Gaudard, *Le fardeau de la mémoire: Le deuil collectif allemand après le national-socialisme* (Paris: Plon, 1997). For a broader perspective on the past and German memory, see Étienne François and Hagen Schulze, eds., *Mémoires allemandes*, trans. Bernard Lortholary (Paris: Gallimard, 2007), abridged from the three-volume German edition (*Deutsche Erinnerungsorte* [Munich: C. H. Beck, 2001]).

77. George Orwell, *Tribune*, February 4, 1944, quoted in Novick, *That Noble Dream*, 290.

78. On Franz Neumann's role in the OSS, see Michael Salter, *Nazi War Crimes, US Intelligence and Selective Prosecution at Nuremberg: Controversies Regarding the Role of the Office of Strategic Services* (New York: Routledge, 2007).

79. Gilles Krugler, "*Historians in Combat:* L'armée américaine et le concept de *Military History Operations*," in "De l'histoire bataille à l'histoire totale," special issue, *Revue historique des armées* 257 (2009): 59-75. This is an original article on a little-known subject. On a related matter, see Noble Frankland, *History at War: The Campaigns of an Historian* (London: Giles de la Mare, 1998), the memoirs of a former Royal Air Force pilot who became director of the Imperial War Museum, serving from 1960 to 1982.

80. The best-known, if not the first, study in the genre is Studs Terkel, "*The Good War*": *An Oral History of World War Two* (New York: Pantheon, 1984).

81. On the history of oral history, see, in French: Philippe Joutard, *Ces voix qui nous viennent du passé* (Paris: Hachette, 1983); Michel Trebitsch, "Du mythe à l'historiographie," in "La bouche de la vérité? La recherche historique et les sources orales," ed. Danièle Voldman, special issue, *Les cahiers de l'Institut d'histoire du temps présent* 21 (November 1992): 13-32, http://www.ihtp.cnrs.fr /spip.php%3Farticle211.html; Florence Descamps, *L'historien, l'archiviste et le magnétophone: De la construction de la source orale à son exploitation* (Paris: Comité pour l'Histoire Économique et Financière de la France, 2001).

82. Novick, *That Noble Dream*, 310. See also Nicolas Werth, "Totalitarisme ou révisionnisme: L'histoire soviétique, une histoire en chantier," in *Le totalitarisme: Le XXe siècle en débat*, ed. Enzo Traverso (Paris: Éditions du Seuil, 2001), 878-96.

83. See Konrad Jarausch, ed., *Zwischen Parteilichkeit und Professionalität: Bilanz der Geschichtswissenschaft der DDR* (Berlin: Akademie Verlag, 1991). See also Stefan Berger, "Historians and Nation-Building in Germany after Reunification," *Past & Present* 148 (1995): 187-222.

84. Several recent studies call that idea into question: on the American case, see Hasia Diner, *We Remember with Reverence and Love: American Jews and the Myth of Silence after the Holocaust, 1945-1962* (New York: New York University Press, 2009); on the French case, see François Azouvi, *Le mythe du grand silence: Auschwitz, les Français, la mémoire* (Paris: Fayard, 2012).

CHAPTER THREE

1. Conrad, *The Quest for the Lost Nation*, 130.

2. Girault, "Pierre Renouvin, la BDIC et l'historiographie française," 7-9.

3. Maurice Agulhon, "Vu des coulisses," in *Essais d'ego-histoire*, ed. Pierre Nora (Paris: Gallimard, 1987), 24.

4. Raoul Girardet, "L'ombre de la guerre," ibid., 163.

5. See Françoise Blum and Rossana Vaccaro, "Madeleine Rebérioux: De l'histoire ouvrière l'histoire sociale," *Cahiers Jaurès* 1, nos. 183-84 (2007): 73.

6. Henk L. Wesseling, "The Annales School and the Writing of Contemporary History," *Review* 1, nos. 3-4 (1978): 185-94, repr. in *Certain Ideas of France: Essays on French History and Civilizatio* (Westport, Conn.: Greenwood Press, 2002), 153-65. See also François Dosse, *L'histoire en miettes Des "Annales" à la "nouvelle histoire"* (Paris: La Découverte, 1987), quoted from the "Pocket" edi tion (1997), 46-47.

7. Cf. Peter Schöttler, "Fernand Braudel, prisonnier en Allemagne face à la longue durée et ar temps présent," paper delivered at the international colloquium "Captivity in Twentieth Centur Warfare: Archives, History, Memory," IHTP/IRSEM (Institut de Recherche Stratégique de l'Écol Militaire), November 17-18, 2011.

8. Fernand Braudel, "L'histoire, mesure du monde," text written in captivity, repr. in Braude *Les ambitions de l'histoire*, ed. Roselyne de Ayala and Paule Braudel, preface by Maurice Aymar (Paris: Éditions de Fallois, 1997), 29.

9. Fernand Braudel, "Personal Testimony," *Journal of Modern History* 44, no. 4 (Decembe 1972), quoted in Braudel, *Les ambitions de l'histoire*, 20-21.

10. Ibid.

11. See Stéphane Audoin-Rouzeau, *Combattre: Une anthropologie historique de la guerre modern (XIXe-XXe siècle)* (Paris: Éditions du Seuil, 2008).

12. Fernand Braudel, "La longue durée," *Annales ESC* (October-December 1958), repr. in *L ambitions de l'histoire*, 190-230, at 223.

13. Braudel, "L'histoire, mesure du monde," 49.

14. Ibid.

15. Fernand Braudel, "La captivité devant l'histoire," *Revue d'histoire de la Deuxième Guerre mon diale* 25 (January 1957): 3-5.

16. [Henri Michel], "Lucien Febvre (1878-1956)," ibid., 2. Michel was undoubtedly the authc of the text.

17. Braudel, "La longue durée," 196-97. On this debate, see François Dosse's fundamental bool which covers several of the same problematics discussed here (he and I have been discussing ther together for a long time): *Renaissance de l'événement: Un défi pour l'historien; Entre sphinx et phéni* (Paris: Presses Universitaires de France, 2010).

18. Ibid., 207, emphasis in the original. The Lévi-Strauss passage is from his article "Diogèn couché," *Les temps modernes* (March 1955).

19. René Rémond, "Plaidoyer pour une histoire délaissée: La fin de la IIIe République," *Revu française de science politique* 7, no. 2 (1957): 253-70, at 253.

20. René Rémond, "Le contemporain du contemporain," in Nora, ed., *Essais d'ego-histoire*, 34

21. Rémond, "Plaidoyer pour une histoire délaissée," 255.

22. Ibid., 256.

23. Ibid., 257.

24. Ibid., 259.

25. Ibid., 260.

26. René Rémond, ed., *Le gouvernement de Vichy 1940-1942: Institutions et politiques* (Paris: A mand Colin, 1972); and René Rémond and Janine Bourdin, eds., *Édouard Daladier, chef de gouve nement* (Paris: Presses de la FNSP, 1977).

27. René Rémond, "France: Work in Progress," in "History Today in USA, Britain, France, Ital Germany, Poland, India, Czechoslovakia, Spain, Holland, Sweden," ed. Walter Laqueur and Georg Mosse, special issue, *Journal of Contemporary History* 2, no. 1 (January 1967): 35-48, at 43-44.

28. René Rémond, "La blessure de 1940 enfin cicatrisée," *Réalités: Revue de Paris* 315 (Apr 1972): 37-41, at 41. My thanks to Olivier Büttner for bringing my attention to this article.

29. Cf. Marie-Claire Lavabre, "Paradigmes de la mémoire," *Transcontinentales* 5 (2007): 139 47, at § 12.

30. Rémond, ed., *Le gouvernement de Vichy*, 17.

31. On this point, see my "La Seconde Guerre mondiale dans la mémoire des Droites françaises," in *Histoires des Droites en France*, ed. Jean-François Sirinelli, vol. 2, *Cultures* (Paris: Gallimard, 1992), 549–620.

32. René Rémond, *Les Droites en France*, 4th ed. (Paris: Aubier-Montaigne, 1982), 10.

33. René Rémond, *Notre siècle: De 1918 à 1988* (Paris: Fayard, 1988), vol. 6 of *Histoire de France*, ed. Jean Favier, 9 [new ed. *Notre siècle: De 1918 à 1991* (Paris: Librairie Générale Française, 1993)].

34. Geoffrey Barraclough, *An Introduction to Contemporary History* (Harmondsworth: Penguin, 1964). I quote from the paperback edition of 1967. My thanks to Martin Conway for bringing my attention to this book, which is almost never cited in French historiography, even though it was translated into French in 1967 and published by Éditions Stock.

35. Geoffrey Barraclough, *History in a Changing World* (Oxford: Basil Blackwell, 1955), 1, quoted in Kenneth C. Dewar, "Geoffrey Barraclough: From Historicism to Historical Science," *Historian* 56, no. 3 (March 1994): 449–64.

36. Barraclough, *An Introduction to Contemporary History*, 20, emphasis in the original.

37. A. J. P. Taylor, "Sales Talk," *New Statesman and Nation*, March 17, 1956, 252, quoted in Dewar, "Geoffrey Barraclough," 457.

38. Barraclough, *An Introduction to Contemporary History*, 23.

39. Barraclough, *History in a Changing World*, 23, quoted in Dewar, "Geoffrey Barraclough," 457. Anecdotally, in 1978 Barraclough played a role in compiling the UNESCO report on the state of the social sciences. He was responsible for history and worked closely with Paul Ricoeur, who wrote the part on philosophy, and with none other than Jean-François Lyotard, responsible for the section on psychoanalysis. See Jacques Havet, ed., *Tendances principales de la recherche dans les sciences sociales et humaines*, 2 vols. (Paris: Mouton/UNESCO, 1978), http://unesdoc.unesco.org/images/0013/001374/137482fo.pdf.

40. Cf. Jan Palmowski and Kristina Spohr Readman, "Speaking Truth to Power: Contemporary History in the Twenty-first Century," in "At the Crossroads of Past and Present: 'Contemporary' History and the Historical Discipline," special issue, *Journal of Contemporary History* 46, no. 3 (July 2011): 485–505.

41. "Editorial Note," *Journal of Contemporary History* 1, no. 1 (January 1966): iii–vi, at iv.

42. Woodward, "The Study of Contemporary History," 1–13.

43. Ibid., 13. The next year, the journal devoted an entire issue, edited by Walter Laqueur and George Mosse, to the state of contemporary history in the world: "History Today in USA, Britain, France, Italy, Germany, Poland, India, Czechoslovakia, Spain, Holland, Sweden," special issue, *Journal of Contemporary History* 2, no. 1 (January 1967).

44. François Dosse, *Pierre Nora: Homo historicus* (Paris: Perrin, 2011), 223.

45. Henri Amouroux, *La vie des Français sous l'Occupation* (Paris: Fayard, 1961).

46. Yves Courrière, *Histoire de la Guerre d'Algérie*, 4 vols. (Paris: Fayard, 1968–1971); Joseph Kessel wrote the preface to the first volume.

47. Benjamin Stora, *La gangrène et l'oubli* (Paris: La Découverte, 1991), 241–42.

48. See the account of Jean Lacouture, *Enquête sur l'auteur* (N.p.: Arléa, 1989), quoted in Guy Pervillé, "L'histoire immédiate selon Jean-François Soulet, Jean Lacouture et Benoît Verhaegen," in "Bilan et perspectives de l'histoire immédiate," special double issue, *Cahiers d'histoire immédiate* 30-31 (Fall 2006-Spring 2007): 6–7.

49. Jean Lacouture, "L'histoire immédiate," in Le Goff, Chartier, and Revel, eds., *La Nouvelle Histoire*, 270–93, at 270.

50. Ibid., 293.

51. Benoît Verhaegen, *Introduction à l'histoire immédiate* (Gembloux: Éd. Duculot, 1974), quoted in Pervillé, "L'histoire immédiate," 7–8.

52. Pierre Nora, "L'événement-monstre," *Communications* 18 (1972): 162–72.

53. Ibid., 164.

54. Ibid., 168.

55. Jacques Le Goff and Pierre Nora, eds., *Faire de l'histoire: Nouveaux problèmes, nouvelles approches, nouveaux objets*, 3 vols. (Paris: Gallimard, 1974). Nora's article is titled "Le retour de l'événement" (1:210-28), Marc Ferro's, "Le film, une contre-analyse de la société?" (3:236-55).

56. Proposal for a program of study, quoted in Dosse, *Pierre Nora*, 282-83. See also Nora, "Présent."

57. Cf. Hirschfeld, "Niederländische Zeitgeschichte: Fragen und Perspektiven der Forschung"; and Pieter Lagrou, "Ou comment se constitue et se développe un nouveau champ disciplinaire," in "L'histoire du temps présent," special issue, *La revue pour l'histoire du CNRS* 9 (2003): 4-15.

58. "Note sur la création d'un Institut du Monde Contemporain," n.d., n.p. This seven-page text was probably written by the future director, François Bédarida, with the assistance of the economist Edmond Lisle, science director of the Département des Sciences Humaines et Sociales at the CNRS in 1977. It was used as the basis for two meetings held the same year at the Hôtel Matignon. I discovered the existence of a copy of it when Anne-Marie Pathé, head of documentation, and I deposited the second set of IHTP archives at the National Archives in 2010. The first set had been placed there in 1998 by Bédarida and Marianne Ranson. Ranson, secretary general at the time, was an active participant in the founding of the IHTP and played a central role there until the late 1990s (AN—Fontainebleau, Ministère de la Recherche, CNRS, IHTP, no. 20110096). The original of this document is undoubtedly in the archives of the General Secretariat of the Government. See also Edmond Lisle, "Les sciences sociales en France: Développement et turbulences dans les années 1970," *La revue pour l'histoire du CNRS* 7 (2002), histoire-cnrs.revues.org/543#text.

59. "Note sur la création d'un Institut du Monde Contemporain," 2.

60. Ibid., 5.

61. Dosse, *Pierre Nora*, 282-83.

62. Hélène Carrère d'Encausse, in inducting René Rémond into the Académie Française on November 4, 1999, would mention that aspect of the new member's career, declaring: "You were behind the creation of the Institut d'Histoire du Temps Présent, for which you served as president from its creation in 1979 until 1990." Rémond and d'Encausse, *Discours de réception de René Rémond à l'Académie Française et réponse d'Hélène Carrère d'Encausse* (Paris: Fayard, 2000), 47. The information also appears in the official biographical note on the Académie Française Web site: http://www.academie-francaise.fr/les-immortels/rene-remond. The praise is in large part deserved, apart from the fact that the position of "president of the IHTP" never existed: during that period, the organization had only a director, in the person of François Bédarida.

63. François Bédarida, *La stratégie secrète de la Drôle de guerre: Le Conseil suprême interallié, septembre 1939-avril 1940* (Paris: Presses de la FNSP/Éditions du CNRS, 1979).

64. Cf. Michel Winock, *Histoire politique de la revue "Esprit," 1930-1950* (Paris: Éditions du Seuil, 1975), 141; and Martine Sevegrand, *"Temps présent," une aventure chrétienne, 1937-1992* (Paris: Éditions du Temps Présent, 2006).

65. François Bédarida, *Histoire, critique et responsabilité*, ed. Gabrielle Muc, Henry Rousso, and Michel Trebitsch (Brussels: Complexe/Paris: IHTP, 2003). I might also mention the seminar Bédarida conducted between 1980 and 1985 titled "Past Historiography and Present Time" at the École Normale Supérieure and the EHESS (recordings and transcription available at the library of the IHTP, SEM 001-0038). See also Christian Delacroix, "L'histoire du temps présent au risque de la demande sociale," in *Concurrence des passés: Usages politiques du passé dans la France contemporaine*, ed. Maryline Crivello, Patrick Garcia, and Nicolas Offenstadt (Aix-en-Provence: Presses Universitaires de Provence, 2006), 271-82.

66. That was the substance of my debate with Gérard Noiriel in 1999-2000, following the publication of his *Les origines républicaines de Vichy*: see "L'histoire du temps présent, hier et aujourd'hui," special issue, *Bulletin de l'IHTP* 75 (July 2000): 23-40, http://www.ihtp.cnrs.fr/spip

/php%Frubrique90.html. The same disagreement lies behind the quarrels between the association Liberté pour l'Histoire, headed by Rémond and later by Nora, which I joined some time after its creation in 2005, and the Comité de Vigilance Face aux Usages Publics de l'Histoire (CVUH) on the subject of the so-called memorial laws.

67. Article 2 of the decision of September 26, 1978, signed by Robert Chabbal, general director of the CNRS, quoted in several documents, especially "Réflexions et perspectives sur l'IHTP," July 8, 1985, personal archives of Henry Rousso.

68. Henry Rousso, *Vichy, l'événement, la mémoire, l'histoire* (Paris: Gallimard, 2001), 32–33.

69. Claude Langlois and Roger Chartier, "Les historiens et l'organisation de la recherche (histoire moderne et contemporaine)," report compiled at the request of Maurice Garden, Direction de la Recherche, Ministère de l'Éducation Nationale, Paris, September 1991, IHTP library, 19.

70. Cf. René Rémond, "L'histoire contemporaine," in *L'histoire et le métier d'historien en France, 1945–1995*, ed. François Bédarida (Paris: Éditions de la Maison des Sciences de l'Homme, 1995), 247–51; and Philippe Poirrier, "L'histoire contemporaine," in *Les historiens français à l'oeuvre 1995–2010*, ed. Jean-François Sirinelli, Pascal Cauchy, and Claude Gauvard (Paris: Presses Universitaires de France, 2010), 73–91.

CHAPTER FOUR

1. Jean-François Lyotard, *The Postmodern Explained: Correspondence, 1982–1985*, trans. Don Barry et al., translation edited by Julian Pefanis and Morgan Thomas (Minneapolis: University of Minnesota Press, 1993; 1st ed. Galilée, 1986), 28–29.

2. Gérard Noiriel, *Sur la "crise" de l'histoire* (Paris: Gallimard, 2005; 1st. ed. Belin, 1996), 167.

3. Hartog, *Régimes d'historicité*, 18.

4. Tocqueville, *De la démocratie en Amérique* (1840), vol. 2, chap. 8, quoted in Arendt, *Between Past and Present*, 7.

5. I have developed some of these points in *La hantise du passé* (*The Haunting Past*).

6. Cf. Henry Rousso, "L'histoire appliquée ou les historiens thaumaturges," *Vingtième siècle: Revue d'histoire* 1 (January–March 1984): 105–21, translated as "Applied History, or the Historian as Miracle-Worker," *Public Historian* 4 (Fall 1984): 65–85..

7. Cf. Roy Rozenberg and David Thelen, *The Presence of the Past: Popular Uses of History in American Life* (New York: Columbia University Press, 1998); Paul Ashton and Paula Hamilton, *History at the Crossroads: Australians and the Past* (Sydney: Halstead, 2010); Jocelyn Létourneau and David Northrup, "Québecois et Canadiens face au passé: Similitudes et dissemblances," *Canadian Historical Review* 92, no. 1 (March 2011): 163–96. On that question, see also the online journal *Histoire engagée*, histoireengagee.ca.

8. Cf. Peter Seixas, ed., *Theorizing Historical Consciousness* (Toronto: University of Toronto Press, 2004), the Centre for the Study of Historical Consciousness at the University of British Columbia, and the journal *Narration, Identity, and Historical Consciousness*.

9. Cf. Gilson Pôrto Jr., ed., *História do tempo presente* (Bauru: Editora da Universidade do Sagrado Coração, 2007); the História do Tempo Presente seminar at the Universidade do Estado de Santa Catarina, which publishes the journal *Tempo et argumento*, edited, notably, by Silvia Maria Favero Arend; and the review *Cadernos do tempo presente* from the Universidade Federal de Sergipe. The international colloquium "Present Time and Contemporaneity," held by the IHTP in Paris on March 24–26, 2011, provided a glimpse of the vitality of the history of the present time in Argentina, Brazil, Chile, and Guatemala. That aspect is the object of a special issue of the online journal *Conserveries mémorielles*, 2013, http://cm.revues.org/index.html.

10. See the remarkable overview by Anne Pérotin-Dumon: *Historizar el Pasado vivo en América Latina* (2007), http://etica.uahurtado.cl/historizarelpasadovivo/es_home.html. For Spain, see

among others Josefina Cuesta, *Historia del presente* (Logroño [La Rioja]: Eudema Universidad, 1993); and Julio Aróstegui Sánchez, *La historia vivida* (Madrid: Ed. Alianza, 2004).

11. This is particularly true of Pierre Laborie, who uses the expression in *Les Français des années troubles: De la guerre d'Espagne à la Libération* (Paris: Desclée de Brouwer, 2001), 8.

12. See especially his articles in *Cahiers d'histoire immédiate* and his *L'histoire immédiate* (Paris: Presses Universitaires de France, 1994) and *L'histoire immédiate: Historiographie, sources et méthodes* (Paris: Armand Colin, 2009).

13. Pervillé, "L'histoire immédiate," 6. On the various labels for contemporary history, see the roundtable discussion held by the IHTP on April 2, 2009, with Philippe Bourdin, Guy Pervillé, Henry Rousso, and Jean-François Sirinelli, facilitated by Patrick Garcia, www.ihtp.cnrs.fr/spip.php%Farticle791.html.

14. William Safire, *Safire's Political Dictionary* (London: Oxford University Press, 1972), 349.

15. Vincent Descombes, "Qu'est-ce qu'être contemporain?," in "Actualités du contemporain," special issue, *Le genre humain* (February 2000): 21–32, at 30–31.

16. Giorgio Agamben, "What Is the Contemporary?" in Agamben, *What Is an Apparatus? and Other Essays*, trans. David Kishik and Stefan Pedatella (Stanford, Calif.: Stanford University Press, 2009), 40 [translation modified], commenting on the second of Nietzsche's *Untimely Meditations*.

17. Marc Augé, *Pour une anthropologie des mondes contemporains* (Paris: Flammarion, 1997; 1st ed. Aubier, 1994), 11. See also Gérard Althabe, Daniel Fabre, and Gérard Lenclud, *Vers une ethnologie du temps présent* (Paris: Éditions de la Maison des Sciences de l'Homme, 1992), and Marc Abelès's writings.

18. Gérard Lenclud, "Observation ethnographique, observation historique," in *La culture, l'esprit: Anthropologie, histoire, psychologie* (Paris: Éditions de l'École des Hautes Études en Sciences Sociales, 2012).

19. Jean Lacouture, "L'histoire immédiate," in Le Goff, Chartier, and Revel, eds., *La nouvelle histoire*, 282.

20. Cf. Pieter Lagrou, "Réflexions sur le rapport néerlandais du NIOD: Logique académique et culture du consensus," in "Srebrenica 1995: Analyse croisée des enquêtes et des rapports," special issue, *Culture & conflits: Sociologie politique de l'international* 65 (2007): 63–79.

21. Christian Bachelier, *La SNCF sous l'Occupation allemande, 1940–1944: Rapport documentaire*, 4 vols. (Paris: IHTP, [1998]). A part of this report (minus the appendices) for which I was responsible is available at the Web site of the Association pour l'Histoire des Chemins de Fer en France, http://www.ahicf.com/une-entreprise-publique-dans-la-guerre-la-sncf-1939-1945,52.

22. "Histoire de France" series, general editors Joël Cornette, Jean-Louis Biget, and Henry Rousso (Paris: Belin, 2009–2012). I have chosen as my criterion the number of volumes for each period, which was a deliberate choice made by the general editors of the series, rather than the number of pages, which varies by the particular author's style and intrinsic choices.

23. Wolfgang Benz, Alfred Haverkamp, and Wolfgang Reinhard, eds., *Gebhardt: Handbuch der deutschen Geschichte*, 24 vols. (Stuttgart: Klett-Cotta, 2004–12). The series bears the name of a German historian, author of textbooks in the late nineteenth century.

24. On the delays in gaining access to the archives considered in other than simply political or administrative terms, see Angelika Menne-Haritz, "Die Verwaltung und ihre Archive: Überlegungen zur Latenz von Zeit in der Verwaltungsarbeit," *Verwaltung & Management* 5, no. 1 (1999): 4–10, English version: "Thoughts on the Latency of Time in Administrative Work and the Role Archives Play to Make it Visible," http://www.staff.uni-marburg.de/~mennehar/publikationen/latency.pdf.

25. Within a vast body of literature, see the lucid exposition by Sophie Coeuré and Vincent Duclert, which approaches the question from a comparative perspective: *Les archives* (Paris: La Découverte, 2001).

26. Jean-Pierre Rioux, "Présentation," *Vingtième siècle: Revue d'histoire* 69 (January 2001): 3–5.

The last sentence has a footnote to René Rémond, *Regard sur le siècle* (Paris: Presses de Sciences Po, 2000) and to Zaki Laïdi, *Le sacre du présent* (Paris: Flammarion, 2000).

27. Fabrice d'Almeida, *Brève histoire du XXIe siècle* (Paris: Perrin, 2007).

28. Eric Hobsbawm, *The Age of Extremes: The Short Twentieth Century, 1914–1991* (London: Michael Joseph, 1994).

29. See especially the writings of the IHTP, particularly those of François Bédarida, already cited, as well as Voldman, ed., "La bouche de la vérité? La recherche historique et les sources orales."

30. Arlette Farge, *Le goût de l'archive* (Paris: Éditions du Seuil, 1989).

31. Hans-Christian Schmid's recent film *Storm* (2009) illustrates this phenomenon very well. It runs through all the postures of the witness before the International Criminal Tribunal for the Former Yugoslavia in The Hague.

32. On the film *Shoah*, see, within a vast body of literature, the deconstructive study by Rémy Besson, "La mise en récit de *Shoah*" (Ph.D. diss., École des Hautes Études en Sciences Sociales, 2012), which analyzes in detail the editing of the film.

33. Renée David, *Traces indélébiles: Mémoires incertaines*, preface by Raymond Aubrac (Paris: L'Harmattan, 2008).

34. I have written at length on this affair in *La hantise du passé*. For a rather unbiased analysis, see Susan Rubin Suleiman, *Crises of Memory and the Second World War* (Cambridge, Mass.: Harvard University Press, 2006), chapter 2.

35. David, *Traces indélébiles*, 13.

36. Fustel de Coulanges, *Questions d'histoire*; see above, chapter 1.

37. Raymond Aron, *Dimensions de la conscience historique* (Paris: Plon, 1964), 100–101.

38. Antoine Prost, "Pour une histoire sociale du temps présent," in Institut d'Histoire du Temps Présent, *Écrire l'histoire du temps présent: En hommage à François Bédarida* (Paris: Éditions du CNRS, 1993), 359.

39. Benjamin, "Theses on the Philosophy of History," thesis 7, p. 256.

40. Peter Catterall, "What (If Anything) Is Distinctive about Contemporary History?" *Journal of Contemporary History* 32, no. 4 (1997): 441–52, at 441–42.

41. Program of July 19, 1957. Cf. Garcia and Leduc, *L'enseignement de l'histoire en France*, 200–205.

42. Fernand Braudel, with Suzanne Baille and Robert Philippe, *Le monde actuel* (Paris: Belin, 1963). The part on civilizations was reissued under the title *Grammaire des civilisations* (Paris: Arthaud, 1987). Cf. Jacques Bouillon, Pierre Sorlin, and Jean Rudel, *Le monde contemporain: Histoire, civilisations* (Paris: Bordas, 1968). This is the book I had in my senior year at the Lycée Florent-Schmitt in Saint-Cloud in 1971–1972. I have only a fuzzy memory of it. But I have not forgotten M. Wagner, the young teacher who had the presence of mind to forget the textbook and the curriculum and to teach us living twentieth-century history. He advised me to pursue this discipline, and I would like to pay tribute to him in this note. Incidentally, in 2005 the name of the Lycée Florent-Schmitt was changed to the Lycée Alexandre-Dumas. It was renamed after several years of polemics, when it was (re)discovered that the musician Florent Schmitt, a resident of Saint-Cloud for a time, had been pro-Nazi, honorary president of the music branch of the Groupe Collaboration during the Occupation. The publication of *La vie musicale sous Vichy* (2001) by the Institut d'Histoire du Temps Présent (I was its director at the time) and Éditions Complexe, a collection edited by the musicologist and historian Myriam Chimènes, seems to have accelerated matters.

43. Tony Judt, *Postwar: A History of Europe since 1945* (New York: Penguin, 2005).

44. Tony Judt, "Rethinking Post-War Europe," *IWMpost* (Institut für die Wissenschaften von Menschen, Vienna), 104 (April–August 2010): 4.

45. See especially François Bédarida, "Penser la Seconde Guerre mondiale," in *Penser le XXe siècle*, ed. André Versaille (Brussels: Complexe, 1990), 115–38, repr. in Bédarida, *Histoire, critique et*

responsabilité, 93-110; Jean-Pierre Azéma, "La Second Guerre mondiale, matrice du temps présent," in Institut d'Histoire du Temps Présent, *Écrire l'histoire du temps présent,* 147-52.

46. Gonzague de Reynolds, "Où va l'Europe?" *La revue universelle,* August 15, 1938. My thanks to Fabien Théofilakis for bringing this text to my attention.

47. Cf. Stéphane Audoin-Rouzeau, Annette Becker, Christian Ingrao, and Henry Rousso, eds., *La violence de guerre, 1914-1945: Approches comparées des deux conflits mondiaux* (Brussels: Complexe; Paris: IHTP, 2002).

48. On that aspect, see the pioneering studies by Jean-Jacques Becker, and those published by the staff at the Historial de la Grande Guerre in Péronne, which opened in 1992, particularly Stéphane Audoin-Rouzeau and Annette Becker, *14-18: Retrouver la guerre* (Paris: Gallimard, 2000).

49. See especially Mosse, *Fallen Soldiers.*

50. Cf. Terkel, *"The Good War."*

51. Thomas L. Friedman, "The End of the West?" *New York Times,* November 2, 2003.

52. See the Web site of the ZZF, http://www.zzf-pdm.de, accessed April 2, 2012. In the pages written in French, the ZZF is called the "Centre de Recherche sur l'Histoire du Temps Présent"; [in those written in English, it is the "Centre for Contemporary History"].

CONCLUSION

1. Ricoeur, *La mémoire, l'histoire, l'oubli,* 26.

2. For the beginning of an explanation, at least a circumstantial one, see Dosse, *Pierre Nora.*

3. Michel Foucault, "La fonction politique de l'intellectuel," *Politique-Hebdo,* November 29, 1976, repr. in *Dits et écrits 1954-1988,* vol. 3, *1976-1979,* ed. Daniel Defert and François Ewald with the collaboration of Jacques Lagrange (Paris: Gallimard, 1994), 109-14. Zygmunt Bauman, *Legislators and Interpreters: On Modernity, Postmodernity, and Intellectuals* (Ithaca, N.Y.: Cornell University Press, 1988).

4. Here I have adopted a hypothesis formulated a few years ago within the context of a reflection on patrimony: introduction to *Le regard de l'histoire: L'émergence et l'évolution de la notion de patrimoine au cours du XXe siècle en France,* ed. Henry Rousso (Paris: Fayard-Monum, Éditions du Patrimoine, 2003), proceedings of the "Entretiens du Patrimoine" conference, 2001. This text has been reprinted in Vincent Auzas and Bogumil Jewsiewicki, eds., *Traumatisme collectif pour patrimoine: Regards sur un mouvement transnational* (Quebec: Les Presses de l'Université Laval, 2008), 13-21.

5. Samuel Pisar, "Auschwitz parle encore aux juifs et aux musulmans," *Le Monde,* January 28, 2012. This article was published on the occasion of the International Day of Commemoration in Memory of the Victims of the Holocaust.

6. Cf. *Le Monde,* April 18, 2012. My thanks to Anne Pérotin-Dumon for drawing my attention to this article within the context of a seminar I conducted at the IHTP in 2011-12 on the relationship between history and justice.

7. Cf. Martin Broszat, "A Plea for the Historicization of National Socialism" (77-87), and Saul Friedländer's reply, "Some Reflections on the Historicization of National Socialism" (88-101), in *Reworking the Past: Hitler, the Holocaust, and the Historians' Debate,* ed. Peter Baldwin (Boston: Beacon, 1990). See also the published correspondence between the two historians: Martin Broszat and Saul Friedländer, "A Controversy about the Historicization of National Socialism," *New German Critique* 44 (Spring–Summer 1988): 85-126.

8. Friedländer, "Some Reflections on the Historicization of National Socialism," 52.

9. François Bédarida and Jean-Pierre Azéma, eds., with Denis Peschanski and Henry Rousso, *Le régime de Vichy et les Français* (Paris: Fayard/IHTP, 1992).

Bibliography

This bibliography lists the references cited in the text, as well as a selection of texts (including some new references for the English-language edition) that reflects the intellectual environment within which this book was conceived. It is also meant to be a working tool and has been divided into three parts to simplify matters: (1) general historical, historiographical, or epistemological studies, as well as texts belonging to the philosophy of history or on history; (2) references on the specific question of contemporaneity and on the definition and practice of a history of the present time, and titles on the history of the twentieth and twenty-first centuries that situate the context for its emergence or which played a particular role in its development, regardless of their intrinsic interest; and (3) a limited selection of texts (from a now substantial international bibliography) on the question of testimony, memory, trauma, and the uses of the past.

THINKING ABOUT HISTORY

Agamben, Giorgio, "What Is the Contemporary?" In *What Is an Apparatus? and Other Essays*, translated by David Kishik and Stefan Pedatella. Stanford, Calif.: Stanford University Press, 2009.

Aït-Touati, Frédérique. *Contes de la Lune: Essai sur la fiction et la science modernes*. Paris: Gallimard, 2011.

Alembert, Jean Le Rond d'. *Réflexions sur l'histoire, lues à l'Académie Française dans la séance publique du 19 janvier 1761*. In *Oeuvres complètes de d'Alembert*. 4 vols. Paris: A. Belin, 1821–22. Vol. 2, part 1: 1–10, online edition by Guido Abbattista, *Cyber Review of Modern Historiography* (January 1997), http://www.eliohs.unifi.it/testi/700/alemb/reflect.html.

Appleby, Joyce, Lynn Hunt, and Margaret Jacob. *Telling the Truth about History*. New York: Norton, 1994.

Arendt, Hannah. *Between Past and Future: Six Exercises in Political Thought*. New York: Viking, 1961.

———. *The Origins of Totalitarianism*. New York: Harcourt, Brace & World, 1966.

———. "Understanding and Politics (The Difficulties of Understanding)." In Arendt, *Essays on Understanding, 1930–1954*, 307–26. New York: Harcourt, Brace, 1994.

Aron, Raymond. *Dimensions de la conscience historique*. Paris: Plon, 1964.

———. *Leçons sur l'histoire: Cours du Collège de France*. Edited by Sylvie Mesure. Paris: Fallois, 1989.

Barret-Kriegel, Blandine. *Les historiens et la monarchie*. 4 vols. Paris: Presses Universitaires de France, 1988.

Bauman, Zygmunt. *Legislators and Interpreters: On Modernity, Postmodernity, and Intellectuals.* Ithaca, N.Y.: Cornell University Press, 1988.

Benjamin, Walter. "Theses on the Philosophy of History." In Benjamin, *Illuminations*, translated by Harry Zohn, 253–64. New York: Schocken, 1968.

Benz, Wolfgang, Alfred Haverkamp, Jürgen Kocka, and Wolfgang Reinhard, eds. *Gebhardt: Handbuch der deutschen Geschichte.* 24 vols. Stuttgart: Klett-Cotta, 2004–12.

Berger, Stefan, ed. *Writing the Nation: A Global Perspective.* New York: Palgrave Macmillan, 2007.

Berger, Stefan, Mark Donovan, and Kevin Passmore, eds. *Writing National Histories: Western Europe since 1800.* New York: Routledge, 1999.

Bloch, Marc. *Apologie pour l'histoire.* Edited by Étienne Bloch. With a preface by Jacques Le Goff. Paris: Armand Colin, 1997 [1st ed. *Apologie pour l'histoire ou Métier d'historien* (1949), with a preface by Lucien Febvre titled "Comment se présentent les manuscrits du *Métier d'historien*"].

———. *Histoire et historiens.* Edited by Étienne Bloch. Paris: Armand Colin, 1995.

Bonnaud, Robert. *Y a-t-il des tournants historiques mondiaux?* Paris: Kimé, 1992.

Bourdé, Guy, and Hervé Martin. *Les écoles historiques.* Paris: Éditions du Seuil, 1990 [1st ed. 1983].

Bouton, Christophe, and Bruce Bégout, eds. *Penser l'histoire: De Karl Marx aux siècles des catastrophes.* Paris: Éditions de l'Éclat, 2011.

Braudel, Fernand. *Écrits sur l'histoire.* Paris: Arthaud, 1990.

———. *Les ambitions de l'histoire.* Edited by Roselyne de Ayala and Paule Braudel. With a preface by Maurice Aymard. Paris: Éditions de Fallois, 1997.

Burguière, André, ed. *Dictionnaire des sciences historiques.* Paris: Presses Universitaires de France, 1986.

———. *L'École des Annales: Une histoire intellectuelle.* Paris: Odile Jacob, 2006.

Carbonell, Charles-Olivier. *Histoire et historiens: Une mutation idéologique des historiens français, 1865–1885.* Toulouse: Privat, 1976.

Carbonell, Charles-Olivier, and Jean Walch, eds., with Roland Marx and Laurent Cesari. *Les sciences historiques: De l'Antiquité à nos jours.* Paris: Larousse, 1994.

Carr, Edward Hallett. *What Is History? The Georges Macaulay Trevelyan Lectures Delivered in the University of Cambridge.* Harmondsworth: Penguin, 1961.

Certeau, Michel de. *L'écriture de l'histoire.* Paris: Gallimard, 1975; Folio Histoire, 2002.

Chateaubriand, François-René de. *Mémoires d'Outre-tombe,* preface by Julien Gracq, introduction, notes, and commentary by Pierre Clarac, revised and corrected by Gérard Gengembre. Paris: Librairie Générale Française, 1999 [1st ed. Liège, 1849].

Chesneaux, Jean. *Habiter le temps: Passé, présent, futur: Esquisse d'un dialogue politique.* Paris: Bayard, 1996.

Cicero. *De oratore.* Translated by E. W. Sutton. Cambridge, Mass.: Harvard University Press, 1942.

Collingwood, Robin George. *Essays in the Philosophy of History.* Edited by William Debbins. New York: McGraw-Hill, 1966.

Cornette, Joël, Jean-Louis Biget, and Henry Rousso, eds. "Histoire de France" series. Paris: Belin, 2009–12.

Correard, Nicolas. "L'hypothèse scientifique comme fabrique de la fiction: Poétiques du discours astronomique au XVIIe siècle." In "Écritures du savoir," special issue, *Acta Fabula*, http://www.fabula.org/revue/document6947.php.

Croce, Benedetto. *Theory and History of Historiography.* Translated by Douglas Ainslie. London: G. C. Harrap, 1921 [originally published in reviews in 1912–13].

Darbo-Peschanski, Catherine. *L'Historia: Commencements grecs.* Paris: Gallimard, 2007.

———. "La politique de l'histoire: Thucydide historien du présent." *Annales ESC* 3 (May–June 1898): 653–75.

Delacroix, Christian, François Dosse, and Patrick Garcia. *Les courants historiques en France XIXe–XXe siècle,* revised and augmented edition. Paris: Gallimard, 2007 [1st. ed. Armand Colin, 1999].

Delacroix, Christian, François Dosse, and Patrick Garcia, eds. *Historicités*. Paris: La Découverte, 2009.

Delacroix, Christian, François Dosse, Patrick Garcia, and Nicolas Offenstadt, eds. *Historiographies: Concepts et débats*. 2 vols. Paris: Gallimard, 2010.

Delacroix, Christian, François Dosse, Patrick Garcia, and Michel Trebitsch, eds. *Michel de Certeau: Les chemins d'histoire*. Brussels: Complexe; Paris: IHTP, 2002.

Despoix, Philippe, and Peter Schöttler, eds. *Kracauer, penseur de l'histoire*. Quebec: Presses de l'Université Laval; Paris: Presses de la Maison des Sciences de l'Homme, 2006.

Dosse, François. *L'histoire en miettes: Des "Annales" à la "nouvelle histoire."* Paris: La Découverte, 1978; Pocket, 1997.

———. *Paul Ricoeur, Michel de Certeau: L'histoire entre le dire et le faire*. Paris: L'Herne, 2006.

———. *Pierre Nora: Homo historicus*. Paris: Perrin, 2011.

———. *Renaissance de l'événement: Un défi pour l'historien; Entre sphinx et phénix*. Paris: Presses Universitaires de France, 2010.

Droysen, Johann Gustav. *Outline of the Principles of History (Grundriss der Historik)*. Translated by E. Benjamin Andrews. Boston: Ginn, 1893 [1st ed. 1858].

Dumoulin, Oliver. "Histoire et historiens de droite." In *Histoire des Droites*, edited by Jean-François Sirinelli. Vol. 2, *Cultures*, 327–89. Paris: Gallimard, 1992.

———. *Le rôle social de l'historien: De la chaire au prétoire*. Paris: Albin Michel, 2003.

Dupuy, Jean-Pierre. *Pour un catastrophisme éclairé: Quand l'impossible est certain*. Paris: Éditions du Seuil, 2002.

Evans, Richard J. *In Defence of History*. London: Granta, 1997.

Farge, Arlette. *Le goût de l'archive*. Paris: Éditions du Seuil, 1989.

Febvre, Lucien. *Combats pour l'histoire*. Paris: Armand Colin, 1992 [1st ed. 1952].

———. "L'histoire dans le monde en ruines." *Revue de synthèse historique* 30, no. 4 (February–June 1920): 1–15.

Force, Pierre. *L'herméneutique chez Pascal*. Paris: Vrin, 1989.

Foucault, Michel. "La fonction politique de l'intellectuel." *Politique-Hebdo*, November 29, 1976, repr. in *Dits et écrits 1954-1988*, vol. 3, *1976-1979*, edited by Daniel Defert and François Ewald with Jacques Lagrange, 109-14. Paris: Gallimard, 1994.

———. *The Order of Things: An Archaeology of the Human Sciences*. New York: Vintage, 1973 [1st ed. 1966].

Fustel de Coulanges, Numa-Denys. "Leçon inaugurale en Sorbonne" (1875). In François Hartog, *Le XIXe siècle et l'histoire: Le cas Fustel de Coulanges*, 341-42. Paris: Presses Universitaires de France, 1988.

———. *Questions d'histoire*. Paris: Hachette, 1893.

Gauchet, Marcel. *La condition historique: Entretiens avec François Azouvi et Sylvain Piron*. Paris: Gallimard, 2005.

———, ed. *Philosophie des sciences historiques: Le moment romantique*. Paris: Éditions du Seuil, 2002.

Goetz, Hanz-Werner. "Historical Consciousness and Institutional Concern in European Medieval Historiography (11th and 12th Centuries)." Paper delivered at the Nineteenth International Congress of Historical Sciences, Oslo, August 6-13, 2000, theme 3: "The Uses and Abuses of History and Responsibility of the Historian, Past and Present," http://www.oslo2000.uio.no /program/papers/m3a/m3a-goetz.pdf, accessed in March 2011.

Goody, Jack. *The Theft of History*. New York: Cambridge University Press, 2006.

Goulemot, Jean-Marie. *Le règne de l'histoire: Discours historiques et révolutions XVIIe–XVIIIe siècles*. Paris: Albin Michel, 1996.

Guenée, Bernard. *Histoire et culture historique dans l'Occident médiéval*. Paris: Aubier-Montaigne, 1980.

Halphen, Louis. *L'histoire en France depuis cent ans*. Paris: Armand Colin, 1914.

Hartog, François. *Évidence de l'histoire: Ce que voient les historiens*. Paris: Gallimard, 2005.

——. *Le XIXe siècle et l'histoire: Le cas Fustel de Coulanges*. Paris: Gallimard, 1988.

——. *Le miroir d'Hérodote: Essai sur la représentation de l'autre*. Paris: Gallimard, 2001.

——. *Régimes d'historicité: Présentisme et expériences du temps*. Paris: Éditions du Seuil, 2003.

——, ed. *L'histoire d'Homère à Augustin: Préfaces des historiens et textes sur l'histoire*. Texts translated by Michel Casevitz. Paris: Éditions du Seuil, 1999.

Hartog, François, and Gérard Lenclud. "Régimes d'historicité." In *L'état des lieux en sciences sociales*, edited by Alexandru Dutu and Norbert Dodille, 18-38. Paris: L'Harmattan, 1993.

Hauser, Henri. "Un comité international d'enquête sur l'histoire des prix." *Annales d'histoire économique et sociale* 2, no. 7 (1930): 384-85.

Herodotus. *The Histories*. Translated by Robin Waterfield. With an introduction and notes by Caroline Dewald. Oxford: Oxford University Press, 1998.

Horace. *Odes*. Translated by James Michie. With the Latin text and an introduction by Rex Warner. New York: Orion, 1963.

Humboldt, Wilhelm von. "On the Historian's Task." *History and Theory* 6, no. 1 (1967): 57-71 [translation of "Über die Aufgabe des Geschichtschreibers" (1821)].

Koselleck, Reinhart. "Le concept d'histoire." In *L'expérience de l'histoire*, edited with a preface by Michael Werner, translated into French by Alexandre Esudier with Diane Meur, Marie-Claire Hoock, and Jochen Hoock, 15-99. Paris: École des Hautes Études en Sciences Sociales / Gallimard / Seuil, 1997 [Translation of "Geschichte." In *Geschichtliche Grundbegriffe: Historisches Lexikon zur politish-sozialen Sprache in Deutschland*, edited by O. Brunner, W. Conze, and R. Koselleck, vol. 2. Stuttgart: Ernst Klett, 1975].

——. *Futures Past: On the Semantics of Historical Time*. Translated by Keith Tribe. Cambridge, Mass.: MIT Press, 1985 [1st ed. Frankfurt am Main, 1979].

——. *Zeitgeschichten: Studien zur Historik*. Frankfurt am Main: Suhrkamp, 2000.

Kracauer, Siegfried, with Paul Oskar Kristeller. *History: The Last Things before the Last*. New York: Oxford University Press, 1969.

Langlois, Charles-Victor, and Charles Seignobos. *Introduction aux études historiques*. With a preface by Madeleine Rebérioux. Paris: Kimé, 1992 [1st ed. 1897].

Laurentin, Emmanuel, ed. *À quoi sert l'histoire aujourd'hui*. Paris: Bayard/France-Culture, 2010.

Lavisse, Ernest, ed. *Histoire de France depuis les origines jusqu'à la Révolution*. 18 vols. Paris: Hachette, 1903-1911; Éditions des Équateurs, 2009-.

——, ed. *Histoire de la France contemporaine depuis la Révolution jusqu'à la paix de 1919*. 9 vols. Paris: Hachette, 1920-22.

Le Goff, Jacques. *Pour un autre Moyen Âge: Temps, travail et culture en Occident; 18 essais*. Paris: Gallimard, 1977 [repr. in *Un autre Moyen Âge* (Paris: Gallimard, 1999)].

——. *Saint Louis*. Paris: Gallimard, 1996 [repr. in *Héros du Moyen Âge, le saint et le roi* (Paris: Gallimard, 2004)].

Le Goff, Jacques, Roger Chartier, and Jacques Revel, eds. *La Nouvelle Histoire*. Paris: Retz, 1978.

Le Goff, Jacques, and Pierre Nora, eds. *Faire de l'histoire: Nouveaux problèmes, nouvelles approches, nouveaux objets*. 3 vols. Paris: Gallimard, 1974 [2011].

Leduc, Jean. *Les historiens et le temps: Conceptions problématiques, écritures*. Paris: Éditions du Seuil, 1999.

Lenclud, Gérard. *La culture, l'esprit: Anthropologie, histoire, psychologie*. Paris: Éditions de l'École des Hautes Études en Sciences Sociales, 2012.

——. "Traversée dans le temps." *Actes de la recherche en sciences sociales* 5 (September 2006): 1053-84.

Le Roy Ladurie, Emmanuel. *Montaillou, village occitan de 1294 à 1324*. Paris: Gallimard, 1975 [new eds. 1982, 1985].

Leterrier, Sophie-Anne. *Le XIXe siècle historien: Anthologie raisonnée*. Paris: Belin, 1997.

"L'histoire anachronique." Special issue, *Les temps modernes* 410 (September 1980).

Löwy, Michael. *Walter Benjamin: Avertissement d'incendie; Une lecture des thèses "Sur le concept d'histoire."* Paris: Presses Universitaires de France, 2001.

Lyotard, Jean-François. *The Postmodern Explained: Correspondence, 1982-1985.* Translated by Don Barry et al. Translation edited by Julian Pefanis and Morgan Thomas. Minneapolis: University of Minnesota Press, 1993 [1st ed. Paris, 1986].

Machiavelli, Niccolò. *Florentine Histories.* Translated by Laura F. Banfield and Harvey C. Mansfield Jr. Princeton, N.J.: Princeton University Press, 1988.

Mallarmé, Stéphane. *Divagations.* In *Igitur; Divagations; Un coup de dés,* edited by Bertrand Marchal. Paris: Gallimard, 2003 [1st ed. 1897].

Marin, Louis. *Pascal et Port-Royal.* Edited by Alain Cantillon et al. Paris: Presses Universitaires de France, 1997.

Marrou, Henri-Irénée. *De la connaissance historique.* Paris: Éditions du Seuil, 1954.

Mercier, Louis-Sébastien. *Du théâtre ou Nouvel essai sur l'art dramatique.* Amsterdam: E. van Harrevelt, 1773.

Momigliano, Arnaldo. *The Classic Foundations of Modern Historiography.* With a foreword by Riccardo Di Donato. Berkeley and Los Angeles: University of California Press, 1990.

Moses, Stéphane. *L'ange de l'histoire: Rosenzweig, Benjamin, Scholem.* Paris: Éditions du Seuil, 1992.

Nietzsche, Friedrich. *Untimely Meditations.* Edited by Daniel Breazeale. Translated by R. J. Hollingdale. New York: Cambridge University Press.

Noiriel, Gérard. *Sur la "crise" de l'histoire.* Paris: Gallimard, 2005. [1st ed. Belin, 1996].

Nora, Pierre, ed. *Les lieux de mémoire.* 7 vols. Paris: Gallimard, 1984-93.

Novick, Peter. *That Noble Dream: The "Objectivity Question" and the American Historical Profession.* Cambridge: Cambridge University Press, 1988.

Paravicini, Werner. "Nietzsche et les sciences historiques: Autour de la Deuxième considération intempestive." *Francia* (Institut Historique allemand de Paris) 29, no. 3 (2002): 151-91.

Pascal, Blaise de. *Pensées.* In *Oeuvres complètes,* with a preface by Henri Gouhier, introduction and notes by Louis Lafuma. Paris: Éditions du Seuil, 1963.

Potočka, Jan. *Essais hérétiques: Sur la philosophie de l'histoire.* Translated by Erika Abrams. With a preface by Paul Ricoeur and an afterword by Roman Jacobson. Paris: Verdier, 2007 [1st ed. 1975].

Plumb, John H. *The Death of the Past.* Boston: Houghton Mifflin, 1969.

Polybius. *Histoire.* Edited by François Hartog. Translated by Denis Roussel. Paris: Gallimard, 2003.

——. *Histories.* Translated by W. R. Paton. 6 vols. London: William Heinemann, 1922-27.

Pomian, Krzysztof. *L'ordre du temps.* Paris: Gallimard, 1984.

——. *Sur l'histoire.* Paris: Gallimard, 1999 [especially "L'histoire de la science et l'histoire de l'histoire," 121-59, repr. from *Annales ESC* 5 (1975)].

Prost, Antoine. "Comment l'histoire fait-elle l'historien?" *Vingtième siècle: Revue d'histoire* 65 (January-March 2000): 3-12.

——. *Douze leçons sur l'histoire.* Paris: Éditions du Seuil, 1996.

Raulff, Ulrich. *Ein Historiker im 20. Jahrhundert: Marc Bloch.* Frankfurt am Main: Fischer, 1995 [*Marc Bloch: Un historien au XXe siècle,* translated by Olivier Mannoni (Paris: Éditions de l'École des Hautes Études en Sciences Sociales, 2005)].

Ricoeur, Paul. *Histoire et vérité.* Paris: Éditions du Seuil, 1957.

——. *Temps et récit.* 3 vols. Paris: Éditions du Seuil, 1983-1985.

Rüsen, Jörn, *History: Narration, Interpretation, Orientation.* New York: Berghahn, 2005.

——, ed. *Meaning and Representation in History.* New York: Berghahn, 2006.

Seignobos, Charles. *La méthode historique appliquée aux sciences sociales.* Paris: Felix Alcan, 1909.

Seixas, Peter, ed. *Theorizing Historical Consciousness.* Toronto: University of Toronto Press, 2004.

Semprun, Jorge. *Mal et modernité.* Paris: Éditions du Seuil, 1997.

Thucydides. *The War of the Peloponnesians and the Athenians.* Edited and translated by Jeremy Mynott. Cambridge: Cambridge University Press, 2013.

Todorov, Tzvetan, *Devoirs et délices: Une vie de passeur, entretiens avec Catherine Portevin.* Paris: Éditions du Seuil, 2002.

———. *Le siècle des totalitarismes.* Paris: Robert Laffont, 2010 [includes, notably, *Face à l'extrême* (Éditions du Seuil, 1991) and *Mémoire du mal, tentation du bien* (Robert Laffont, 2000)].

Veyne, Paul. *Comment on écrit l'histoire.* Paris: Éditions du Seuil, 1971.

Voltaire. *La philosophie de l'histoire: Texte intégral d'après l'édition de 1765.* With a preface by Catherine Volpilhac-Auger. Geneva: Slatkine, 1996.

THINKING ABOUT CONTEMPORANEITY

Agulhon, Maurice. "Vu des coulisses." In *Essais d'ego-histoire*, edited by Pierre Nora, 9–59. Paris: Gallimard, 1987.

Almeida, Fabrice d'. *Brève histoire du XXIe siècle.* Paris: Perrin, 2007.

Althabe, Gérard, Daniel Fabre, and Gérard Lenclud. *Vers une ethnologie du temps présent.* Paris: Éditions de la Maison des Sciences de l'Homme, 1992.

"At the Crossroads of Past and Present: 'Contemporary' History and the Historical Discipline." Special issue, *Journal of Contemporary History* 46, no. 3 (July 2011).

Amouroux, Henri. *La vie des Français sous l'Occupation.* Paris: Fayard, 1961.

Aron, Robert, with Georgette Elgey. *Histoire de Vichy, 1940–1944.* Paris: Fayard, 1954.

Aróstegui Sánchez, Julio. *La historia vivida.* Madrid: Ed. Alianza, 2004.

Audouin-Rouzeau, Stéphane. *Combattre: Une anthropologie historique de la guerre moderne (XIXe–XXe siècle).* Paris: Éditions du Seuil, 2008.

Audouin-Rouzeau, Stéphane, and Annette Becker. *14–18: Retrouver la guerre.* Paris: Gallimard, 2000.

Audouin-Rouzeau, Stéphane, Annette Becker, Christian Ingrao, and Henry Rousso, eds. *La violence de guerre, 1914–1945: Approches comparées des deux conflits mondiaux.* Brussels: Complexe; Paris: IHTP, 2002.

Augé, Marc. *Où est passé l'avenir?* Paris: Éditions du Seuil, 2001.

———. *Pour une anthropologie des mondes contemporains.* Paris: Aubier, 1994; Flammarion, 1997.

"Aus Politik und Zeitgeschichte." *Das Parlament* 51–52 (December 2002): 3–54.

Azéma, Jean-Pierre. "La Seconde Guerre mondiale matrice du temps présent." In Institut d'Histoire du Temps Présent, *Écrire l'histoire du temps présent: En hommage à François Bédarida*, 147–52. Paris: Éd. du CNRS, 1993.

Babelon, Ernest. *Le Rhin dans l'histoire.* 2 vols. Paris: Ernest Leroux, 1917–18.

Bachelier, Christian. *La SNCF sous l'Occupation allemande, 1940–1944: Rapport documentaire.* 4 vols. Paris: IHTP, 1998.

Barraclough, Geoffrey. *History in a Changing World.* Oxford: Basil Blackwell, 1955.

———. *An Introduction to Contemporary History.* Harmondsworth: Penguin, 1964.

Becker, Jean-Jacques. *Dictionnaire de la Grande guerre.* Brussels: André Versaille éditeur, 2008.

———. "La Grande guerre et la naissance de la BDIC." *Matériaux pour l'histoire de notre temps* 100 (October–December 2010): 5–6.

———. *Même si la cause était mauvaise . . . Mémoires d'un historien, 1936–1968.* Paris: Larousse, 2009.

Bédarida, François. *Histoire, critique et responsabilité.* Edited by Gabrielle Muc, Henry Rousso, and Michel Trebitsch. Brussels: Complexe; Paris: IHTP, 2003.

———. *La stratégie secrète de la Drôle de guerre: Le Conseil suprême interallié, septembre 1939–avril 1940.* Paris: Presses de la FNSP/Éditions du CNRS, 1979.

———. "Penser la Seconde Guerre mondiale." In *Penser le XXe siècle*, edited by André Versaille, 115–38. Brussels: Complexe, 1990.

Bédarida, François, ed. *L'histoire et le métier d'historien en France, 1945-1995*. Paris: Éditions de la Maison des Sciences de l'Homme, 1995.

Bédarida, François, and Jean-Pierre Azéma, eds., with Denis Peschanski and Henry Rousso. *Le régime de Vichy et les Français*. Paris: Fayard/IHTP, 1992.

Benedict, Ruth. *The Chrysanthemum and the Sword: Patterns of Japanese Culture*. Boston: Houghton Mifflin, 1946.

Berg, Nicolas. *Der Holocaust und die westdeutschen Historiker: Erforschung und Erinnerung*. Göttingen: Wallstein Verlag, 2003.

Berger, Stefan. "Historians and Nation-Building in Germany after Reunification." *Past & Present* 148 (1995): 187-222.

Berger, Stefan, and Chris Lorenz. *Nationalizing the Past: Historians as Nation Builders in Modern Europe*. London: Palgrave Macmillan / European Science Foundation, 2010.

"Bilan et perspectives de l'histoire immédiate." Special double issue, *Cahiers d'histoire immédiate* 30-31 (Fall 2006-Spring 2007).

Blanc, Louis. *Histoire des dix ans, 1830-1840*. Paris: Pagnerre, 1842 [facsimile ed., Coeuvres-et-Valsery: Ressouvenances, 2012].

Bloch, Marc. *La société féodale*. Paris: Albin Michel, 1939.

———. *L'histoire, la guerre, la Résistance*. Edited by Annette Becker and Étienne Bloch. Paris: Gallimard, 2006 [includes *L'étrange défaite: Témoignage écrit en 1940* (Paris: Société des Éditions Franc-Tireur, 1946)].

Blum, Françoise, and Rossana Vaccaro. "Madeleine Rebérioux: De l'histoire ouvrière à l'histoire sociale." *Cahiers Jaurès* 1, nos. 183-84 (2007): 65-80.

Bouillon, Jacques, Pierre Sorlin, and Jean Rudel. *Le monde contemporain, histoire, civilisations*. Paris: Bordas, 1986 [textbook for the senior year of secondary school].

Boockmann, Hartmut. *Der Historiker Hermann Heimpel*. Göttingen: Vandenhoeck & Ruprecht, 1990.

Bourgeois, Émile. *Manuel historique de politique étrangère*. Vol. 4, *La politique mondiale (1878-1919): Empires et nations*. Paris: Belin, 1926.

Bourlet, Michaël. "Les officiers de la section historique de l'état-major de la Grande guerre." *Revue historique des armées* 231, no. 2 (2003): 4-12.

Braudel, Fernand. "La captivité devant l'histoire." *Revue d'histoire de la Deuxième Guerre mondiale* 25 (January 1957): 3-5.

———. "La longue durée." *Annales ESC*, 13, no. 4 (October-December 1958): 725-53 [repr. in *Les ambitions de l'histoire*, edited by Roselyne de Ayala and Paule Braudel, with a preface by Maurice Aymard, 190-320. Paris: Éditions de Fallois, 1997].

———. *La Méditerranée et le monde méditerranéen à l'époque de Philippe II*. Paris: Armand Colin, 1949.

———. *L'identité de la France*. Vol. 1, *Espace et histoire*. Vols. 2 and 3, *Les hommes et les choses*. Paris: Arthaud-Flammarion, 1986-1987.

———. "Personal Testimony." *Journal of Modern History* 44, no. 4 (December 1972): 448-67 [repr. as "Ma formation d'historien" in *Les ambitions de l'histoire*, edited by Roselyne de Ayala and Paule Braudel, with a preface by Maurice Aymard, 9-29 (Paris: Éditions de Fallois, 1997)].

Braudel, Fernand, in collaboration with Suzanne Baille and Robert Philippe. *Le monde actuel*. Paris: Belin, 1963 [repr. in part under the title *Grammaire des civilisations* (Paris: Arthaud, 1987)].

Brinton, Crane. "The 'New History' and 'Past Everything.'" *American Scholar* 8, no. 2 (1939): 144-57.

Broszat, Martin. "Aufgaben und Probleme zeitgeschichtlichen Unterrichts: Am Beispiel der nationalsozialistischen Zeit." *Geschichte in Wissenschaft und Unterricht* 8 (1957): 529-50.

———. "A Plea for the Historicization of National Socialism." In *Reworking the Past: Hitler, the Holocaust, and the Historians' Debate*, edited by Peter Baldwin, 77-87. Boston: Beacon, 1990.

Broszat, Martin, and Saul Friedländer. "A Controversy about the Historicization of National Socialism." *New German Critique* 44 (Spring-Summer 1988): 85-126.

Callu, Agnès, ed. *Le mai 68 des historiens: Entre identités narratives et histoire orale.* Villeneuve d'Ascq: Presses Universitaires du Septentrion, 2010.

Capuzzo, Paolo, Chiara Giorgi, Manuela Martini, and Carlotta Sorba, eds. *Pensare la contemporaneità: Studi di storia per Mariuccia Salvati.* Rome: Viella, 2001.

Catterall, Peter. "What (If Anything) Is Distinctive about Contemporary History?" *Journal of Contemporary History* 32, no. 4 (1997): 441–52.

Cavani, Liliani, dir. *The Night Porter.* 1974.

Chablat-Beylot, Agnès, and Amable Sablon du Corail. "Les archives de la Grande guerre: Mise en ligne d'un guide." *Revue historique des armées* 254 (2009): 132–34.

Chabord, Marie-Thérèse. "Le Comité d'histoire de la Deuxième Guerre mondiale et ses archives." *La gazette des archives* 116 (1982): 5–19.

Chaouat, Bruno. *L'ombre pour la proie: Petites apocalypses de la vie quotidienne.* Villeneuve d'Ascq: Presses Universitaires du Septentrion, 2012.

"Che cos'è il presente?" Special issue, *Psiche: Rivista di cultura psicoanalitica* 1 (January–June 2014).

Chimènes, Myriam, ed. *La vie musicale sous Vichy.* Paris: IHTP/Éditions Complexe, 2001.

Coeuré, Sophie, and Vincent Duclert. *Les archives.* Paris: La Découverte, 2001.

Conrad, Sebastian. *The Quest for the Lost Nation: Writing History in Germany and Japan in the American Century.* Berkeley and Los Angeles: University of California Press, 2010 [1st ed. Göttingen, 1999].

Cordier, Daniel. *Jean Moulin: La République des catacombes.* Paris: Gallimard, 1999 [reissued in 2 vols. 2011].

Courrière, Yves. *Histoire de la Guerre d'Algérie.* 4 vols. Paris: Fayard, 1968–71.

Courtois, Stéphane, Nicolas Werth, Jean-Louis Panné, et al. *Le livre noir du communisme: Crimes, terreur, répression.* Paris: Robert Laffont, 1997.

Crémieux-Brilhac, Jean-Louis. *La France libre: De l'appel du 18 juin à la Libération.* Paris: Gallimard, 1996 [reissued in 2 vols. 2001].

Cuesta, Josefina. *Historia del presente.* Logroño (La Rioja): Eudema Universidad, 1993.

Darbo-Peschanski, Catherine. "La politique de l'histoire: Thucydide historien du présent." *Annales ESC* 3 (May–June 1989): 653–75.

Delacroix, Christian. "L'histoire du temps présent au risque de la demande sociale." In *Concurrence des passés: Usages politiques du passé dans la France contemporaine*, edited by Maryline Crivello, Patrick Garcia, and Nicolas Offenstadt, 271–82. Aix-en-Provence: Presses Universitaires de Provence, 2006.

Delage, Christian, and Vincent Guigueno. *L'historien et le film.* Paris: Gallimard, 2004.

Descamps, Florence. *L'historien, l'archiviste et le magnétophone: De la construction de la source orale à son exploitation.* Paris: Comité pour l'Histoire Économique et Financière de la France, 2001.

Descombes, Vincent. "Qu'est-ce qu'être contemporain?" In "Actualité du contemporain." Special issue, *Le genre humain* (February 2000): 21–32.

Dewar, Kenneth C. "Geoffrey Barraclough: From Historicism to Historical Science." *Historian* 56, no. 3 (March 1994): 449–64.

Douzou, Laurent. *La Résistance française, une histoire périlleuse: Essai d'historiographie.* Paris: Éditions du Seuil, 2005.

———, ed. *Faire l'histoire de la Résistance.* Rennes: Presses Universitaires de Rennes, 2008.

Dujardin, Philippe. "De quoi sommes-nous contemporains? Essai d'anthropologie politique." *Cahiers sens public* (November–December 2009): 11–91.

Durkheim, Émile. *"L'Allemagne au-dessus de tout": La mentalité allemande et la guerre.* Paris: Armand Colin, 1915.

Duruy, Victor. "Lettre au général Coffinières de Nordeck." In *Notes et souvenirs,* 122–25. Paris: Hachette, 1901.

Duverger, Maurice. *La démocratie sans le peuple*. Paris: Éditions du Seuil, 1967.

Febvre, Lucien. "Avant-Propos." *Cahiers d'histoire de la guerre* 1 (January 1949): 1-3.

———. "Par manière de préface." *Cahiers d'histoire de la guerre* 3 (February 1950).

Ferro, Marc. "Le film, une contre-analyse de la société?" In *Faire de l'histoire*, edited by Jacques Le Goff and Pierre Nora, 3:236-55. Paris: Gallimard, 1974.

Frankland, Noble. *History at War: The Campaigns of an Historian*. London: Giles de la Mare, 1998.

Frei, Norbert. "The Federal Republic of Germany." In *Contemporary History: Practice and Method*, edited by Anthony Seldon. Oxford: Basil Blackwell, 1988.

———, ed. *Was heißt und zum welchen Ende studiert man Geschichte des 20. Jahrhunderts?* Göttingen: Walstein Verlag, 2007.

Friedländer, Saul. *Pie XII et le IIIe Reich*. Paris: Éditions du Seuil, 1964 [new ed. 2010].

Furet, François. *Le passé d'une illusion: Essai sur l'idée communiste au XXe siècle*. Paris: Robert Laffont/Calmann-Lévy, 1995.

Galimi, Valeria. "De l'histoire de la Résistance à l'histoire du XXe siècle: L''Istitut nazionale per la storia del movimento di Liberazione in Italia' et le réseau des Instituts associés." In "L'histoire du temps présent, hier et aujourd'hui," special issue, *Bulletin de l'Institut d'histoire du temps présent* (July 2000), http://www.ihtp.cnrs.fr/spip/php%3Frubrique89.html.

Girardet, Raoul. "L'ombre de la guerre." In *Essais d'ego-histoire*, edited by Pierre Nora, 139-71. Paris: Gallimard, 1987.

Girault, René. "Pierre Renouvin, la BDIC et l'historiographie française des relations internationales." *Matériaux pour l'histoire de notre temps* 49-50 (1998): 7-9.

Guibert de Nogent. *Histoire des Croisades*. Book 4. In *Collections des mémoires relatifs à l'histoire de France depuis la fondation de la monarchie française jusqu'au 13e siècle*, edited by François Guizot. Paris: J.-L.-J. Brière Libraire, 1825.

Hamel, Jean-François. *Revenances de l'histoire: Répétition, narrativité, modernité*. Paris: Éditions de Minuit, 2006.

Hartog, François. "Le présent de l'historien." *Le débat* 158 (January 2010): 18-31.

Hartog, François, Pauline Schmitt, and Alain Schnapp, eds. *Pierre Vidal-Naquet: Un historien dans la cité*. Paris: La Découverte, 1998.

Havet, Jacques, ed. *Tendances principales de la recherche dans les sciences sociales et humaines*. 2 vols. Paris: Mouton/New York: UNESCO, 1978.

Heimpel, Hermann. *Der Mensch in seiner Gegenwart: Acht historische Essais*. Göttingen: Vandenhoeck & Ruprecht, 1975 [1st ed. 1954].

Hirschfeld, Gerhard. "Niederländische Zeitgeschichte: Fragen und Perspektiven der Forschung." *Jahrbuch des Zentrums für Niederlande-Studien* 16 (2005): 141-57.

"Historians on the Twentieth Century." Special issue, *Journal of Contemporary History* 2, no. 1 (January 1967).

Hobsbawm, Eric. *The Age of Extremes: The Short Twentieth Century, 1914-1991*. London: Michael Joseph, 1994.

Hudemann, Rainer. "Frankreich-Histoire du Temps présent zwischen nationalen Problemstellungen und internationaler Öffnung." In *Zeitgeschichte als Problem: Nationale Traditionen und Perspektiven in Europa*, edited by Alexander Nützenadel and Wolfgang Schieder, 175-200. Göttingen: Vandenhoeck & Ruprecht, 2004, https://docupedia.de/zg/Frankreich_-_Histoire_du_Temps_présent?oldid=80318.

Hürter, Johannes, and Hans Woller. *Hans Rothfels und die deutsche Zeitgeschichte*. Munich: Oldenbourg Wissenschaftsverlag, 2005.

Husson, Édouard. *Comprendre Hitler et la Shoah: Les historiens dans la République fédérale d'Allemagne et l'identité allemande depuis 1949*. Paris: Presses Universitaires de France, 2000.

Iggers, Georg G. *Historiography in the Twentieth Century: From Scientific Objectivity to the Postmodern Challenge*. Middletown, Conn.: Wesleyan University Press, 1997.

——. *New Directions in European Historiography*. Middletown, Conn.: Wesleyan University Press, 1975.

Institut d'Histoire du Temps Présent. *Écrire l'histoire du temps présent: En hommage à François Bédarida*. Paris: Éditions du CNRS, 1993.

——. *Histoire et temps présent*. Paris: IHTP/CNRS, 1980 [mimeograph].

Isaac, Jules, *Jules Isaac, un historien dans la Grande guerre: Lettres et carnets, 1914–1917*. Edited with notes by Marc Michel. With an introduction by André Kaspi. Paris: Armand Colin, 2004.

Jäckel, Eberhard. *Umgang mit der Vergangenheit: Beiträge zur Geschichte, 133–50*. Stuttgart: Deutsche Verlags-Anstalt, 1989.

Jarausch, Konrad, ed. *Zwischen Parteilichkeit und Professionalität: Bilanz der Geschichtswissenschaft der DDR*. Berlin: Academie Verlag, 1991.

Jarausch, Konrad, and Martin Sabrow, eds. *Verletztes Gedächtnis: Erinnerungskultur und Zeitgeschichte im Konflikt*. Frankfurt-am-Main: Campus Fachbuch, 2002.

Jeanneney, Jean-Noël. *Concordances des temps: Chronique sur l'actualité du passé*. Paris: Éditions du Seuil, 1987.

Jong, Louis de. *Het Koninkrijk der Nederlanden in de Tweede Wereldoorlog (The Kingdom of the Netherlands during World War II)*. 14 parts in 29 volumes. The Hague: Martinus Nijhoff, 1969–1991.

Jouhaud, Christian. *Les pouvoirs de la littérature: Histoire d'un paradoxe*. Paris: Gallimard, 2000.

Journal of Contemporary History 1, no. 1 (January 1966).

Judt, Tony. *Postwar: A History of Europe since 1945*. London: Penguin, 2005.

——. "Rethinking Post-War Europe." *IWMpost* (Institut für die Wissenschaften von Menschen, Vienna) 104 (April–August 2010): 4.

Kassow, Samuel D. *Who Will Write Our History? Rediscovering a Hidden Archive from the Warsaw Ghetto*. New York: Vintage, 2009.

Krugler, Gilles. "*Historians in Combat*: L'armée américaine et le concept de *Military History Operations*." In "De l'histoire bataille à l'histoire totale," special issue, *Revue historique des armées* 257 (2009): 59–75.

Laborie, Pierre. *Les Français des années troubles: De la guerre d'Espagne à la Libération*. Paris: Desclée de Brouwer, 2001.

Lacouture, Jean. "L'histoire immédiate." In *La Nouvelle Histoire*, edited by Jacques Le Goff, Roger Chartier, and Jacques Revel, 270–93. Paris: Retz, 1978.

Lacretelle, Charles de. *Histoire de France depuis la Restauration*. 4 vols. Paris: Delaunay, 1829–35.

——. *Histoire de la Révolution française*. 8 vols. Paris: Treuttel et Würtz, 1821–26.

Lagrou, Pieter. "Historiographie de guerre et historiographie du temps présent: Cadres institutionnels en Europe occidentale, 1945–2000." *Bulletin du Comité international d'histoire de la Deuxième Guerre mondiale* 30–31 (1999–2000): 191–215, http://www.ihtp.cnrs.fr/spip/php %3Farticle515.html.

——. *Mémoires patriotiques et occupation nazie: Résistants, requis et déportés en Europe occidentale, 1945–1965*. Brussels: Complexe; Paris: IHTP-CNRS, 2003.

——. "Ou comment se constitue et se développe un nouveau champ disciplinaire." In "Histoire du temps présent," special issue, *La revue pour l'histoire du CNRS* 9 (2003): 4–15.

Laïdi, Zaki. *Le sacre du présent*. Paris: Flammarion, 2000.

Lanzmann, Claude, dir. *Shoah*. 1985.

Laqueur, Walter, and George Mosse, eds. "History Today in USA, Britain, France, Italy, Germany, Poland, India, Czechoslovakia, Spain, Holland, Sweden." Special issue, *Journal of Contemporary History* 2, no. 1 (January 1967).

Le Journal ou Histoire du temps présent; contenant toutes les Declarations du Roy vérifiées en Parlement, & tous les Arrets rendus, les Chambres assemblées, pour les affaires publiques. Depuis le mois d'avril 1651, jusques en juin 1652. Paris: Gervais Alliot & Emmanuel Langlois, 1652.

Le Moigne, Nicolas. "L'histoire du temps présent à l'allemande: L'*Institut für Zeitgeschichte* de Munich." *Bulletin de la mission historique française en Allemagne* 40 (2004): 186–92.

"L'histoire du temps présent." Special issue, *Documents: La revue des questions allemandes* 4 (September–October 2000).

"L'histoire du temps présent." Special issue, *La revue pour l'histoire du CNRS* 9 (November 2003).

"L'histoire du temps présent, hier et aujourd'hui." Special issue, *Bulletin de l'Institut d'histoire du temps présent* 75 (July 2000), http://www.ihtp.cnrs.fr/spip.php%Frubrique89.html.

Lisle, Edmond. "Les sciences sociales en France: Développement et turbulences dans les années 1970." *La revue pour l'histoire du CNRS* 7 (2002), histoire-cnrs.revues.org/543#text.

Martens, Stefan. "Frankreich zwischen 'Histoire contemporaine' und 'Histoire du temps présent.'" *Vierteljahrshefte für Zeitgeschichte* 4 (2007): 583–616.

Meinecke, Friedrich. *Die deutsche Katastrophe: Betrachtungen und Erinnerungen.* Wiesbaden: Brockhaus, 1946.

Menne-Haritz, Angelika. "Die Verwaltung und ihre Archive: Überlegungen zur Latenz von Zeit in der Verwaltungsarbeit." *Verwaltung & Management* 5, no. 1 (1999): 4–10. [English version: "Thoughts on the Latency of Time in Administrative Work and the Role Archives Play to Make it Visible," http://www.staff.uni-marburg.de/~mennehar/publikationenen/latency.pdf.]

[Michel, Henri]. "Lucien Febvre (1878–1956)." *Revue d'histoire de la Deuxième Guerre mondiale* 25 (January 1957): 2.

Michel, Henri. "Une enquête sur la Résistance par la Commission d'histoire de l'Occupation et de la Libération de la France." *Cahiers d'histoire de la guerre* 2 (June 1949): 45–55.

Möller, Horst, and Ugo Wengst, eds. *50 Jahre Institut für Zeitgeschichte: Eine Bilanz.* Munich: Oldenbourg Verlag, 1999.

Morin, Edgar. *La rumeur d'Orléans.* Paris: Éditions du Seuil, 1969.

Mosse, George. *Fallen Soldiers: Reshaping the Memory of the World Wars.* London: Oxford University Press, 1990.

Neumann, Franz. *Behemoth: The Structure and Practice of National Socialism.* London: Gollancz, 1942.

Niethammer, Lutz, with Axel Doßmann. *Kollektive Identität: Heimliche Quellen einer unheimlichen Konjunktur.* Hamburg: Rowohlt, 2000.

Niethammer, Lutz, with Dirk van Laak. *Posthistoire: Has History Come to an End?* New York: Verso, 1992 [1st ed. 1989].

Noiriel, Gérard. *Les origines républicaines de Vichy.* Paris: Hachette, 1999.

———. *Qu'est-ce que l'histoire contemporaine?* Paris: Hachette, 1998.

Nora, Pierre. "L'événement-monstre." *Communications* 18 (1972): 162–72 [repr. in "Le retour de l'événement," in *Faire de l'histoire*, edited by Jacques Le Goff and Pierre Nora (Paris: Gallimard, 1974), 1:210–28].

———. *Les Français d'Algérie.* Paris: Julliard, 1961 [new ed. Christian Bourgois, 2012].

———. "Présent." In *La Nouvelle Histoire*, edited by Jacques Le Goff, Roger Chartier, and Jacques Revel, 467–72. Paris: Retz, 1978.

Nützennadel, Alexander, and Wolfgang Schieder, eds. *Zeitgeschichte als Problem: Nationale Traditionen und Perspektiven der Forschung in Europa.* Göttingen: Vandenhoeck & Ruprecht, 2004.

Ophuls, Marcel, dir. *Le chagrin et la pitié* [*The Sorrow and the Pity*]. 1969.

Palmowski, Jan, and Kristina Spohr-Readman. "Speaking Truth to Power: Contemporary History in the Twenty-first Century." In "At the Crossroads of Past and Present: 'Contemporary' History and the Historical Discipline," special issue, *Journal of Contemporary History* 46, no. 3 (July 2011): 485–505.

Pavone, Claudio, ed. *Novecento: I tempi della storia.* Rome: Donzelli, 2008 [1st ed. 1997].

———. *Prima lezione di storia contemporanea.* Rome: Laterza, 2007.

Patel, Kiran Klaus. "Zeitgeschichte im digitalen Zeitalter: Neue und alte Herausforderungen." *Vierteljahrshefte für Zeitgeschichte* 3, no. 59 (July 2011): 331–51.

Paxton, Robert O. *Vichy France: Old Guard and New Order, 1940–1944.* New York: Knopf, 1972.

Pérotin-Dumon, Anne. *Historizar el Pasado vivo en América Latina.* 2007, http://etica.uahurtado.cl/historizarelpasadovivo/es_home.html.

Pervillé, Guy. "L'histoire immédiate selon Jean-François Soulet, Jean Lacouture et Benoît Vergaegen." In "Bilan et perspectives de l'histoire immédiate," special double issue, *Cahiers d'histoire immédiate* 30-31 (Fall 2006-Spring 2007): 5-9.

Peschanski, Denis, Michael Pollak, and Henry Rousso, eds. *Histoire politique et sciences sociales*. Brussels: Complexe; Paris: IHTP, 1991.

Pirenne, Henri. *Histoire de Belgique*. 7 vols. Brussels: Lamertin, 1900-1932.

Pisar, Samuel. "Auschwitz parle encore aux juifs et aux musulmans." *Le Monde*, January 28, 2012.

Plumyène, Jean, and Raymond Lasierra. *Les fascismes français, 1923-1963*. Paris: Éditions du Seuil, 1963.

Poirrier, Philippe. "L'histoire contemporaine." In *Les historiens français à l'oeuvre 1995-2010*, edited by Jean-François Sirinelli, Pascal Cauchy, and Claude Gauvard, 73-91. Paris: Presses Universitaires de France, 2010.

Poliakov, Léon. *Le bréviaire de la haine*. Paris: Calmann-Lévy, 1951.

———. "Une grande institution française: Le Comité d'histoire de la 2e Guerre mondiale." *La revue du Centre de Documentation juive contemporaine* (April 1956): 19-22.

Pôrto, Gilson Jr, ed. *História do tempo presente*. Bauru, Brazil: Editora da Universidade do Sagrado Coração, 2007.

Postel-Vinay, Karoline. "Dire l'histoire à l'échelle du monde." *Esprit* (June 2007), http://www.esprit.presse.fr/archive/review/article.php?code=14083.

Poznanski, Renée. "La création du Centre de documentation juive contemporaine en France (avril 1943)." *Vingtième siècle: Revue d'histoire* 63 (July-September 1999): 51-64.

Prost, Antoine. "L'histoire du temps présent: Une histoire comme les autres." In "Bilan et perspectives de l'histoire immédiate," special double issue, *Cahiers d'histoire immédiate* 30-31 (Fall 2006-Spring 2007): 21-28.

———. "Pour une histoire sociale du temps présent." In Institut d'histoire du temps présent, *Écrire l'histoire du temps présent: En hommage à François Bédarida*. Paris: Éditions du CNRS, 1993.

Rabinbach, Anson. *In the Shadow of Catastrophe: German Intellectuals between Apocalypse and Enlightenment*. Berkeley and Los Angeles: University of California Press, 1997.

Rasmussen, Anne. "La 'science française' dans la guerre des manifestations, 1914-1918." *Mots: Les languages du politique* 76 (2004): 9-23.

Raulff, Ulrich. *De l'origine à l'actualité: Marc Bloch, l'histoire et le problème du temps présent*. Sigmaringen: Jan Thorbecke Verlag, 1997.

Rémond, René. "France: Work in Progress." In "Historians on the Twentieth Century." Special issue, *Journal of Contemporary History* 2, no. 1 (January 1967): 35-48.

———. "La blessure de 1940 enfin cicatrisée." *Réalités: Revue de Paris* 315 (April 1971): 37-41.

———. "Le contemporain du contemporain." In *Essais d'ego-histoire*, edited by Pierre Nora, 293-349. Paris: Gallimard, 1987.

———. *Les Droites en France*. Paris: Aubier-Montaignes. 4th ed. 1982 [1st ed. *La Droite en France de 1815 à nos jours: Continuité et diversité d'une tradition politique* (Paris: Aubier, 1954)].

———. "L'histoire contemporaine." In *L'histoire et le métier d'historien en France, 1945-1995*, edited by François Bédarida, 247-51. Paris: Éditions de la Maison des Sciences de l'Homme, 1995.

———. *Notre siècle: De 1918 à 1988*. Vol. 6 of *Histoire de France*, edited by Jean Favier. Paris: Fayard, 1988 [new ed. *Notre siècle: De 1918 à 1988* (Paris: Librairie Générale Française, 1993)].

———. "Plaidoyer pour une histoire délaissée: La fin de la IIIe République." *Revue française de science politique* 7, no. 2 (1957): 253-70.

———, ed. *Le gouvernement de Vichy 1940-1942: Institutions et politiques*. Paris: Armand Colin, 1972.

Rémond, René, and Janine Bourdin, eds. *Édouard Daladier, chef de gouvernement*. Paris: Presses de la Fondation Nationale des Sciences Politiques, 1977.

Rémond, René, and Hélène Carrère d'Encausse. *Discours de réception de René Rémond à l'Académie française et réponse d'Hélène Carrère d'Encausse*. Paris: Fayard, 2000.

Renouvin, Pierre. *Les origines immédiates de la guerre: 28 juin-4 août 1914*. Paris: Alfred Costes, 1925.

Reynolds, David. "The Origins of the Two 'World Wars': Historical Discourse and International Politics." *Journal of Contemporary History* 38, no. 1 (January 2003): 29–44.

Reynolds, Gonzague de. "Où va l'Europe?" *La revue universelle*, August 15, 1938.

Rioux, Jean-Pierre. "20-01-84." *Vingtième siècle: Revue d'histoire* 1 (January 1984): 5–6.

——. "Présentation." *Vingtième siècle: Revue d'histoire* 69 (January 2001): 3–5.

Rosenstone, Robert A. *Visions of the Past: The Challenge of Film to Our Idea of History.* Cambridge, Mass.: Harvard University Press, 1995.

Rothfels, Hans. "Zeitgeschichte als Aufgabe." *Vierteljahrshefte für Zeitgeschichte* 1 (January 1953): 1–8.

Rousso, Henry. "Histoire du temps présent." In *Le dictionnaire des sciences humaines*, edited by Sylvie Mesure and Patrick Savidan, 555–58. Paris: Presses Universitaires de France, 2006.

——. "L'histoire du temps présent, vingt ans après." In "L'histoire du temps présent, hier et aujourd'hui," special issue, *Bulletin de l'Institut d'histoire du temps présent* 75 (July 2000): 23–40.

Sabrow, Martin, Ralph Jessen, and Klaus Grosse Kracht, eds. *Zeitgeschichte als Streitgeschichte: Grosse Kontroversen nach 1945.* Munich: C. H. Beck, 2003.

Safire, William. *Safire's Political Dictionary.* London: Oxford University Press, 1972.

Salvati, Mariuccia. *Il Novecento: Interpretazioni e bilanci.* Rome: Laterza, 2004.

Sauvageot, Jacques, Alain Geismar, and Daniel Cohn-Bendit. *La révolte étudiante: Les animateurs parlent.* Paris: Éditions du Seuil, 1968.

Schmid, Hans-Christian, dir. *Storm.* 2009.

Schöttler, Peter. "After the Deluge: The Impact of the Two World Wars on the Historical Work of Henri Pirenne and Marc Bloch." In *Nationalizing the Past: Historians as Nation Builders in Modern Europe*, edited by Stefan Berger and Chris Lorenz, 404–25. London: Palgrave Macmillan / European Science Foundation, 2010.

——. "Fernand Braudel, prisonnier en Allemagne face à la longue durée et au temps présent." Paper delivered at the international colloquium "Captivity in Twentieth-Century Warfare: Archives, History, Memory," Institut d'Histoire du Temps Présent / Institut de Recherche Stratégique de l'École militaire, November 17–18, 2011.

——. "La 'Zeitgeschichte' allemande, entre révisionnisme, conformisme et autocritique." Paper delivered at the international colloquium "Present Time and Contemporaneity," Paris, Institut d'Histoire du Temps Présent, March 24–26, 2011.

——, ed. *Geschichtsschreibung als Legitimationswissenschaft 1918–1945.* Frankfurt am Main: Suhrkamp, 1997.

——. ed. *Marc Bloch, Historiker und Widerstandskämpfer.* Frankfurt am Main: Campus, 1999.

Seldon, Anthony, ed. *Contemporary History: Practice and Method.* Oxford: Basil Blackwell, 1988.

Seton-Watson, Robert William. "The Historian as a Political Force in Central Europe." Inaugural lecture upon the creation of the chair in Slavonic Studies at the University of London on November 2, 1922, School of Slavonic Studies, University of London, King's College, 1922.

——. "Plea for the Study of Contemporary History." *History (Journal of the Historical Association)* 14, no. 53 (April 1929): 1–18.

Sevegrand, Martine. *"Temps présent," une aventure chrétienne, 1937–1992.* Paris: Éditions du Temps Présent, 2006.

Sirinelli, Jean-François. *Comprendre le XXe siècle français.* Paris: Fayard, 2005.

——, ed. *Histoires des Droites en France.* 3 vols. Paris: Gallimard, 1992.

Sirinelli, Jean-François, Pascal Cauchy, and Claude Gauvard, eds. *Les historiens français à l'oeuvre 1995–2010.* Paris: Presses Universitaires de France, 2010.

Solchany, Jean. *Comprendre le nazisme dans l'Allemagne des années zéro (1945–1949).* Paris: Presses Universitaires de France, 1997.

Soulet, Jean-François. *L'histoire immédiate: Historiographie, sources et méthodes.* Paris: Armand Colin, 2009.

———. *L'histoire immédiate*. Paris: Presses Universitaires de France, 1994.

Stoop, Paul. "Das 'Rijksinstituut voor Oorlogsdocumentatie' in Amsterdam." *Jahrebibliographie der Bibliothek für Zeitgeschichte* 58 (1986): 455-64.

Stora, Benjamin. *Les guerres sans fin: Un historien, la France et l'Algérie*. Paris: Stock, 2008.

Taine, Hippolyte. *Les origines de la France contemporaine*. 6 vols. Paris: Hachette, 1875-93.

Taylor, Alan J. P. "Sales Talk." *News Statesman and Nation*, March 17, 1956.

Tillion, Germaine. *Le harem et les cousins*. Paris: Éditions du Seuil, 1966.

Toulongeon, Emmanuel de. *Histoire de France depuis la Révolution de 1789 écrite d'après les mémoires et manuscrits contemporains, recueillis dans les depôts civils et militaires*. Paris: Didot, 1803.

Traverso, Enzo. *L'histoire comme champ de bataille: Interpréter les violences du XXe siècle*. Paris: La Découverte, 2011.

———, ed. *Le totalitarisme: Le XXe siècle en débat*. Paris: Éditions du Seuil, 2001.

Trebitsch, Michel. "Du mythe à l'historiographie." In "La bouche de la vérité? La recherche historique et les sources orales," edited by Danièle Voldman, special issue, *Les cahiers de l'Institut d'histoire du temps présent* 21 (November 1992): 13-32, http://www.ihtp.cnrs.fr/spip.php %Farticle211.html.

———. "L'histoire contemporaine: Quelques notes sur une histoire énigmatique." In *Périodes: La construction du temps historique*, edited by Olivier Dumoulin and Raphaël Valéry, 135-44. Paris: Éditions de l'École des Hautes Études en Sciences Sociales, 1991.

Verhaegen, Benoît. *Introduction à l'histoire immédiate*. Gembloux: Éd. Duculot, 1974.

Versaille, André, ed. *Penser le XXe siècle*. Brussels: Complexe, 1990.

Vidal de La Blache, Pierre. "La frontière de la Sarre d'après les traités de 1814 et 1815." *Annales de Géographie* 28, no. 154 (1919): 249-67.

Vidal-Naquet, Pierre. *Mémoires*. Vol. 1, *La brisure et l'attente, 1930-1955*. Paris: Seuil/La Découverte, 1995.

Vierteljahrshefte für Zeitgeschichte 1 (January 1953).

Vingtième siècle: Revue d'histoire 1 (January-March 1984).

Virilio, Paul. "Les illusions du temps zéro." *Esprit* 260 (January 2000): 97-104.

Voldman, Danièle, ed. "La bouche de la vérité? La recherche historique et les sources orales." Special issue, *Les cahiers de l'Institut d'histoire du temps présent* 21 (November 1992).

Weber, Eugen. *Action Française: Royalism and Reaction in Twentieth Century France*. Stanford, Calif.: Stanford University Press, 1962.

Werth, Nicolas. "Totalitarisme ou révisionnisme: L'histoire soviétique, une histoire en chantier." In *Le totalitarisme: Le XXe siècle en débat*, edited by Enzo Traverso, 878-96. Paris: Éditions du Seuil, 2001.

Wesseling, Henk L. "The Annales School and the Writing of Contemporary History." *Review* 1, nos. 3-4 (Winter-Spring 1979): 185-94 [repr. in his *Certain Ideas of France: Essays on French History and Civilization* (Westport, Conn.: Greenwood Press, 2002)].

Winock, Michel. *Histoire politique de la revue "Esprit," 1930-1950*. Paris: Éditions du Seuil, 1975.

Wirsching, Andreas. "'Epoche der Mitlebenden'—Kritik der Epoche." *Zeithistorische Forschungen/ Studies in Contemporary History* 8 (May 2011), http://www.zeithistorische-forschungen.de /16126041-Wirsching-1-2011.

Woodward, Llewellyn. "The Study of Contemporary History." *Journal of Contemporary History* 1, no. 1 (January 1966): 1-13.

TESTIMONY, PRESENCE, AND THE USES OF THE PAST

Andrieu, Clarie, Marie-Claire Lavabre, and Danielle Tartakowski, eds. *Politiques du passé: Usages politiques du passé dans la France contemporaine*. Aix-en-Provence: Presses Universitaires de Provence, 2006.

Ashton, Paul, and Paula Hamilton. *History at the Crossroads: Australians and the Past*. Sydney: Halstead, 2010.

Assmann, Aleida. *Der lange Schatten der Vergangenheit: Erinnerungskultur und Geschichtspolitik*. Munich: C. H. Beck, 2006.

Assmann, Jan. *Das kulturelle Gedächtnis: Schrift, Erinnerung und politische Identität in frühen Hochkulturen*. Munich: C. H. Beck, 1992.

Auzas, Vincent, and Bogumil Jewsiewicki, eds. *Traumatisme collectif pour patrimoine: Regards sur un mouvement transnational*. Quebec: Les Presses de l'Université Laval, 2008.

Azouvi, François. *Le mythe du grand silence: Auschwitz, les Français, la mémoire*. Paris: Fayard, 2012.

Becker, Annette. *Maurice Halbwachs: Un intellectuel en guerres mondiales 1914–1945*. Paris: Noêsis, 2003.

Besson, Rémy. "La mise en récit de *Shoah*." Ph.D. diss., Écoles des Hautes Études en Sciences Sociales, 2012.

Blaive, Muriel, Christian Gerbel, and Thomas Lindenberger, eds. *Clashes in European Memory: The Case of Communist Repression and the Holocaust*. Innsbruck: Studien Verlag, 2011.

Broog, Mooli. "In Blessed Memory of a Dream: Mordechai Shenhavi and Initial Holocaust Commemoration Ideas in Palestine, 1942–1945." Shoah Resource Center, http://www.yadvashem.org/odot_pdf/Microsoft%20Word%20-%205423.pdf

Brückner, Pascal. *La tyrannie de la pénitence: Essai sur le masochisme occidental*. Paris: Grasset, 2006.

Courtois, Stéphane, Nicolas Werth, Jean-Louis Panné, et al. *Le livre noir du communisme: Crimes, terreur, répression*. Paris: Robert Laffont, 1997; "Bouquins" edition, 1998.

Crivello, Maryline, Patrick Garcia, and Nicolas Offenstadt, eds. *Concurrence des passés: Usages politiques du passé dans la France contemporaine*. Aix-en-Provence: Presses Universitaires de Provence, 2006.

Cru, Jean Norton. *Du témoignage*. Paris: Gallimard 1931 [reissued Jean-Jacques Pauvert, 1967].

———. *Témoins: Essai d'analyse et de critique des souvenirs des combattants édités en français de 1915 à 1928*. Paris: Les Étincelles, 1929 [reissued Presses Universitaires de Nancy, 1993].

David, Renée. *Traces indélébiles, mémoires incertaines*. With a preface by Raymond Aubrac. Paris: L'Harmattan, 2008.

Davoine, Françoise, and Jean-Max Gaudillière. *Histoire et trauma: La folie des guerres*. Paris: Stock, 2006.

Diner, Hasia. *We Remember with Reverence and Love: American Jews and the Myth of Silence after the Holocaust, 1945–1962*. New York: New York University Press, 2009.

Dulong, Renaud. *Le témoin oculaire: Les conditions sociales de l'attestation personnelle*. Paris: Éditions de l'École des Hautes Études en Sciences Sociales, 1998.

Fassin, Didier, and Richard Rechtman. *L'empire du traumatisme: Enquête sur la condition de victime*. Paris: Flammarion, 2007.

Ferro, Marc. *Le ressentiment dans l'histoire: Comprendre notre temps*. Paris: Odile Jacob, 2007.

François, Étienne, and Hagen Schulze, eds. *Deutsche Erinnerungsorte*. Munich: C. H. Beck, 2001. Abridged version translated into French by Bernard Lotholary as *Mémoires allemandes*. Paris: Gallimard, 2007.

Frank, Anne. *The Diary of Anne Frank: The Critical Edition*. Edited by David Barnouw and Gerrold van der Stroom. Translated by Arnold J. Pomerans and B. M. Mooyaart-Doubleday. New York: Doubleday, 1989.

Frei, Norbert. *Vergangenheitspolitik: Die Anfange der Bundesrepublik und die NS-Vergangenheit*. Munich: C. H. Beck, 1997.

———, ed. *Martin Broszat, der "Staat Hitlers" und die Historisierung des Nationalsozialismus*. Göttingen: Wallstein Verlag, 2007.

Friedländer, Saul. "Some Reflections on the Historicization of National Socialism." In *Reworking the Past: Hitler, the Holocaust, and the Historians' Debate*, edited by Peter Baldwin, 88–101. Boston: Beacon, 1990.

Friedman, Thomas L. "The End of the West?" *New York Times*, November 2, 2003.

Fussel, Paul. *The Great War and Modern Memory*. London: Oxford University Press, 1975.

Gallerano, Nicola, ed. *L'uso pubblico della storia*. Milan: Franco Angeli, 1995.

———. *Le Bicentenaire de la Révolution française: Pratiques sociales d'une commémoration*. With a preface by Michel Vovelle. Paris: CNRS Éditions, 2000.

Garcia, Patrick, and Jean Leduc. *L'enseignement de l'histoire en France de l'Ancien régime à nos jours*. Paris: Armand Colin, 2003.

Gaudard, Pierre-Yves. *Le fardeau de la mémoire: Le deuil collectif allemand après le national-socialisme*. Paris: Plon, 1997.

Gildea, Robert. *The Past in French History*. New Haven: Yale University Press, 1994.

Halbwachs, Maurice. *La mémoire collective*, critical edition by Gérard Namer. Paris: Albin Michel, 1997.

———. *Les cadres sociaux de la mémoire*, critical edition by Gérard Namer. Paris: Albin Michel, 1994.

Homans, Peter, ed. *Symbolic Loss: The Ambiguity of Mourning and Memory at Century's End*. Charlottesville: University Press of Virginia, 2000.

Institut Universitaire de Formation des Maîtres. *L'histoire entre épistémologie et demande sociale*. Créteil: Institut Universitaire de Formation des Maîtres, 1994.

Isaac, Jules. "De la véracité dans les récits de guerre qui émanent des combattants et des garanties que nous en avons: Entretien tenu au siège de l' 'Union' le 16 novembre 1930 à propos du livre de M. Jean Norton Cru 'Témoins.'" *Bulletin de l'Union pour la vérité* (February–March 1931): 68-69.

Jarausch, Konrad, and Thomas Lindenberger, eds., with Annelie Ramsbrock. *Conflicted Memories: Europeanizing Contemporary Histories*. New York: Berghahn, 2007.

Jaspers, Karl. *The Question of German Guilt*. Translated by E. B. Ashton. New York: Fordham University Press, 2000 [1st ed. Zurich, 1946].

Jeanneney, Jean-Noël. *Le passé dans le prétoire*. Paris: Éditions du Seuil, 1998.

Jockusch, Laura. *Collect and Record! Jewish Holocaust Documentation in Early Postwar Europe*. London: Oxford University Press, 2014.

Joutard, Philippe. *Ces voix qui nous viennent du passé*. Paris: Hachette, 1983.

Lagrou, Pieter. *Mémoires patriotiques et Occupation nazie: Résistants, requis et déportés en Europe occidentale, 1945-1965*. Brussels: Complexe; Paris: IHTP-CNRS, 2003.

———. "Réflexions sur le rapport néerlandais du NIOD: Logique académique et culture du consensus." In "Srebrenica 1995: Analyse croisée des enquêtes et des rapports." Special issue, *Culture & conflits: Sociologie politique de l'international* 65 (2007): 63-79.

"La responsabilité sociale de l'historien." Special issue, *Diogène* 168 (October–December 1994).

Lavabre, Marie-Claire. "Du poids et du choix du passé." In *Histoire politique et sciences sociales*, edited by Denis Peschanski, Michael Pollak, and Henry Rousso, 265-78. Brussels: Complexe; Paris: IHTP, 1991.

———. "Paradigmes de la mémoire." *Transcontinentales* 5 (2007): 139-47.

———. "Usages du passé, usages de la mémoire." *Revue française de science politique* 44, no. 3 (June 1994): 480-93.

Lavabre, Marie-Claire, and Dominique Damamme, eds. "Expertises historiennes." Special issue, *Sociétés contemporaines* 39 (2000).

Lemoine, Hervé. *La Maison de l'histoire: Pour la création d'un Centre de recherche et de collections permanentes dédié à l'histoire civile et militaire de la France*. Status report. Paris: Ministère de la Culture, 2008.

Létourneau, Jocelyn, and David Northrup. "Québecois et Canadiens face au passé: Similitudes et dissemblances." *Canadian Historical Review* 92, no. 1 (March 2011): 163-96.

Lowczyk, Olivier. *La fabrique de la paix: Du comité d'études à la Conférence de la paix*. Paris: Économica, 2010.

Malcolm, Janet. *The Journalist and the Murderer*. New York: Vintage, 1990.

Marès, Antoine. "Louis Léger et Ernest Denis: Profil de deux bohémisants français au XIXe siècle." In *La France et l'Europe centrale, 1867-1914*, edited by Bohumila Ferenuhová, 63-82. Bratislava: Academic Electronic Press, 1995.

Margalit, Avishai. *The Ethics of Memory*. Cambridge, Mass.: Harvard University Press, 2002.

Martin, Jean-Clément. "Histoire, mémoire et oubli: Pour un autre régime d'historicité." *Revue d'histoire moderne et contemporaine* 47 (October-December 2000): 784-804.

"Mémoire, histoire." Special issue, *Revue de métaphysique et de morale* 1 (March 1998).

Morin, Mélissa S., and Patrick-Michel Noël, eds. "Les représentations du passé: Entre mémoire et histoire." *Conserveries mémorielles* 9 (2011), http://cm.revues.org/808.

Mosse, George. *Fallen Soldiers: Reshaping the Memory of the World Wars*. London: Oxford University Press, 1990.

Nielson, Jonathan M. *American Historians in War and Peace: Patriotism, Diplomacy and the Peace Conference, 1918-1919*. Palo Alto, Calif.: Academia Press, 2011.

Ory, Pascal. *Une nation pour mémoire, 1889, 1939, 1989, trois jubilés révolutionnaires*. Paris: Presses de la Fondation Nationale des Sciences Politiques, 1992.

Pollak, Michael. *L'expérience concentrationnaire: Essai sur le maintien de l'identité sociale*. Paris: Métailié, 1990.

Prost, Antoine, and Jay Winter. *Penser la Grande guerre: Essai d'historiographie*. Paris: Éditions du Seuil, 2004.

Rémond, René. *Regard sur le siècle*. Paris: Presses de Sciences Po, 2000.

Rey, Jean-Michel. *L'oubli dans les temps troublés*. Paris: Éditions de l'Olivier, 2010.

Ricoeur, Paul. *La mémoire, l'histoire, l'oubli*. Paris: Éditions du Seuil, 2000.

Ringelblum, Emmanuel. *Notes from the Warsaw Ghetto: The Journal of Emmanuel Ringelblum*. Edited and translated by Jacob Sloan. New York: Schocken, 1974 [1st ed. 1958].

Robin, Régine. *La mémoire saturée*. Paris: Stock, 2003.

Rousseau, Frédéric. *Le procès des témoins de la Grande guerre: L'affaire Norton Cru*. Paris: Éditions du Seuil, 2003.

Rousso, Henry. *La hantise du passé: Entretien avec Philippe Petit*. Paris: Textuel, 1997. Translated by Ralph Schoolcraft as *The Haunting Past: History, Memory, and Justice in Contemporary France*, preface by Philippe Petit, foreword to the English-language edition by Ora Avni. Philadelphia: University of Pennsylvania Press, 2002.

———. "La Seconde Guerre mondiale dans la mémoire des Droites françaises." In *Histoires des Droites en France*, edited by Jean-François Sirinelli. Vol. 2: *Cultures*, 549-620. Paris: Gallimard, 1992.

———. "L'histoire appliquée ou les historiens thaumaturges." *Vingtième siècle: Revue d'histoire* 1 (January-March 1984): 105-21. Translated as "Applied History, or the Historian as Miracle-Worker," *Public Historian* 4 (Fall 1984): 65-85.

———, ed. *Le regard de l'histoire: L'émergence et l'évolution de la notion de patrimoine au cours du XXe siècle en France*. Proceedings of the "Entretiens du Patrimoine" conference, 2001. Paris: Fayard-Monum, Éditions du Patrimoine, 2003.

———. *Le syndrome de Vichy de 1944 à nos jours*. Paris: Éditions du Seuil, 1987 and 1990.

———. *Vichy, l'événement, la mémoire, l'histoire*. Paris: Gallimard, 2001.

Rozenberg, Roy, and David Thelen. *The Presence of the Past: Popular Uses of History in American Life*. New York: Columbia University Press, 1998.

Salter, Michael. *Nazi War Crimes, US Intelligence and Selective Prosecution at Nuremberg: Controversies Regarding the Role of the Office of Strategic Services*. New York: Routledge, 2007.

Segev, Tom. *The Seventh Million: The Israelis and the Holocaust*. Translated by Haim Watzman. New York: Henry Holt, 2000.

Stora, Benjamin. *La gangrène et l'oubli*. Paris: La Découverte, 1991.

Stroom, Gerrold van der. "The Diaries, *Het Achterhuis,* and the Translations." In Anne Frank, *The Diary of Anne Frank: The Critical Edition,* edited by David Barnouw and Gerrold van der Stroom, translated by Arnold J. Pomerans and B. M. Mooyaart-Doubleday, 59–78. New York: Doubleday, 1989.

Suleiman, Susan Rubin. *Crises of Memory and the Second World War.* Cambridge, Mass.: Harvard University Press, 2006.

Terkel, Studs. *"The Good War": An Oral History of World War Two.* New York: Pantheon, 1984.

Traverso, Enzo. *Le passé, mode d'emploi: Histoire, mémoire, politique.* Paris: La Fabrique, 2005.

Trémeaux, Jean-Claude. *Deuils collectifs et création sociale.* With a preface by René Kaës. Paris: La Dispute, 2004.

Vidal-Naquet, Pierre. *Les Juifs, la mémoire et le présent.* Paris: Éditions du Seuil, 1995.

Wieviorka, Annette. *L'ère du témoin.* Paris: Plon, 1999.

Wilson, Keith, ed. *Government and International Historians through Two World Wars.* New York: Berghahn, 1996.

Wilson, Richard Ashby. *Writing History in International Trials.* Cambridge: Cambridge University Press, 2011.

Winter, Jay. *Sites of Memory, Sites of Mourning: The Great War in European Cultural History.* Cambridge: Cambridge University Press, 1995.

Yerushalmi, Yosef. *Zakhor, Jewish History and Jewish Memory.* Seattle: University of Washington Press, 1982.

Index

Société d'Histoire de la Révolution de 1848, 59

Société d'Histoire Moderne (1901), 59

Société Nationale des Chemins de Fer Français (SNCF), 160

Society for the History of the War, 69

Sorbonne, 59, 69, 107, 171

SOREL, Albert, 50–51

SOREL, Charles, 35

SOT, Michael, 204n3

SOULET, Jean-Francois, 153

South Africa, 145

South Korea, 92, 127

Soviet Union (USSR), 9, 40, 63, 73, 87, 92, 98, 102, 103, 145, 150, 168, 178, 182

Spain, 12

Sparta, 23

Srebrenica, 160

STALIN, Joseph, 1, 94, 185

STERNHALL, Zeev, 171

STORA, Benjamin, 130

Strasbourg, 10, 66

SUETONIUS, 60

Suez, 183

Switzerland, 92

TACITUS, 40

TAINE, Hippolyte, 16, 60

TAYLOR, A. J. P., 123–24

Témoignage Chrétien movement, 1

Tempo et Argumento (journal), 217n9

Temps présent (journal), 139

TERKEL, Studs, 213n80

THIERS, Adolphe, 44, 46

THOMPSON, Paul, 192

THUCYDIDES, 3, 14, 18, 23, 24, 34, 47, 71, 82, 123

TILLION, Germaine, 130

TOCQUEVILLE, Alexis Clérel de, 46, 59, 122, 152

Tokyo trials, 92

TOULONGEON, Francois-Emmanuel, 47

Toulouse-Le Mirail, University of, 154

TOUVIER, Paul, 119

Troy, 31

Turkey, 83

Twentieth Century (journal), 141, 165

Twenty-first Century (journal), 166

Ukraine, 150

United Kingdom, 51–52, 64, 65, 92, 125, 137, 177, 182

United States, 51, 52, 64, 67, 69, 74, 92, 98, 100, 102, 115, 137, 144, 153, 161, 177, 192

Université de Paris X Nanterre, 165

USSR. *See* Soviet Union

VERHAEGEN, Benoît, 131

Versailles, Treaty of, 65

Vichy, 1, 90, 91, 97, 118, 119, 120, 179, 193

VIDAL DE LA BLACHE, Paul, 63

VIDAL-NAQUET, Lucien, 40

VIDAL-NAQUET, Margot, 40

VIDAL-NAQUET, Pierre, 40

Vienna, 87

Vietnam, 183

VIOLANTE, Luciano, 198

VOLDMAN, Danièle, 141, 165

VOLTAIRE, 18, 42, 43

WAGNER, M., 219n42

Warsaw, 84

WEBER, Eugen, 124, 136

WESSELING, Henk, 109, 214n6

West Germany, 10, 94, 95

WHITE, Hayden, 149

WIENER, Alfred, 124

Wiener Library (London), 124

WIESENTHAL, Simon, 145

WILLIAM II, 65

Williams College (Mass.), 71

WINOCK, Michael, 165

WINTER, Jay, 66

WOODWARD, Llewellyn, 51, 207n86

Yad Vashem, 84

YERUSHALMI, Yosef Hayim, 33

Yugoslavia, 92, 145, 160, 182

ZANCARINI, Jean-Claude, 204n3

Zentrum für Zeithistorische Forschung (ZZF), 185